The Archaeology
of the Holocaust

The Archaeology of the Holocaust

Vilna, Rhodes, and Escape Tunnels

Richard A. Freund

ROWMAN & LITTLEFIELD
Lanham · Boulder · New York · London

Dedicated to the memory of the Jews and
Judaism of Greece and Lithuania—
may their names be for a blessing!

Published by Rowman & Littlefield
An imprint of The Rowman & Littlefield Publishing Group, Inc.
4501 Forbes Boulevard, Suite 200, Lanham, Maryland 20706
www.rowman.com

6 Tinworth Street, London SE11 5AL

British Library Cataloguing in Publication Information Available

Library of Congress Cataloging-in-Publication Data Available

978-1-5381-0266-4 (cloth)
978-1-5381-0267-1 (electronic)

∞™ The paper used in this publication meets the minimum requirements of American
National Standard for Information Sciences—Permanence of Paper for Printed Library
Materials, ANSI/NISO Z39.48-1992.

Printed in the United States of America

Contents

List of Photos

Preface

$\mathcal{T}$he *Archaeology of the Holocaust: Vilna, Rhodes, and Escape Tunnels* takes you inside a paradigm shift in Holocaust studies and archaeology. You will join me in one of the first applications of a technological and method-ological revolution in archaeology and Holocaust studies using noninvasive geoscience as a precursor to any excavation, but most especially at Holo-caust sites. According to many in my research group, we have worked in six countries and at as many as forty-five different sites from a variety of periods. Using complementary noninvasive geoscience technologies (each technology confirming the other's results), along with GPS "smart" but intelligible digital mapping of a site, ensures that accurate results can be immediately transmitted to local governments for action, whether that be follow-up excavations or marking of the site.

Jews are particularly sensitive to the issues of disturbing Jewish burials, and have developed very specific views regarding the violation of Holocaust sites. Jewish law is quite explicit in its condemnation of moving or tam-pering with burials. This book documents a more-"appropriate" method for examining and documenting Holocaust sites with mass burials using geoscience. You'll read about how we now use technologies to ensure that we do not desecrate the victims a second time by digging up their remains in an attempt to document the Holocaust. It is a methodology which has served my group well, not only in Holocaust-era sites, but also in holy sites in many places where traditional archaeology just cannot be done. I contend that if all archaeology was done using this methodology—in a systematic way, before ground is broken—far more would ultimately be achieved, with less excavation required.

(Left to right) Professor Richard Freund, with 2018 University of Hartford students and colleagues: Abigail Dunkin, Justin Lockhart, Professor Susan Cardillo, Taylor Ugrinow, Dima Karakitukova, and Kyle Conti, standing in front of the recently placed sign at the site of the Great Synagogue of Vilna, Lithuania, discovered under an elementary school in downtown Vilnius in 2015, using GPR and ERT. (Courtesy of Richard Freund, the Vilna Excavations Project at the University of Hartford)

OVERVIEW

I include a short introduction to the major ideas that led up to the Holocaust, such as anti-Judaism and anti-Semitism; the stages of Nazi anti-Semitism that led up to the violence; and ultimately, the so-called "Final Solution." This book introduces and suggests way of integrating testimonies into Holocaust studies in general, but, more importantly, how to use testimonies in field investigation. Learning how to critically read testimonies and integrate them into the science is key to this new frontier in Holocaust studies which this book chronicles.

Following this introduction are chapters on the Kahal Shalom and Kahal Grande Synagogues in Rhodes (and even a sense of where the earliest synagogues of Rhodes might still lay buried); the Great Synagogue and Shulhoyf of Vilna, at Ponar; the Lithuanian killing fields at Forts IX, VII, and IV in Kovno, and at HKP 562, a labor camp on the outskirts of Vilnius; Sobibor, a Nazi death camp in eastern Poland; Otwock, Poland; Rasu Prison, Vilnius; and our searches for mass burial sites in the Rokiskis region of Lithuania, where the use of testimonies was integral to our work.

To my mind, survivor testimonies represent the largest untapped body of information for scientific research of the Holocaust. These testimonies from different sources were compared one to another and placed alongside the testimonies of bystanders and perpetrators, and critically evaluated. You will read how the survivors, perpetrators, and bystanders provide detailed maps and descriptions of sites that no longer exist. All of these people's maps and descriptions give the scientific work greater context, setting this work apart from other books on the archaeology of the Holocaust that deal separately with archaeological evidence and the testimonies that give the evidence context. The testimonies are not just footnotes in our work; they are integral to our assessment of the project from start to finish. I take them seriously—as if they are just as important as the archaeological artifacts themselves—while recognizing the unique nature of the Holocaust and trauma memory in general.

Significantly, I wrote this book with access to survivors, bystanders, rescuers, and perpetrators who can (and did) speak for themselves. I personally spoke and engaged with them. Future researchers may only have access to video and audio accounts. I see this book as presenting a methodology of how to use the testimonies effectively—not just slavishly following them for the facts, but as guidelines for the scientific work.

I have had the opportunity to personally speak to and understand many of these sites that we are permitted to work on through the eyes of the individuals who lived through the events that took place there. These testimonies preserve more than just the events; the fact that I still have the ability to go to the field to do our work and sometimes go back to these "living" sources and ask questions is a key difference between this book and any other that will be written in the future, when we will no longer have living witnesses. This book is also different from other works on the archaeology of the Holocaust because rather than only being concerned with understanding the fate of anonymous Jews among the six million who were killed, I researched sites with very specific information about both the location and the individuals involved.

DOCUMENTING JEWISH LIFE BEFORE AND AFTER THE HOLOCAUST

This book not only makes a significant contribution to Holocaust and genocide studies, but also to Judaic studies and history in general. In order to understand what has been lost in a genocide, I think we must provide the cultural history of the people and what they believed—who they were, how they lived, what they ate, drank, and dreamed about. In this book I include the cultural history of Sephardic and Ashkenazic Jewries in my chapters on Rhodes and Vilna. All too often people forget that the Holocaust extended far beyond the traditional boundaries of Europe, ranging from North Africa and throughout the Mediterranean, from the Middle East and Asia, to all parts of Europe. It took more than two millennia to build the Jewish culture of Rhodes and Greek Jewry, and it was lost in a matter of months. The five hundred years of Vilna and Lithuanian Jewry was lost in the span of three years. The Jews were in Poland for a thousand years before suffering the loss of their Jewish population. Knowing what was lost—the religious customs, the languages, the literature, music, art, food, and dance, the institutions, the intellectual and personal capital of the Jews of these countries—this is often forgotten in the quest for details about the Holocaust. The archaeology of the Holocaust is only meaningful when we understand what came before.

The Archaeology of the Holocaust is intended to capture the revolution in archaeology and Holocaust studies today, and I hope it will inspire people to study their own family's stories, and look for answers. The study of the archaeology of Native American life in the United States inspired a whole generation of Native Americans to seek their own stories, and engage with archaeologists and anthropologists to help tell them. I think this book, with its photos, maps, scans, and evolving technologies, will help to inspire a revolution around the world in the study of the Holocaust. Scholars and family members alike can learn how to engage with geoscientists, archaeologists, and anthropologists to do preliminary work without destroying the evidence for future generations.

This book is geared toward the general public, as well as students from many different disciplines, including geoscience, archaeology, geology, geography, computer science, anthropology, engineering, architecture, chemistry, biology, history, religion, Judaic studies, philosophy, international studies, and communications—just some of the majors of students we have taken to the field. It is also intended to allow faculty and professionals in these different disciplines to seriously think about how a new methodology can change the field. I introduce the history of geoscience, and early efforts after World War II to forensically identify and archaeologically confirm details of the Holocaust.

WHY MATERIAL CULTURAL HISTORY MATTERS

I mention several times in this book that unlike the public perception of archaeology—that it's only about coins, glass, metal objects, ceramic pots, walls, and architecture—at the end of the day, all archaeology is about people. What I mean by this is that all of these artifacts lead us back to understand the people who made and used them; they are not just an end in and of themselves.

In the case of Rhodes, I introduce the history of pre-Sephardic and Sephardic Jewry and its languages and customs, focusing on the sites where Jews lived before the Holocaust, and that may yet be excavated in the future. The literature and culture of Greek Jewry through the ages helped to make the 2,300-year-old settlement there unique. In the case of Lithuania, I introduce the early history of the Ashkenazic—specifically, Litvak or Lithuanian—Jewry. The languages and customs of the Jews who settled in Vilnius gave Vilna the designation of "Jerusalem of the North."

The most important part of this book is its unique integration of science, history, photos, maps, and testimonies, elements which are rarely included together. I developed the content with a team of colleagues who collaborated with local archaeologists, historians, and scientists over the past twenty years, bringing together researchers from many different disciplines to work together and teach in the field. Our work has been vetted by the best and the brightest in each field, and our results presented all over the world at lectures and museums, as well as at conferences on history, religion, Judaic studies, geology, anthropology, geoscience, geography, and communications.

For full disclosure, I am an American Jew of Lithuanian descent. Some, but not all, of my Israeli colleagues who worked on this project can also trace their roots back to Lithuania. For the most part, the US and Lithuanian students who participated in our work come from diverse ethnic and religious backgrounds. The students and my colleagues all share a unique relationship in the field, teaching—and learning—about one of the most horrific periods in human history, while also learning a lot about each other.

I hope this book will heal some old wounds, and perhaps open some eyes. I have seen that our research can bring closure to some, and inspire others to think about what science can do for Holocaust studies. What I have realized is just how much we do not know about what actually happened in the Holocaust. I have personally witnessed how audiences in Israel, Latin America, Europe, and North America have been affected after watching how this transformational scientific work can give new hope, and perhaps even act as a deterrent for those who may harbor particularly "violent" thoughts about certain races, religions, ethnic origins, or people with different sexual orientations in their own societies, and think they can exact violence upon them and get away with it.

If one thing can be learned from this book, it is that science will find ways of unearthing the truth, even after seventy-five years, or more. I hope it will educate and inspire, and perhaps serve as a cautionary tale for future generations.

Acknowledgments

$\mathcal{W}$hen students ask how the program at the University of Hartford—which has included geoscience and archaeology for the past twenty years—is different from other programs that teach about archaeology, they are immediately met with my question: "Would you ever consider having major surgery without first going to a radiologist?" We are living in an age when we can choose to use technology to avoid "surprises" in medicine, so why not in archaeology? A hundred years ago X-ray technology did not exist, so surgeons used their intuition and training to determine how and where to cut. Today, it is not necessary. So, too, I think, in archaeology.

I started with what I call, the five "-IVES" that motivated me to write this book. Even in its most sophisticated incarnations, traditional archaeology tends to be destructIVE, expensIVE, labor-intensIVE, ineffectIVE, and offensIVE. With this book, I am encouraging a new approach that uses technology to deal with all of the finds, including—most importantly, in the case of the Holocaust—the people who died. So here are my new "–IVES" from my geoscientist colleagues: noninvasIVE, inexpensIVE, pedagogically intensIVE, productIVE, and sensitIVE.

Without my colleagues in the field, none of my work would have been possible.

The Maurice Greenberg Center for Judaic Studies has had archaeology as part of its educational mission since it was founded in 1985 by Arnold C. and Beverly Greenberg. The first director of the Greenberg Center, and first endowed Maurice Greenberg professor, Jonathan Rosenbaum, created an educational center that included summer excavations in Israel, and the first administrator, Arlene Neiditz, who continues to serve on the Greenberg Center Board of Visitors, continues to support these efforts. Four chairs of the Board of Visitors (including the present chair, Dane Kostin) and four presidents of the University of Hartford provided support for student scholarships, which allow the center to send students from every part of the university to excavate. I particularly want to point out the efforts of Dr. Walter Harrison (1997–2017), who accompanied me on the historic 2000 Millennium Tour to Israel (when I met Pope John Paul II) and visited all of our excavation sites; and Susan Gottlieb, who had the task of signing up every staff member and student participant during every summer and winter term, and ensuring that all bills were paid. In 2018, Dr. Greg Woodward, the new president of the University of Hartford, continued this tradition as he opened the new high-tech Greenberg Center for the public, which includes archives, film and displays on archaeology, and the largest Holocaust studies collection in the region. The projects are "teaching" excavations in Rhodes, Vilna, and elsewhere, and they represent the highest values of a liberal arts institution. Teaching geoscience, archaeology, and history in the field is a major goal, and mentoring of students in the field is an equally important goal.

The Greenberg Center began the University of Hartford Rhodes project in 2014, and the Vilna project in 2015, as a regular part of the archaeology and Holocaust studies coursework. The Greenberg Center has been involved with forty different archaeological sites over the past thirty-five years, including some of the most important sites in Israel, Spain, Poland, Greece, and now, Lithuania. The 2015 and 2016 projects in Rhodes brought together four universities, both students and faculty, and GPR-SLICE, in Los Angeles, to study the Holocaust.

I wish to thank Rabbi Albert Ringer of the Netherlands, who first introduced me to the issues of the Kahal Shalom Synagogue in Rhodes; Rabbi Marc D. Angel, rabbi emeritus of Congregation Shearith Israel in New York City, whose work I consulted; University of Hartford students Nicole Awad and Emily Galica; Tel Aviv University archaeology graduate student Vanessa Workman; Rachel Polinsky, from Clark University; Phillip Foglia, from Stockton University, New Jersey; and Jonathan Luczak and Jackelyn Seamans, from the University of Wisconsin–Eau Claire. I also want to thank my colleagues, Professor Harry Jol from the University of Wisconsin–Eau Claire, who provided the ground-penetrating radar (GPR) equipment and analysis; and Philip Reeder, dean and professor of the Bayer School of Natural and Environmental Sciences at Duquesne University, Pennsylvania, who was the chief cartographer. Their work is featured in the exhibitions, and I have published many of the pieces together in different conference papers, along with the students.

I wish to acknowledge my colleagues from the Fourth Archaeological Ephorate (the licensing authority of Greece) in Rhodes, Dr. Angeliki Katsioti, Dr. Natasha Psarologaki, and Maria Michalidou, director of the Ephorate, for their help, as well as the director of the Rhodes Jewish Museum, Carmen Cohen. I would like to thank Aron Hasson of Los Angeles, who facilitated receiving some of the items displayed at the University of Hartford. The cover and the poster for the exhibition are thanks to the family photo of Esther Fintz Menascé, whose book, *A History of Jewish Rhodes* (Los Angeles: Rhodes Jewish Historical Foundation, 2014, p. 236), was a central pillar of the exhibition. Her great-grandparents, Nissim and Rachel Cohen, appear in their finery in the exhibition catalog and poster. The artifacts in the exhibition were on loan from the Rhodes Jewish Historical Foundation, Los Angeles, thanks to Aron Hasson's good efforts.

Fieldwork with students, as well as a study abroad program in the summer term, winter term, and even during spring break, has been a hallmark of the program of the Greenberg Center. The two exhibitions on Rhodes and Vilna were intended to tell the story of each of these communities, and included the history of the Holocaust, archaeology, the history of the Jews of Rhodes and Vilna, and the people of Rhodes and Vilna, before and after the Holocaust. Rhodes's long Jewish history goes back 2,300 years, and Vilna's Jewish history goes back 500 years. Students did individual research projects in each location.

The University of Hartford exhibition on Rhodes was called "It Was Paradise: Jewish Rhodes," and included concerts, lectures, and a whole course offered through May 1, 2016. It was made possible through the generous support of the Avzaradel-Capuano Family Fund at the University of Hartford, established by Angele and Benjamin di Liscia, of Boca Raton, Florida. The di Liscias have also provided unique family photos of Rhodes, and made a donation in support of the Rhodes archaeological project in 2016.

I would also like to thank Norman and Carole Korowitz of Mount Sinai, New York, for their generous contribution in support of the 2015 excavations. I have to thank the director of the Museum of Jewish Civilization, Professor Avinoam Patt, Philip D. Feltman Professor of Modern Jewish History at the Greenberg Center; the curator of the Museum, Dreanna Hadash of Omaha, Nebraska; and the administrator of the Museum, Susan Gottlieb, of the Greenberg Center. The exhibition is both a tribute to the people who came before, and the history of the lives that were cut short by the Nazis.

I want to thank the twelve Rhodesli (descendants of Jews from Rhodes) whom I interviewed: Rachel (Israel) Goodman, Los Angeles; Arthur Benveniste, Los Angeles; Selma (Franco) Jaffee, Los Angeles; Esther Fintz Menascé, Italy; Guiseppe Mallel, Italy; Boaz (Bernard) Turiel, New Jersey; members of the Kehilat Chalom congregation in Buenos Aires, Argentina; Aron Hasson, Los Angeles; Gareth Kantor, South Africa; Benjamin di Liscia, Boca Raton, Florida; Beni Avzaradel, Zimbabwe; and Isaac Habib, South Africa. They transmitted much about the depth of the unique brand of spirituality and Sephardic life that developed in the past four hundred years on the island.

We also filmed testimonies of Eastern European Jews who live/d in Hartford at the University of Hartford to preserve the unique Ashkenazic and especially Litvak (Lithuanian + other modern states in the area) customs and life from before the Holocaust. Many people participated in the seasons of Lithuanian work from 2015 to 2018 and deserve my thanks. They are: Dr. Jon Seligman of the Israel Antiquities Authority; Zenonas Baubonis and Mantas Daubaras of the Kultūrospaveldo išsaugojimo pajėgos (Cultural Heritage Conservation Authority of Lithuania); Professor Harry Jol of the University of Wisconsin–Eau Claire; Paul Bauman and Alastair McClymont, WorleyParsons, Advisian Division, Calgary, Alberta, Canada; Dean and Professor Philip Reeder of Duquesne University; Professor Jean Marc Dreyfus, Manchester University; Dr. Dean Goodman, GPR-SLICE, Los Angeles; Dr. Vladimir Levin of the Centre for Jewish Art, Hebrew University of Jerusalem; Dr. Gintautas Zabielas, Vilnius University; Ramunas Smigelkas, Vilnius University; Rokas Vengalis, Institute of History, Vilnius; Rokas Kraniaukas, Klaipedia University; Adriajana Filinaitė and the Mayor and Municipality of Kaunas and it's Cultural Heritage Department, and people who helped me either in the field or through their personal insights: including Ken Bensimon, William Freund, Mantas Šikšnianas, and Zigmas Vitkus.

Sponsors and contributors to the work include: the University of Hartford's Maurice Greenberg Center for Judaic Studies, College of Arts & Sciences, University of Hartford; the Grae Family Vilna Excavations Project at the University of Hartford; Duquesne University; the US Commission for the Preservation of America's Heritage Abroad; US Embassy in Vilnius, Lithuania; Fondation pour la Mémoire de la Shoah, Paris, France; Targum Shelishi, USA; Faina Kukliansky, president of the Jewish Community of Lithuania; Martynas Uzpelkis, Jewish Community of Lithuania; Markas Zingeris, director of the Vilna Gaon Jewish State Museum; Jurate Zakaite, director, Fort IX; Vladimir Orlov, director, Fort VII; Ada (Gens) Ustjanauskas, daughter of Jacob Gens (Gens served as director of the Jewish Council of the Vilna Ghetto); Irene Bernhard, granddaughter of Jacob Gens; Mayor of Vilnius, Remigijus Šimašius; Adviser to the President of Lithuania, Marija Dautartaite; Consul General of Lithuania, Julius Pranevicius (NYC); Dr. Michael Good, son and grandson of Pearl and Samuel Esterowicz, of the Vilna Ghetto and HKP 562, and author of *The Search for Major Plagge* (Fordham University Press, 2005); Jonathan Good, grandson and great-grandson of Pearl and Samuel Esterowicz of the Vilna Ghetto and HKP 562; Simcha Jacobovici, Yaron Niski, Felix Golubev, Ric Bienstock of Associated Producers; Irina Guzenberg, senior researcher emeritus of the Vilna Gaon Jewish

State Museum; Mira Van Doren, the Vilna Project NYC; Sondra Litvaityte, Consulate of Lithuania; and the Jewish Federation of Greater Hartford.

I want to acknowledge the efforts to promote my work at my own university, starting with the provost, Fred Sweitzer, of the College of Arts and Sciences, Katherine Black, and the university team that included Paula Ribeiro, Lynn Baronas, and Mary Ingarra. Mary began her work at the University of Hartford almost at the same time as the discovery of the tunnel became world news. She fielded the vast majority of press questions while I was in Lithuania, and worked with me on the Connecticut Center for Advanced Technology, Inc. of East Hartford (CCAT) project to create a free app from iTunes entitled "Archaeology Quest: Vilna," which will give people around the world a sense of what Vilna and the University of Hartford have in common. The CCAT people who deserve thanks are Kevin Knott, Carl Fazzina, Herbert Liezer, and Melanie Harrison Wadden.

As I write these acknowledgments, I am flying to Rokiskis, Lithuania, to begin a search for Matilda Olkin, a young poet killed by the Nazis. This is thanks to Philip and Aldora Shapiro, who introduced me to author Laima Vince. I am working with University of Hartford School of Communications professor Susan Cardillo and her students Taylor Ugrinow and Kyle Conti.

As I correct these acknowledgements I have returned from Rokiskis, Lithuania, where we searched for (and found) the burial place of Matilda Olkin and her extended family in a forest in northwest Lithuania. She was a young Jewish teenage poetess killed at the very beginning of the Nazi incursion there. This work was made possible thanks to the generosity of Philip and Aldona Shapiro, Dr. Joan Silber of the US Commission for America's Heritage Abroad and many local researchers and people. I want to acknowledge in particular the assistance of the RKM museum, especially Nijole Sniokiene and Giedrius Kujelis, the municipality and mayor of Rokiskis, my archaeological colleague Romas Jarockis, the playwright Neringa Daniele, the translator of Matilda's diary, Laima Vince and the "protector of the diary," Irena Veisaite. I am now working with University of Hartford School of Communications Professor Susan Cardillo and her students, Taylor Ugrinow and Kyle Conti on the documentary "Finding Matilda: The Anne Frank of Lithuania" and it required all of these people to tell this story and make this documentary possible. In particular I want to thank Ronald Leopold, Director of the Anne Frank House who helped us shape the story in Amsterdam and Smithsonian magazine writer, Matthew Shaer, who wrote the article "Finding Her Voice" on our work in the November 2018 that touched upon many elements of the story.

My ultimate praise is reserved for the co-directors of *Holocaust Escape Tunnel*, Kirk Wolfinger and Paula Apsell, who championed this film even as I was in the field working on a rare discovery that happened in front of the cameras. It takes a sixth sense to know that this kind of film about a Holocaust-era escape by a ragtag group of Jews in a Lithuanian forest will capture the imagination of millions of people. Paula Apsell and Melanie Wallace stood by this project through its many events leading up to the national premiere. Owen Palmquist, who was in the field writing the documentary as it was unfolding, deserves special praise, as does my colleague, Dr. Avinoam Patt, a rare historian of the Holocaust who understands the significance of sharing material and literary culture with the general public. But for this film, the discovery of the escape tunnel would have been a mere footnote in a book on the Holocaust in Lithuania.

West Hartford, CT
December 2018

What If: Geoscience and Archaeology

The reason we do anything is because we assume that there will be knowable results. "What if" geoscience and archaeology is what stirred me a quarter-century ago to pursue a new way of doing fieldwork with students. I noted that my millennial students were fascinated by work in the field, but they wanted to see immediate results. They were interested in using technology to yield more-precise areas for excavating, and they loved the idea of discovery. Millennial students became extraordinary workers in the field when they knew that they could help to predict where they might find that next discovery using technology. I call this "what if" geoscience and archaeology because that is what I told them: *What if* they could help to pinpoint the places where the discoveries would be made, and then make those discoveries? This is a totally different way of thinking about the field experience. A generation ago, archaeologists went to the field because "it was there." They did not know whether they would find anything; the process of seeking alone was sufficient to provide the challenge. When I did not find anything over a summer or a digging season, I would say to myself, "Maybe next year."

After my first use of geoscience in the field in search of an archaeological goal, I said to myself, "*What if* I could predict what is below the surface with reasonable accuracy, and only then excavate? *What if* I could find a group of scientists who were interested in sharing their expertise with students and nonscientist staffs to convince them that this is a better way of doing excavations?"

That is how "what if" geoscience and archaeology was born, and it had unintended consequences. It transformed the millennial students who were in the field with us as much as it transformed the staff. The same "what if" geoscience and archaeology that predicted the existence of remains also allowed me the solace of not having to excavate them. Thus, "what if" geoscience and archaeology bred the next stage of development: noninvasive archaeology of the Holocaust, in which the goal was not so much to excavate each site, but rather, to identify, map, and mark it.

WHY SCIENCE IS THE NEXT FRONTIER
FOR THE STUDY OF THE HOLOCAUST

George Santayana is credited with saying "Those who cannot remember the past are doomed to repeat it." Memory—that faculty by which we record and store our past actions—is fleeting, as we all know. The sheer volume of actions in an individual lifetime is astonishing, and imperfectly remembered. It is hard enough to learn from our own mistakes; how, then, can we hope to learn from the past actions of others? I speculate that Santayana was speaking not of the individual memory, but of societal memory—the collective memory of a civilization's constituents. How can we record and store the actions of a society's past? The task is daunting, but we are not without tools. Archaeology is a tool that lets us peer into the past, find actions stored in societal memory, even though they may be lost to individual memory, and bring that knowledge into the present.

I study the Holocaust as an archaeologist to make a permanent record that will serve as a resource for current and future generations. I study and teach about the Holocaust as a professor of Jewish history to ensure that people understand there are texts, oral accounts, video accounts, and physical evidence of the Holocaust. I hope that by making such a record, history will not be repeated—but I am a skeptic. I doubt the permanency of memory. I think that society must continually figure out new and better ways to document the past. Over the course of this book, I will take you on my archaeological journey of the Holocaust, perhaps to give you new insight, not only into what is known, but *how* it is known. Although this journey is specific to fieldwork, it is through fieldwork that I made some remarkable discoveries. I hope to unfold the mystery and excitement as I experienced it, so that you too will reach the same conclusions by the end of these chapters. A generation from now, when there are no more survivors to tell their stories, perhaps science will provide a memory that will be meaningful to future generations.

To a certain generation, the mere mention of archaeology conjures up images of pyramids and mummies and Indiana Jones. Such is the stuff of Hollywood. Even to the less imaginative, archaeology means excavations. Modern archaeologists—particularly when studying the Holocaust, as will become meaningful later—do not begin with a shovel and pick. The groundwork, so to speak, actually begins aboveground, not in it. Whether I am researching an ancient or a modern Holocaust site, I must complete extensive geo-imaging before I will consider excavation.

Archaeology is one of the most destructive sciences on Earth. Most people know that the scientific method requires a scientist to be able to repeat an experiment to prove that the original result is neither an anomaly nor flawed. In archaeology, that is not possible. Much like an oenologist must destroy a fine bottle of wine to enjoy it, an archaeologist at an excavation must destroy the subject to study it. While it is true that a dig is careful and systematic—studiously recording each find, no matter how small, and diligently moving and reconstructing the finds to a laboratory for later examination—nevertheless, the process is irreversible. The experiment can never be repeated. It is scientific, but destructive. Archaeology can entail multiple seasons of slow and deliberate physical work done by many laborers, often never knowing what is below the surface, with expensive and intensive testing of materials from unknown periods. It has always seemed to me like performing surgery, but without an MRI, X-ray, or CT scan to help direct the surgeon.

My work is a mild corrective of this method. Although not limited to studying the Holocaust, this "noninvasive" archaeology is designed to meet the special challenges associated with studying such important events. My research group has employed this methodology in the study of more than forty sites worldwide, in many different time periods, from the Bronze Age through the modern period. We have found that it provides important data before an excavation even begins, giving the researcher an edge. The researcher can locate an artifact specifically and do "pinpoint excavations," or leave the artifact in the ground until such time as the excavations can be done more effectively. Noninvasive subsurface imaging is inexpensive, not very labor-intensive, and an important alternative when excavations cannot be done at all.

While I mention the technology extensively in this book, that is not really the point. The technology, which is evolving even as I write this, is only a tool to help document the Holocaust, and without trained and sensitive geoscientists, it is far less productive in the field. Documenting the Holocaust does not mean just listening to Holocaust testimony, looking for the Holocaust site location mentioned in the testimony, and digging up remains and artifacts. It is not just looking at the period of the Holocaust from 1933 to 1945. The method I am suggesting here is a hybrid, combining all of the evidence. It includes documents and photographs from the Nazis, as well as from local governments and regular people at those sites. It also includes illustrations, photographs, and film of the period and the sites, from before the

Holocaust era. It includes maps, both hand-drawn by people from the period, and those professionally done. Often many of these items are key to understanding and authenticating the hundreds of thousands of witness testimonies from victims, perpetrators, and bystanders.

A comprehensive investigation of a Holocaust-era site involves an understanding of the life and culture of the Jews and other ethnic and religious groups in a place from before the Holocaust, and having the right scientific technologies and methodologies to establish the facts of what happened. I have said many times to students in the field that you cannot know what was lost in the Holocaust unless you study the culture and life from before the Holocaust. When I am studying a Holocaust site, I feel like a crime-scene detective: I want to establish the facts of the case using traditional, critical-thinking detective skills and the latest technological advancements to pin down as much of the story as possible with scientific facts. More important, just as modern sleuthing requires a myriad of scientific subspecialties to uncover a crime, so, too, the modern scientific study of the Holocaust requires many new subspecialties, including archaeology and geoscience.

The research group which I established at the University of Hartford combines these tools. Some of the staff members have worked together for as long as twenty-five years, their collaboration developing organically. In as many as forty different archaeological sites worldwide, the group has shared its information and developed the research questions as a team. I often feel more like the conductor of an orchestra than the director of a research group; there are so many experts in different fields, so many different instruments working harmoniously in concert to produce the results.

I am limited in my abilities to know everything at a single site, often because of circumstances beyond my control. It is often the case, particularly at Holocaust sites, that traditional archaeology is not possible. In the archaeology of the Holocaust I must document the Holocaust without excavating bodies. One of the basic rules established for examining Holocaust sites is that the human remains of the victims must stay unexcavated. I have told my students that in the case of the Holocaust, you do not want to victimize the victims a second time by digging up their remains. In fact, it is more complex than that. Jews have a clear prohibition, developed over the past two thousand years, against the disinterring of the dead unless there are rabbinically supervised mitigating circumstances.

I wanted to find a way of collecting the data without victimizing the dead. It was ingrained in me from early on that the sanctity of the burial often means that I must leave the dead in their place. Early in the formation of what became rabbinic Judaism, the physical remains of a Jew were seen as a "holy sanctuary." The body was "on loan" for his or her time on Earth, and then returned "to the dust." Today, at funerals, mourners intone the words that are a take on the book of Genesis's story about the creation of Adam: "from dust you came—to dust you shall return"[1] to mean that in-ground burial of a body with its parts is key. It can be related to the idea of the physical resurrection of the dead which Jews, Christians, and Muslims share. It is an important part of everything you will read about in this book, which differentiates the work I do from earlier work. I am committed to gathering as much information from below the ground as possible using subsurface geoscience imaging, and only in rare instances is it recommended to excavate at the site of mass burials (usually only under the supervision of Rabbinic authorities).

I think the use of subsurface imaging for examining Holocaust sites is singularly progressive, but I am not the first to see the importance of gathering information using archaeology at a Holocaust site. There are books that provide a general overview of the archaeology of the Holocaust.[2] This book is about the work that my research group has done—a personal account about how my work developed. The accomplishments I write about here would have been impossible without the achievements of many past archaeological examinations, so, like Isaac Newton, "If I have seen further than others, it is by standing upon the shoulders of giants." In this book, I will tell you about some discoveries of those who came before, and also my own discoveries about the Holocaust; I will tell you of the process by which I came to make the discoveries; and of how future researchers can follow in my footsteps.

I am first and foremost a researcher; I want to use the work of those who came before, but I also need to know that the findings and conclusions of past research are indeed accurate and scientifically valid. My group, therefore, usually goes to places where work has been done before, and we attempt to shed new light on old examinations, or we work to corroborate old evidence. Past research, even when I may disagree with old methodology, provides me with important precedents at most sites. All of the work I do in foreign countries is vetted and licensed by and affiliated with local archaeological and scientific institutes. I share my team's information with them, and they, ultimately, are the ones who must follow up with the plans of the local population. They are my collaborators, past, present, and future, in the "great chain of scientific knowledge."

A SHORT HISTORY OF MAPPING THE ARCHAEOLOGY OF THE HOLOCAUST

This is a book about many different types of discoveries. The discoveries are usually not of gold and silver, or even rare jewels or art, but rather elements that illuminate an entire history. Maps tell us much more than just what direction to go. They tell us where others have been, and where we are. The discovery of a map of the archaeology of a Holocaust-era site—Fort IX, Kaunas, Lithuania—made me think about how little is known of the history of archaeological work done by others at Holocaust sites. I need to know what others have done in order to know what I must do.

Discovery #1: One of the first scientific archaeological excavation maps of a Holocaust site from Fort IX, Kaunas (Kovno), Lithuania. (Courtesy of Richard Freund, the Vilna Excavations Project at the University of Hartford)

It is rare for me to be surprised by a discovery. Nevertheless, the map pictured opposite—a discovery that my colleague Alastair McClymont, a geophysicist from Canada, and I happened upon during our meetings with the director of Fort IX in Kaunas, Lithuania, in October 2016—gave me a jolt. Fort IX was originally a nineteenth-century defensive stronghold that was later used by the Germans as a killing site during the Holocaust. We had traveled there to prepare ourselves for a summer 2017 project on the fort's enormous campus. It is one thing to get a permit to do a geophysical subsurface mapping project on a massive site connected with events from the Holocaust era, and quite another to figure out where exactly you want to do the work.

The Fort IX site today is imposing, with scores of sprawling acres featuring lush green lawns and trees. The nineteenth-century fort sits near an open field and a late-twentieth-century Soviet-style monument where the killing of as many as fifty thousand people took place during the Holocaust in Kaunas (1941–1944). Kaunas—*Kovno* in Yiddish—is the old capital of the Lithuanian state. It had a sizable population of Jews for more than four hundred years, including some of the greatest rabbis and *yeshivot* (institutions of higher rabbinic learning), well into the early twentieth century. It was virtually annihilated in the span of three years. The site of Fort IX is one of the Lithuanian equivalents of the Auschwitz extermination camp, without the gas chambers and the crematoria. All of the killing was done by locals and Nazis, with guns, and the burning, by makeshift "Burning Brigades." (Nazi-ordered *Aktion* 1005 created these squads of Jews, brought especially to killing sites to burn the "evidence" of the killings.)

My first task in October 2016 was to figure out what geoscience problem I wanted to solve at Fort IX. When the director brought out the map and the archaeological field diaries, I immediately wanted to know what past researchers had excavated, and why. This map is one of the most important documents I have ever encountered in studying the history of the archaeology of the Holocaust. This complete excavation map shows the results of more than a decade's worth of archaeological digs performed by skilled Soviet excavators at the Fort IX site, including the field notes they took to help identify what they discovered. These excavators had the opportunity less than twenty years after the Holocaust to systematically examine a killing field. It was Soviet-financed and -inspired research performed over the course of a decade, following the last war crimes trial.

I had a number of native speakers look at the diaries and help me distinguish the markings on the map, which show archaeological ditches in the field that during 1941–1944 included the dead bodies of the murdered victims, and later, their burned remains. It shows a series of pits that were dug in Fort IX in 1941 and used first for the killing and then for the burning of the victims by the Burning Brigades. The pits were systematically excavated by

Soviet archaeologists from the late 1950s until 1971. It appears that they were interested in seeing what evidence was still extant at the site. This map serves as a symbol of what the earliest forms of Holocaust archaeology attempted to do: document a Holocaust site with a site map, collect the artifacts from the pits (mainly human remains, cremated ash, personal effects), and display the artifacts in the developing museum collection at Fort IX. On the one hand, this map was used to document what happened, and where, but on the other, in the case of the Soviet officials in 1960s Kaunas, it apparently served as a catalyst in local purges and trials. The site had only been selectively excavated, as was the technique of the time: sampling in different areas of the field in a way that could be easily graphed onto a map so work could proceed from year to year, with open small "squares" (actually, rectangles) for excavation and collection of artifacts.

When the director of Fort IX took out the map and showed me the small notebooks that served as the archaeologists' field diaries, I was astonished, and immediately discerned their significance. Less than two decades after the Soviets entered Kaunas, Lithuania, they were interested enough to conduct a scientific excavation that lasted for more than a decade, and this was a record of their work. Often when a new government takes over a place where there has been a genocide, there is little interest in conducting a thorough forensic examination, except perhaps for initial "show trials." Here, trained Soviet archaeologists had been funded to investigate the exterminations long after the show trials of the late 1940s. At the end of the investigation, some of the artifacts that were found were used to create a small museum, and, ultimately, a large and imposing Soviet-style monument was created near the killing fields. These records constitute something of a Magna Carta for serious Holocaust archaeology, a standard rarely found at other Holocaust sites.

Archaeological studies of specific periods and sites are common. Roman archaeological studies look at the places where a specific period occupation of Romans can be distinguished. Native American archaeology is usually distinguished by traditional tribal designations which are a remembered and documented part of the tribe's history. Holocaust archaeology is not limited to one location. In this book I have chosen to evaluate places where I have specifically worked: Poland, Lithuania, and Greece. The circumstances of the history of the archaeology is presented here because there were precedents, especially in Europe, of archaeological and anthropological methodologies used to investigate what happened. I decided to include a short history of archaeological and forensic investigations at the start of this book so you could see how I assessed what I needed to do in my own work.

Fort IX's early work gave me a perspective on who did what, and why, in Holocaust archaeology before I began my own investigations. It was at

Fort IX, on December 25, 1943, that members of a Burning Brigade of Jews made a daring escape from their Nazi captors. The Fort IX director in the 1950s undertook systematic excavations of the large field used for killing and burning the bodies, presumably to identify the site of the killing and document what happened there, but also to indicate what parts of the massive fort should not be developed in the future. It is clear that although the Soviets were not totally interested in documenting and memorializing what happened at Fort IX, they do not seem to want to build on top of what they knew had been a massive burial and cremation site. The museum is close by, and this "killing field" ultimately was graced with a massive Soviet sculpture in the 1980s. While the archaeological work was not published, it still exists in the maps and original field journals. These journals contain smaller maps with sections from the larger map, including coordinates to indicate the corresponding loci, revealing the archaeological method that was used. This qualifies as a true excavation rather than merely a "crime-scene investigation."

Fort IX is one of the now fifteen different projects my research group has undertaken in Lithuania. The type of information that my group uncovered at Fort IX is both significant and chilling, and stands as good evidence to build upon in my own work. A systematic archaeological excavation, with multiple seasons and ongoing work and analysis of the finds, began here in the late 1950s under the Soviets in limited areas, and continued through the early 1960s. The field journals of those who directed the excavations on the "battlefield," as it was called by the inmates, reveal how archaeology was done during this period. As a museum with clear, documented remains, along with restored and memorialized artifacts discovered on-site and displayed in its museum space, Fort IX has an important place in the history of Holocaust archaeology. Others have gone before me with their attempts to document, display, and memorialize what happened at this site; I just represent the next stage of their pioneering work. I have brought geoscience techniques to areas they excavated, and to areas they did not.

THE ORIGINS OF HOLOCAUST ARCHAEOLOGY

The Holocaust archaeology that emerged in the period directly after the end of the war was part of the effort to build war crimes cases in the Soviet sphere of influence, usually against local populations and their leaders. It is similar to what could be called the "forensic anthropology" used in the study of ancient disasters, from the natural disaster at Pompeii to the man-made destruction of Napoleon's armies. Holocaust archaeology started almost immediately after the Soviets re-took countries, from Poland to the Ukraine, in 1945 and 1946, and preceded trials and punishment. It continued in what I see as four waves: from 1945 to the early 1960s; from the 1960s to the 1990s; from the 1990s to the early 2000s; and from the mid-2000s to the present.

Those working in each wave of Holocaust archaeology have had different motivations and used different techniques. The information gleaned from the work also had different purposes. In the first wave, from 1945 through the early 1960s, Holocaust archaeology was part of war crimes investigations and the start of reconstruction in Soviet-bloc areas. Soviet leadership used Holocaust archaeology as a way to consolidate power by seeking out collaborators and prosecuting war crimes. The Nazi death camps are distinguished by what could not be done rather than what was done. The death camps located in Poland, which housed victims, gas chambers, and crematoria, were often destroyed by the Nazis themselves, such as Treblinka in 1943, or Auschwitz, where records and buildings were destroyed in late 1944 and early 1945.

The early Soviet efforts to use forensic science to prove "war crimes" were very important as well. Within two weeks of the liberation of Auschwitz, a technical commission of forensic experts from many fields used in anthropological and archaeological research—chemistry, engineering, medicine, and transport—was sent to collect evidence. Their purpose was to document the crimes, but in many ways they set the stage for future archaeology of the Holocaust. Standard military-style excavation was used at many locations, as legal teams jockeyed to amass physical evidence for presentation at war crimes commissions in the East and the West.

It was difficult for the Soviets to collect evidence early on in the post–World War II era. Treblinka, Sobibor, and Belzec had been either destroyed or buried by the Germans. The evidence collected at death camps and mass burial sites sat unprotected after the war at most of these sites, subject to pilfering from the local population. Nevertheless, the Soviets used "excavations" in these early days to establish war crimes investigation committees in Poland, with local populations in attendance. In the name of legal proceedings, excavations continued through 1947, were reinitiated in the 1960s, and systematized according to modern archaeological methodology in the 1990s. Now, in the 2000s, they regularly include geoscience to minimize physical destruction of the site.

On October 10, 1945, an investigation commission led by a judge from Zamosc, Poland, came to the Belzec death camp, and after hearing oral testimonies, authorized the opening of nine pits for forensic examination. The evidence revealed that thousands of people had been killed and cremated, their bones crushed beyond recognition. This is essentially the way Holocaust archaeology began. The open sites were excavated by heavy equipment to move the piles of ashes and bones into centralized areas—first, behind fences, and later, into brick-and-mortar or cement enclosures. These commission reports are important archaeological documents. The unearthed remains were put into a specially constructed concrete crypt at Belzec, similar to the one at Sobibor.

During my own work at Sobibor, I was able to see the development of how the evidence of the Holocaust was displayed. Marek Bem, then the director of the museum at Sobibor, showed me photographs of earlier versions of the concrete crypt. At Sobibor, there was a viewing station in the concrete enclosure that held the ashes and bones found at the site. Initially, the viewing station was large, but over the years it was minimized, and finally closed. It was originally installed to allow people to see the remains (usually just ashes, with some complete bones), to serve as visual proof that killing had indeed taken place there. In the first steps toward a systematic Holocaust archaeology, the idea of making sure that visitors "saw" the remains was important. This practice stopped in the third period of Holocaust archaeology, as some—both archaeologists and survivors who visited—thought this was offensive and scientifically unnecessary.

The second investigation at Belzec, in April of 1946, essentially dealt with the last actions in the camp, including the destruction of evidence, the dismantling of gas chambers, the removal of fences, and the planting of trees. The idea this time was not only to investigate for war crimes trials, but also to begin "reconstruction."

Many people see this early archaeology as crude and not scientifically significant, but the information is nonetheless unique. It was the photographs of the 1946 commission at Ponar that gave me a sense that all of the bodies had not been burned. In my own work at Ponar in 2016, I was aided by photos in locating the sites where other burial pits might be located. The photos were taken during this first period of work by the Soviet commission of 1946, and provided them with the evidence they needed to conduct trials of locals. On August 31, 1946, the "Extraordinary State Commission to Investigate and Establish War Crimes of the German Fascist Invaders" (previously created in the USSR in 1942) visited Ponar, to investigate the burial pits. They concluded that 100,000 people, including 70,000 Jews, were killed, and their remains burned. The commission's findings provided important evidence of the mass burial pits that I would investigate seventy years later. This is a strong argument in favor of using the Soviet-era records, despite what seem to be political motivations in their creation.

In 2017 I worked at the Fort IX site in Kovno (Kaunas), and the systematic excavations there are from the next period of Holocaust archaeology, the 1960s and 1970s. I have matched my own work against the Soviet archaeologists' map and field diaries, to see what was still in the ground, and to verify the accuracy of their work. The biggest issue in this second period of Holocaust archaeology is the creation of memorials and neatly crafted sites that often did not preserve the original entrances, walkways, buildings, and burial sites. At the sites where I have been working—Sobibor, Kaunas, Vilnius, Silute, and Rokiskis, which I'll describe in more detail in later chapters—I have discovered that the memorials were deliberately reengineered to provide the visitor a more topographically harmonious arrangement. The testimonies of survivors confirmed that they were disoriented by the new arrangements, to the point where they could not always locate key parts of the site where they had been held. I found this to be the case in Ponar, Fort VII, and Fort IV. In addition to the changing of the highways and train tracks (very important, since many of the killing sites required trains to bring the victims from the larger cities), the development of new infrastructure has made the original site unrecognizable even for survivors. At Ponar, for example, the placement of the parking lot, entrance, pathways, memorials, and lighting make the experience confusing for survivors.

Needless to say, it is complicated to begin archaeological and geoscience work seventy years after the event, especially if there is no earlier work to use as a basis for comparison. The Soviet commission exhumed the last layers of some of the pits and performed forensic investigations (for example, at the Ponar site, they created a schematic); they photographed some of their work, and then wrote an extensive report that resulted in legal entanglements for some people who were locally involved. Their records are invaluable, despite the fact that they are incomplete and directed toward goals that were not necessarily scientific or research-oriented.

The second wave of Holocaust archaeology extends from the 1960s through the end of the 1990s. This period encompasses a Soviet follow-up effort to reconstruct modern cities and the allied infrastructures of sites all over Europe. The streets and buildings where many Holocaust events unfolded were systematically overbuilt. In the case of the Great Synagogue of Vilna, a new elementary school was built on top of the synagogue's remains; I call this "Postwar Rebuilding, Part II." But it was in this period that a major effort was first made to create new memorials, especially Jewish memorials, to Holocaust victims. I would also call this the "Memorialization Period, Part I."

One of the characteristic traits I found in the second wave of Holocaust archaeology involves the use of "excavations" in the course of creating memorials, specifically at the death camps in Poland, often at the expense of the original camp designs. Areas for large-scale, Soviet-style, concrete-block memorials were originally designed and implemented with little regard for the destruction of the elements still in the ground, and little or no mention of religious affiliation was made. At the death camp of Belzec, for example, acres of territory were bulldozed and fenced off from the original camp and marked as a memorial. Monuments were placed above the original mass burial sites (the remains had been reinterred elsewhere at the camp), and symbolic tombs to commemorate what had happened there were created for visitors. Landscaping is often one of the enemies of Holocaust archaeology. An attempt to provide aesthetically pleasing landscaping often makes it difficult to perform even noninvasive archaeology. Auschwitz and Treblinka are examples of death camps that have been almost totally reengineered.

The destruction of the camps at the end of the war, whether by the Nazis or the Allies, made many of the death camps problematic sites for traditional archaeological projects. The Chelmno death camp, for example, was the first place at which gas was used for mass executions, and therefore, an important target location for Holocaust archaeology. Unfortunately, when the archaeology team, led by Lucja Nowak of the Konin Regional Museum, began working in Chelmno in 1986, they discovered that there was very little that could be visibly identified on the surface to help direct the work. Inevitably in this period, excavations uncovered burial sites. It is during this era that for the first time, survivors and Jewish and rabbinic communities began to vocally demand accountability with regard to the desecration of the graves.

The third wave of Holocaust archaeology can be identified as the 1990s through the early 2000s, and marks the first use of new geoscience technology, such as ground-penetrating radar (GPR). I call this phase "Geoscience, Part I"; however, nonscientific efforts to establish sites with memorials that reflect the ethnic/racial and religious backgrounds of victims, separate from national identities, are also part of this period. I call this "Memorialization, Part II." It is during this period that the US Commission for the Preservation of America's Heritage Abroad began its work to create a series of systematic and meaningful memorials to the Jewish victims using many of the elements from the sites.

One of the biggest changes that happened in the 1990s was the understanding of Jewish sensitivity for the dead by local, non-Jewish archaeologists and authorities, and Jewish activism from abroad. Jewish concerns over the exhumation of the dead became an issue at the follow-up excavation in Belzec (by Dr. Andrzej Kola, in the 1990s), and in areas where rabbinic supervision had begun in other areas of Poland. The other issue was the extrapolation factor that was used by traditional archaeology to assess elements such as burials. In many cases the idea was not to excavate mass burials, but to sample and gain data about how many burials existed in a single location. Traditional archaeological method in this period determined the composition of the subsurface core by boring a hole and collecting samples. Excavation teams at the death camp in Belzec attempted to calculate the numbers of dead using standard core samples of the victims' traces (e.g., wax/fat, oil, soil, sand, charcoal, burned bone, etc.), and extrapolating from the ground samples by applying standard statistical analysis. This was all done in the name of "science," but was perceived as controversial, and in the end did very little to answer any of the more-pressing questions of what happened at the location. This method became the source of much controversy.

The fourth wave of Holocaust archaeology extends from the mid-2000s to the present. It is during this period, which I call "Geoscience, Part II," that I performed the work that I recount in this book. This Holocaust archaeology is motivated both by protection of sites and research for the sake of research. During this phase, the Vilna Gaon Jewish State Museum at Ponar commissioned a lidar study. Lidar—which stands for "light detection and ranging," and is also known as LIDAR, LiDAR, and LADAR—measures distance to a target by illuminating the target with pulsed laser light and measuring the reflected pulses with a sensor. Lidar is used to "see" beneath the tree canopy to find previously unidentified burial pits in the forest. Here, geoscience is employed with full knowledge of Jewish sensitivities, and is sometimes supervised by a coordinated rabbinic effort, thereby creating a holistic archaeological, educational, and memorialization process. Holocaust sites should be more than pilgrimage destinations that simply memorialize the dead in some anonymous way; they should inform and educate visitors as to what actually happened at the location.

WHAT WE LEARNED IN POLAND
AND APPLIED IN LITHUANIA

For the past decade I have closely followed the discoveries and work being done at Sobibor by my colleagues, Yoram Haimi and Wojciech Mazurek. I have been an ongoing part of a film documentation project there since 2008, which will chronicle the work from start to finish. A discovery of a pendant from a relative of Anne Frank's made international news in 2017. It is amazing to me that a single small pendant can make international news, but it points to the issue that is at the heart of Holocaust-era archaeology: The public can only understand the tragedy of the Holocaust through the lens of individual cases. In this case, the triangular metal pendant of Karoline Cohn found in 2017 had her birthday—July 3, 1929—inscribed on it, along with the Jewish Star of David and even her city of origin, Frankfurt. It is similar to the pendant that Anne Frank wore as well. An artifact like this tells us a story about a named individual and connects her with the entire tragedy of the Holocaust. It was fourteen-year-old Karoline Cohn that died at Sobibor, not just one anonymous representative of the six million Jews.

Tracing a single pendant to a person who lived and died at the camp reminded me how much I have learned from Yoram and Wojciech over the past decade. The pendant is just one of the thousands of small artifacts that they have uncovered during the excavations of the Sobibor death camp. My own work in Rhodes and Lithuania uncovered small artifacts usually left behind as Jews moved toward their deaths; part of my work is not only to document the places, but also to tell the world about the individuals whose personal items were found, to give these people back their identities. In addition, I have learned that most of the evidence may not always be found at the main site; I needed to also investigate the surrounding area, to visit the sub-camps and the nearby villages and cities, to understand the full extent of the Holocaust at a place like Sobibor.

I began my search with two such areas: the city of Wlodawa, and the village of Luta.

THE HOLOCAUST IS MUCH MORE THAN DEATH CAMPS: THE SUB-CAMP OF LUTA, POLAND

The Holocaust happened at more than the infamous death camps in Poland. Beyond the six major camps—Auschwitz-Birkenau, Belzec, Chelmno, Majdanek, Sobibor, and Treblinka—there were hundreds of concentration camps that became killing centers, and thousands of sites that were transformed from labor and concentration camps into extermination centers by the end of the war.

I decided to look at one labor sub-camp at Luta, Poland. This was not a simple task. The people who now live on the land where these labor sub-camps existed often are very tentative about allowing serious Holocaust-era research on their property, and are often not even aware of what happened there. I was aided in Poland by the office of the chief rabbi, who has been working with locals to interview local (non-Jewish) landowners around the death camps to see whether they will tell what they know about the Holocaust era.

In Luta, in 2008, I interviewed a local landowner and conducted a GPR survey which confirmed what the local landowner had told us. His land had been a labor sub-camp for Sobibor during the Holocaust. The prisoners worked on the land, and when the escape happened at Sobibor, all of the workers were killed and buried on his land. His interview was both one of

Taking testimony in Luta, Poland. (Left to right) Jan's wife, Richard Freund, Jan, and Lukasz Biedka (translator). (Courtesy of Richard Freund, the Sobibor Documentation Project at the University of Hartford)

the most chilling and inspiring of my work in Sobibor. I visited a series of sites around the Nazi death camp in the villages that were in close contact with the camp, both when it was being built and during its operation. One of my goals in locating the labor sub-camps that surrounded a large camp like Sobibor was to understand what role the locals played in their maintenance. Often, as in the case of Jan, the Polish landowner seated in this photo, it was quid pro quo: The locals were asked to help Nazis and others to service the camp, and in exchange, the camp provided workers to work the land of local farmers to provide food.

Another of my goals was to learn what the locals in the greater Sobibor area actually knew about the Holocaust, and when they knew it. This second goal was facilitated by a local non-Jewish farmer who came forward and provided information about his own site and that of Sobibor. I had known that locals were pressed into service to make the operation at Sobibor work, but I learned that Sobibor also provided workers in a labor unit to work in the local area of Luta. Thanks to the chief rabbi of Poland, and my translator, Lukasz Biedka, a psychiatrist from Warsaw, I was able to make an appointment to visit with Jan, a local farmer who wanted to tell his own Sobibor story.

Luta is a small town fifteen miles outside of Sobibor. Jan had seen the labor units from Sobibor working in his family's fields by the Bug River, and he had also seen the laborers killed in the field nearby after the rebellion. He knew what was happening, and like many, he remembered it all. When I decided to bring my equipment to work in the Sobibor camp, I was asked to do a few different tasks, one of which was to survey the field in back of Jan's home. He recounted what happened to the labor units that were killed after the escape from the main camp. His land had become a killing field for the Germans after the rebellion at Sobibor, and for sixty years he did not speak about it.

Jan is not Jewish, and when I met him a decade ago, he was in his eighties. He was happy to tell me the story of his life and what he knew about the inner workings of Sobibor. He wanted to tell his story because of a young girl he had met before the war. She was a Jewish child he had known in school, and largely constituted his memory of the Jews who had lived side by side with other Poles in this region. He had a soft place in his heart for this girl, and knew she had been taken away.

Jan was a young man in 1942–1943, but he had a horse and cart. Carts like the one Jan described were used at the camp mostly to bring the weak and the infirm directly to the gas chambers, especially in the early months of the camp's existence. (There was probably some form of a light-gauge rail system built to handle delivery more efficiently, but it is unlikely that this was operational in the earliest period.) Jan was told to bring his horse and cart to the Sobibor camp in 1942. He says that he did not know exactly why he was being pressed into service, but he was a teenager, and fearful of what might happen to him if he did not listen to the Nazis and their collaborators. When he arrived at the camp, he says that he was overwhelmed by the smell of burning bodies. He fell from his cart, and when he awoke, he was alone. This profoundly unnerving experience was seared into his memory. He expressed regret that he did nothing at the time to stop the carnage taking place within his own area.

HOLOCAUST ARCHAEOLOGY INCLUDES CITIES NEAR DEATH CAMPS: WLODAWA, POLAND

An important part of my Sobibor project was gathering as much information as I could about the site. I began my work in Poland in the large city of Wlodawa, located about fifteen miles from Sobibor, to determine the relationship between this city and the construction of the camp. I was also interested in seeing the level of Jewish culture and interaction in a town that was so close to Sobibor.

It is estimated that before World War II, more than two-thirds of all businesses in Wlodawa were owned or run by Jews. In fact, Jews made up more than 70 percent of the population (about 7,000 of the 10,000 people in the town). Written records of Jewish settlement in Wlodawa go back to the sixteenth century. Many types of Jewish organizations had branches in town by the end of the nineteenth century. It was a good blend of Polish and Polish-Jewish life, and beginning in the twentieth century, there were secular Jewish groups and religious Jewish groups: Bund, Agudath Israel, and Poalei Zion organizations existed, among many others, and there was a *bet midrash* (study house) and a *bais yaakov* (literally "House of Jacob," which was a school for girls). It was a microcosm of Jewish life in Poland and Lithuania. I came away with a deeper understanding of how much everyone in Wlodawa must have known about Jewish culture, and how most non-Jews in Wlodawa must have known Jews.

I discovered that Wlodawa was on the main train route to Sobibor. I knew that everyone in the city would have seen the trainloads of Jews passing through on the train line, and I wanted to know what was left of the historic presence of the Jews there. The director of the Sobibor Museum, Marek Bem, was responsible for the restoration of the synagogue and study house located in the middle of the city. Marek was very proud of the synagogue's restoration. Visiting the meticulously reconstructed synagogue of Wlodawa in 2008 was almost eerie in comparison with the empty forest site or Sobibor. It had not been destroyed during the war because it was an example of excellent architecture, and was well built. The moment I arrived in Wlodawa, I knew I had been transported back to a pre–World War II era. Little had changed—except for the fact that the city had been mostly Jewish before 1939, and now there is a meticulously reconstructed synagogue with no Jews to populate it.

In a strange twist to my interest in Wlodawa, a few years later, as I was finishing my book *Digging through History* in 2011, I met the granddaughter of a Jewish woman who left Wlodawa on the eve of the Holocaust. Her stories provided me with background on the city that added to my own research. She agreed that it was a very Jewish city in the pre-Holocaust era, with a proud past, and it had been changed almost overnight into a non-Jewish city during the Holocaust. The restoration of the Wlodawa synagogue seemed excessive, even by archaeological reconstruction standards, for a city which no longer had any Jews. In my work in Spain I had had a similar insight. Most of the restored areas of the medieval Jewish presence in Spain had taken on local importance, despite the fact that there were no longer any Jews living in those cities. In one of the two different Jewish restaurants I visited in Segovia, Spain, I asked why the Jewish sites had local interest, and the restaurant owner said that it was just their unique touristic theme.

When I visited with the chief rabbi of Poland, Rabbi Michael Schudrich, on the Sabbath before I began work at Sobibor, he told me that to understand the whole story, going to the cities and villages around the death camps was just as important as studying the camps themselves. The Polish sites were restored to attract Polish and non-Polish tourism, but also to educate Poles about their own history. I began to see how problematic it must be for modern-day Poles to view their own history in this way, but it also must be slightly comforting to see Jewish tourists from families connected to Wlodawa coming to visit, in much the same way that modern Spaniards view Jewish tourists coming to see the sites of medieval Jewish remains. For Poles, making sure that the World War II stories of Polish citizens are known and recorded has become a form of national therapy.

WHY TESTIMONIES ARE ONLY PART OF THE STORY

Artifacts found *in situ* (in their original location) are incredibly important, especially when there are testimonies from survivors of the burial pits as to what happened, and photos of the trenches. With written testimonies, these artifacts can make the difference between not understanding a site, and understanding the details of what happened there. They can change the way we "read" the literature and the site. Being able to excavate the site today as opposed to the period immediately after World War II makes Sobibor a Holocaust archaeology laboratory.

When I was working on the so-called *Himmelfahrstrasse* (literally, "the way to heaven," an extremely negative euphemism for the victims' journey from the train tracks of Sobibor to the gas chambers), which I surveyed in 2008, there were hundreds of small objects found along the hundred-foot-long, barbed-wire-enclosed walk. The artifacts were sometimes simple items, like cups and eyeglasses, but I was often stymied by the presence of items I could not easily understand; for example, there were scores of small keys along the path to the gas chambers. They appeared so random and small, and not associated with any other artifact discovered along the walk.

The ability to speak with survivors and listen carefully to their insights made our work more enlightening. Selma Engel-Wijnberg, a Dutch Jewish Holocaust survivor, lived in Connecticut near the University of Hartford, and was willing to share her insights with us personally. She escaped successfully from Sobibor, largely, she said, because of Chaim, who later would become her husband. As I finished the galley proofs for this book in December 2018 she passed at the age of 96. Her obituary was featured all over the world and I feel obligated to acknowledge her contributions to archaeology of the Holocaust. Almost a decade ago when we began the Sobibor work she joined me on stage at an event at the University of Hartford, where we were puzzling over artifacts that had been discovered in the excavations there: many small metal objects that had been discovered along the walk that led from the trains and the processing areas to the gas chambers. The objects were bewildering to us. So many of these similar small metal objects were scattered along the path with no explanations. My encounter with Selma nearly floored me with the simplicity of her explanations: She looked at the photos and immediately told me these were the keys to suitcases the prisoners had come with and left at the terminal. They had locked the suitcases thinking they would come back and get them later, after their "shower." As they got closer to the gas chambers and could see the burning fires behind them, they must have realized there would be no going back to get their things. Their first instinct was to drop or hide the keys. Without the field archaeology, the keys would not have been found. Without the testimonies of the survivors, the reason for the keys being there would not have been known. Archaeologists need these testimonies, and the testimonies need the tools of archaeology.

I spoke with another Sobibor survivor, Thomas "Toivi" Blatt, after I gave a talk on Sobibor in Los Angeles, in 2012. A fiery young man during the rebellion, Blatt gave me a personal tour of the Holocaust museum in Los Angeles, and was very generous with his time. He wanted me to tell him why Sobibor was different from other death camps. At the time I did not know what he meant, but I would soon find out.

It was Blatt who told me about the Sobibor escape tunnel project—a tunnel that was not used, but which I now know was part of the regular Soviet soldier plan to escape. Blatt investigated and wrote about its history in his two books, *Sobibor: The Forgotten Revolt* and *From the Ashes of Sobibor*. It is really thanks to Blatt's personal connection with Sobibor that he was able to gather so much information about the camp. His story of the revolt was immortalized in the television film, *Escape from Sobibor*, which premiered in 1987. His documentation was invaluable for understanding the events and different characters, and has informed the general public about what actually happened on that October day in 1943.

THE LONG VIEW: GETTING A HIGHER PERSPECTIVE WITH GEOSCIENCE

Archaeologists say that getting a "big perspective" on a site is a crucial part of their understanding. According to all of the survivor maps, the killing and burning fields at Sobibor were located in front of what is today the cement enclosure for the ashes. Originally, ashes filled the field, and the first step in the memorialization process was collecting them into an enclosure. A window

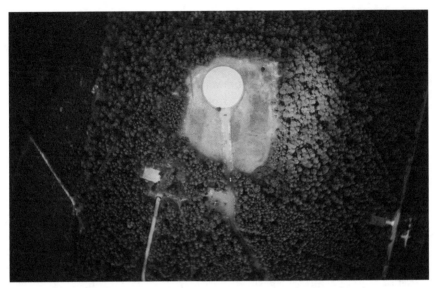

The site of Sobibor's ash heaps inside of a round cement enclosure, taken from a camera attached to a helium balloon. (Courtesy of Paul Bauman, WorleyParsons, Inc., on behalf of the Sobibor Documentation Project at the University of Hartford)

in the front of the enclosure afforded a view of the bones and ashes from cremation. The viewing station was ultimately removed about thirty years ago, and the ashes and bones are now sealed from view.

The "big picture" can encompass understanding a site's use across generations, or it can include learning about a site from many different periods and angles to see how it logistically fits together. In the archaeology of the Holocaust, it is critical to see the site from the moment a victim left the trains to the final conclusion, the burning of the corpses. In the photograph of Sobibor's ash heaps, you see the created memorial walkway which paralleled the so-called *Himmelfahrstrasse*, the footpath which ran from the train tracks, passing by other parts of the camp en route to the area where the gassing took place, to the open area where the bodies were stacked on metal railroad tracks and burned. Holocaust archaeology needs to establish a perspective for both academics and the public to understand the size of a Holocaust site, which, it turns out, could often be quite compact.

Perhaps surprisingly, most of the sites where hundreds of thousands of people were murdered are so small due to the need for efficiency. The mechanism of systematized murder as perpetrated by the Nazis—bringing victims to the death camp in cattle cars, moving them through the processing areas, marching them to the gas chambers, and ultimately hauling the bodies to the incinerators—was more efficient if the distances were short. This compact area also made it possible to plan and execute escapes.

Over the years, I have been confronted by Holocaust deniers who use the case of Sobibor to support their denial. They insist that there is simply not enough room inside the forested area to burn the remains of 250,000 people. In almost every excavation I have performed, aerial photos—taken from cameras attached to drones, kites, or even helium balloons—have revealed an orchestrated movement of prisoners from one side of the camp to the other. It is often impossible to get airplane or helicopter flyover photographs of a site, so using helium weather balloons is one great, inexpensive solution to the vexing problem of getting the big picture when it comes to archaeology.

At Sobibor, I could see the killing fields where the cremation area formed a very clear, defined, non-forested space. Low-altitude aerial photography allowed me to measure the size of the mass burial plots in the open field. The aerial photos show these areas are defined by deeper green hues in the vegetation. This conclusion is supported by coring activities done by previous archaeologists in 2001 (Dr. Andrzej Kola's excavation at Belzec, for example), according to Marek Bem, the director of the Sobibor park and museum. GPR profiles of the site also support this conclusion.

In the field, there is a large cement circle, filled with the ashes collected from the area. This is the most prominent monument at the site. However, not all of the ashes collected were deposited into the circle, only the layers above the ground level. In Lithuania, I encountered a single burial pit that was seventy-two feet in diameter and twelve feet deep, filled with ashes. If I had not used flyover photographs of the Ponar burial pits from 1944, I would never have known they were there. When the UltraGPR collected thousands of readings at an isolated site in the forest of Ponar we realized we had uncovered a new unmarked burial pit. Using this noninvasive device we were able to detect a massive burial pit that we calculated may contained the remains of as many as 8,000 people.

The aerial photographs appear to clearly show the contours of the Sobibor death camp, which can easily be distinguished from the surrounding forest by the subtle change in tree-canopy height and homogeneity. The soil around this area is not able to support vegetation because of the chemical decomposition below. Magnetic gradient data in the open field identified a number of buried metal anomalies which are relatively close to the surface. One anomaly that was particularly large and carefully aligned was identified at the junction of two tentatively identified mass burial plots. According to Marek Bem, this anomaly may indicate the locations of steel rails used in cremating human remains. The *EM38* (an instrument used for geophysical measurement) showed indications of buried metal, close to the surface, to the southwest, south, and southeast of the circular monument. Excavations since then have revealed much of the infrastructure of the death camp around this anomaly.

I knew that I wanted to refute the assertion by Holocaust deniers that this area was too small to have served as the place where 250,000 people were put to death. First of all, the deniers base their estimates of camp size on the small maps made by the survivors, which are not drawn to scale. In reality, if you have the full perspective, you realize there was ample space to house the systematic extermination machine that was Sobibor. The camp took up more than twenty acres, and the areas were all divided into standard quadrants. I knew that aerial photographs would prove this. I did have some photographic comparisons to go on, thanks to random photos that were taken of the camp in the 1940s. A researcher named Alex Bay provided me with photographs from the US Naval Archives, taken in the 1940s, before the camp was covered with heavy forest. (The same archives also provided us with flyover photographs of Ponar, from 1944.) These photos were invaluable, but only because I was able to get the same perspective for my work.

The fact that I was in Poland, on the border with Ukraine, made it more interesting when it came to finding an easy and effective way to obtain aerial photographs. Flyovers with a plane or helicopter would have involved enormous challenges, so I turned to balloons as a solution. Approximately 350 aerial photographs were taken at elevations varying from twenty meters to approximately four hundred meters aboveground, from cameras mounted on the tether of helium-filled balloons. The vast majority were taken with the camera lens looking directly downward, though some shots were taken at oblique angles. All digital photographs were delivered, unedited, to the museum and the archaeological team before my departure from Sobibor.

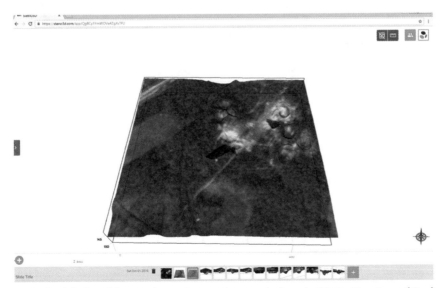

Ponar burial pits with an enhanced area of research done in 2016. (Courtesy of Paul Bauman, WorleyParsons, Inc. on behalf of the Sobibor Documentation Project at the University of Hartford)

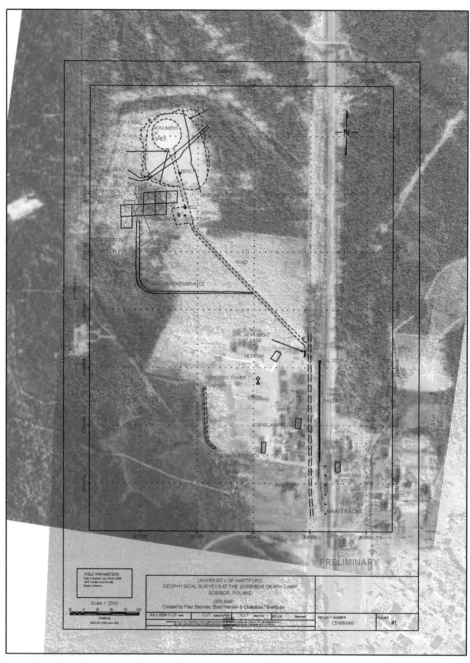

Superimposing the 1940s photograph on my own grids, created during my work at Sobibor. (Courtesy of Paul Bauman, WorleyParsons, Inc., on behalf of the Sobibor Documentation Project at the University of Hartford)

In 1944, the Nazis produced a number of flyover photos of the areas around Vilnius, including the Ponar burial pits. Today, much of the area is surrounded by forest, and a good perspective on the burial pits is not easily accessible, even with lidar technology. The work I did in the Ponar forest not only involved the search for an escape tunnel, but also for the pits that are now in the forest, surrounding the neatly paved areas built for the park. I took the 1944 photos supplied by the US Naval Archives and superimposed my own work onto the historical photos to help direct studies in the field. I used the same method I employed in the Sobibor work in Lithuania, to find additional Ponar burial pits.

This is a metaphor of my work in geoscience and archaeology. The photographs which the Nazis used in 1944 to direct their troop movements now serve as evidence of their crimes against humanity. I use modern techniques of detection on top of old crime scenes, and from this emerges new knowledge. The evidence of the Holocaust is still there, waiting to be uncovered, even three-quarters of a century later.

· 2 ·

Discoveries in the Archaeology of the Holocaust

*W*hat constitutes a discovery in the archaeology of the Holocaust? You may think of great archaeological discoveries as gold and silver coins and artifacts, massive pieces of elaborately decorated architecture, or inscribed pieces, but in the archaeology of the Holocaust, there is a totally different expectation. A discovery here is something that you simply did not know before; often it is just understanding how to do work that has never been adequately done before at sites associated with the Holocaust. In each chapter, I will introduce you to something that either I did not know before, or to the method by which I uncovered a "secret" that I could not easily have discovered before.

The biggest discovery I have made concerns the use of technology in the archaeology of the Holocaust. The technology is not an end in and of itself, but rather a step in the right direction toward future research of the Holocaust. In each case, I have uncovered new evidence that makes it harder to forget what happened at each site. In general, I have one unique presentation of the data which will appear in every chapter. It is the recognition that *All archaeology is about people.* It is based upon two methodological choices: The first is using oral (mostly video or audio recordings of Holocaust survivors and bystanders) and written survivor and bystander testimonies seriously (but not literally) to guide me in the field. I access as many of the records, photographs, and testimonies about a site as I can, and then compare them to one another, looking for clues that will help to pinpoint discernible locations at a site. This information provides a direction in the field for the equipment. I am attempting to do this work while some of the survivors who gave this testimony are still able to provide greater insights to a site. A few years from now, these people will no longer be among the living, and their testimonies alone will have to provide all of the direction for future studies. I need to find

The 2015 geoscience discovery of the Great Synagogue of Vilna under the elementary school. (Left to right) Professor Harry Jol and Nicole Awad. (Courtesy of Richard Freund, the Vilna Excavations Project at the University of Hartford)

out how to use these testimonies to do fieldwork now, while I can still ask questions of the survivors.

What makes this book unique is the combination of testimonies and the background of those who lived in these places—the examination of their lives in comparison to what I am uncovering. It is the affirmation that archaeology is really about people's lives, not just about the artifacts. I include among those people whose lives are significant not just the survivors of the Holocaust, but also the locals living at the sites, as well as my colleagues and students. If I examine the students, the staff, the survivors, or the people I encounter in the field, it is because they are all part of the story. When I highlight a colleague, it is because he or she is part of the archaeology of the Holocaust.

As far as I can calculate, my colleague Dr. Harry Jol has saved me thousands of hours, years of work in the field, and spawned many different projects, all because he was open to investigating how ground-penetrating radar (GPR) could solve different types of archaeological mysteries. Harry is a North American geoscientist working on problems of geomorphology (the study of the changing physical features of the Earth and their relationship to adjacent geology), coastlines, and large bodies of water, using GPR as a guide. When I first worked with him, it was on a Sea of Galilee shoreline problem

I had encountered, and this was a direct continuation of his previous work. Slowly, he became engaged with my work in other parts of the world.

I do not know whether Harry was prepared for the work on geoscience and archaeology of the Holocaust, but he and his students have been invaluable to my projects in Rhodes and Lithuania. He could have chosen to say that these other projects were not of interest, not part of his expertise, or, simply, not the standard research he was interested in. (Over the years I have had biologists, chemists, statisticians, and psychologists turn me down to work in the field. Although I see all of these fields as interrelated in understanding a site, they simply could not see how they could contribute to our research program.) Harry examined how he could add to the questions and information already known at each location. It is his scientific and intellectual curiosity that made him see these projects as worthy successors to his earlier geomorphological work.

What do I see when I look at the photo of Harry and Nicole? I see a geoscience discovery in the making, of the Great Synagogue of Vilna, without having to destroy the elementary school on top. This is what I call "noninvasive archaeology." In each chapter, I will show you a discovery like this. You cannot see this discovery (yet), but Harry and my student Nicole Awad saw it on the tiny display of their computer screen as they passed over it. They saw for the first time the comprehensive view of the remains of the medieval and the premodern Synagogue of Vilna, Lithuania, one of the great religious institutions of the world, a magnificent brick-and-stone edifice which survived for hundreds of years into the mid-twentieth century. It is that moment of discovery, today mostly on computer screens, that recalls what Howard Carter, the Egyptologist, must have felt when he opened the tomb of Tutankhamun. Today, thanks to the use of noninvasive technologies, scientists will be able to make many new discoveries on computer screens, remotely. Only later will they need to find ways to uncover the actual evidence. Someday those future discoveries might be made by someone who is reading this book.

The Great Synagogue I was looking for was destroyed, but not entirely lost. One could say that it was inadvertently hidden. This photo is, for me, the epitome of what I have been doing with geoscience and archaeology for the past twenty years, at more than forty sites. My work is collaborative between universities, various disciplines, private industry, the general public, governments, and ministries, and it involves students at every juncture. Every year I assemble my "Mission Impossible" team; we generally meet at conferences and in the field to review past projects and proposed future projects, and to present our research for others to evaluate. In the photo, Nicole and Harry are doing a GPR survey in front of an elementary school in downtown Vilnius, which is built directly upon the remains of the Great Synagogue and Shulhoyf (the synagogue courtyard) of Vilna. The sign above their heads in the center of the photo reads "Jew Street." The photo gives you the same set of clues that I started with. Here is a mid-twentieth-century brick-and-mortar school built upon a cement foundation by the Soviets, on the edges that remain of the historical "Jew Street." A student and a mentor perform a simple test to see what remains below the surface. As it turns out, it's quite a lot.

I often tell students that I do not choose the archaeological sites where we end up working each year. In a strange way, the sites choose us. I usually have multiple proposals from different countries and various sites (within a country), and I have to vet the possibilities of using our limited time and resources to do one project or another. I attempt to discern what I could do at each one, develop a hypothesis, find in-country colleagues to work with, secure funding and a permit to do the work, and then go to the field to test the hypothesis.

Despite years in the field, I frequently find that when I get to the site and start researching, the hypothesis changes. In this case, back in 2015, I wanted to see the edges of the Great Synagogue. Although it was gutted in 1945, many of the walls were left standing. Today there are no walls. The Soviets, who did not want a resurgence of Jewish (or any other religious) expression, demolished the standing walls, plowed them under, and in their attempt to leave no standing remnant, ended up ironically preserving everything below for posterity. The Lithuanian archaeologists who opened three archaeological squares at the site of the Great Synagogue back in 2011 discovered that there were indeed many artifacts from the Great Synagogue visible in their pits. They could not use traditional archaeological methods, since they had no idea how much of the Great Synagogue still remained. My group is helping to provide a more-comprehensive plan of what is left at the same time as we are excavating to test our observations. The Great Synagogue is now one of the most extensive joint excavation projects associated with Jewish life in Lithuania, and will continue for the foreseeable future.

My University of Hartford research group is slightly different from "for-profit" research groups. This is because once I decide to take on a project, I must commit to a fund-raising, grant-writing track in order to finance the work. Our group does not take salaries, and it shares data with local authorities. I work with local archaeologists and in-country licensing bodies, and I share the research with them from start to finish. I have tried to keep the research an open, collegial exchange in hopes that someone from another discipline can provide a suggestion for future research. One major goal is to involve the students in every aspect of the work, from planning to publication. Students also pay for the privilege of going to the field to do this work.

The study of the Holocaust is not done just for cultural, historical, or religious reasons. I want to mention early on that most of the researchers and students who participate in these field projects are not Jewish; their interest in doing the work is for the sake of research. Students are required to pursue a subproject of the work, and over the years have written on a single find, on a methodological issue, or created illustrations of artifacts. Their work is often incorporated into the lead researchers' final publication. Most students do public and conference presentations, and, for the most part, collaborate with me on my own public presentations. I do this research because I think it will help Holocaust scholars to document in a new way what has been up to now mostly a literary and historical discipline. I see this work as pioneering, not only for Holocaust studies, but for the study of genocides worldwide. I tell students that uncovering the truth about the Holocaust might act as a sort of deterrent to future genocides by continually demonstrating that perpetrators cannot "get away with" their crimes.

CHOOSING GREECE AND LITHUANIA

The reasons for choosing to work on Holocaust-era projects in Rhodes and Vilna are not self-evident. These are two populations that were almost totally wiped out during the Holocaust, their central institutions destroyed. I was admittedly more interested in understanding the buildings and material culture that existed in the pre–World War II era using geoscience and archaeology, but I came to know that understanding the life of Jews in Rhodes and Vilna helped shape the targets that I worked on while in-country. Often, the sites I work on are chosen for me by the local authorities, and I have to decide whether or not to participate. My rule of thumb is to accept when I can add to the body of knowledge on a site; if I think I can, then I do it. In the cases of both Greece and Lithuania, I did not sit down and just decide to go to Rhodes or Vilna. I was invited to look at problems already perceived by the locals and not easily solved with traditional archaeology. When I thought I could use geoscience to solve some of the problems without excavation, that is what I recommended. In the case of some of the sites, excavations were mandated.

It is often individuals who begin the process; many times ideas for projects come from students, community members, faculty, or, in some cases, my neighbors. For example, I was giving a lecture on ancient synagogues in England in 2012, and was asked a question by an audience member, rabbi Albert Ringer of Amsterdam. He had visited Rhodes and noticed an unusual architectural feature in the Kahal Shalom Synagogue in Old Town Rhodes. He wanted to know why there were two arks on the eastern wall, with a door in between that was really out of place. I think he thought I could give him a simple architectural reason for the almost unprecedented configuration, but I could not. The door opened onto a courtyard from which people could walk into the middle of prayer service (and fully interrupt the services by doing so). It did not make any sense. The two arks, one on each side of the door, presented some balance, but even these seemed to belie some unseen purpose. Under normal circumstances, the rabbi would have asked the people of the congregation, but the entire Jewish community of Rhodes was rounded up in July 1944 by the Nazis, and all of the synagogues were either damaged or destroyed. This is a puzzle that might be solved by using tools of the archaeology of the Holocaust.

During the past six years of working on this question, both on- and off-site, I have collected several answers that are included in this book. I have additional answers, thanks to my work on the synagogues of Lithuania. It took years of research, but I know more now about why the synagogue was configured this way than I did in 2012 (without excavating), and I also answered questions about what happened in Rhodes and Vilna during the Holocaust using noninvasive archaeology.

In 2014, I came to Rhodes for a conference commemorating the seventieth anniversary of the roundup of the Jews. On July 23, 1944, the Jews of Rhodes and Kos were rounded up and taken—first, by boat, to Athens, and then, by train, to Auschwitz. At the conference, I spoke about what should be done to understand the earlier iterations of the Kahal Shalom Synagogue (and other synagogues destroyed on the island), and what I thought might be done with the research on the synagogues of Rhodes. The Jewish community of Greece, based in Athens, invited my group to work on the synagogues, and we have been working with the Rhodes administrator, Carmen Cohen, since then. The Ephorate of Antiquities of Rhodes provided permits and supervising archaeologists, and my group came to know the small number of full-time Jewish residents on the island of Rhodes. The true wellspring of knowledge, however, came from the worldwide network of Rhodes's Jews that I met in Buenos Aires, Los Angeles, New York, and various other locations in Africa and Europe while researching what I needed to know about the religious life of the Jews of Rhodes.

In the fall of 2014, I met Dr. Jon Seligman of the Antiquities Authority of Israel at an archaeology conference in Omaha, Nebraska. He asked if my research group might be interested in joining him and his colleagues in an effort to excavate the Great Synagogue of Vilna. In 2015 I found myself in Rhodes and Vilna. Thus was born the initial stages of this book. I try to be mindful of how I can use each site under investigation to teach my students about geoscience, archaeology, and the history of the location. In the case of Rhodes and Vilna, I was able to teach about local and Jewish history, and, ultimately, about how the Holocaust ended two great Jewish civilizations in the course of a few years.

I did not start out to excavate the two great, emblematic synagogues of the Jews in Rhodes and Vilna at the same time, but that is what happened. The Great Synagogue of Rhodes was a significant symbol of Sephardic Jewry, and the Great Synagogue of Vilna was a significant symbol of Ashkenazic Jewry. In the course of three years, I mapped the subsurface of the areas where two of the greatest institutions of the Jewish people stood, and asked the same questions: What happened here? What can be learned from these synagogues about the life of the people in different periods before the Holocaust? And, of course, why is this important?

These two great synagogues of the Jewish people were important places for investigation. Having worked on both sites back to back, I realized that the technology drove the urgency of the task, and not the other way around. I did not know how excavatable the two sites would be, but at least I knew that there were archaeological authorities in both places to help, and Jewish communities worldwide which were interested in the work. The results of excavations always depend upon whether there are actually materials that can be excavated, and whether the local partners want to continue with field excavations after I have left. Also, it is important to see whether there are sponsors interested in funding the work. This is not always a given. Often there are materials to excavate, and the local authorities want to excavate, and just as often there is no interest in excavating after I have finished mapping the subsurface of a site.

I often choose a place in the field that is offered because my group is interested in the historical questions that can be resolved with geoscience; but just as often I choose a place about which we know very little, but would like to learn more. Often I find that local authorities know very little about the proposed site, and they, too, are interested in learning more about what lies buried beneath the surface, without the obligation to do labor-intensive and often-disruptive excavations. Filing our maps with the state—which indicate where things are buried—serves as a deterrent for further development, or at least will guide informed development by the municipality. This is not what a traditional archaeologist is taught to do. The work I do, however, is noninvasive, and therefore not as problematic for archaeological authorities to approve. Local municipalities are more willing to allow this kind of work because they sense that the intention is to ensure that Holocaust victims are not victimized by later development. I have encountered archaeological authorities that are interested in knowing what is in the subsurface, but are not dedicated to long-term and expensive excavations (and reconstruction projects) of the medieval synagogues, ritual baths, Jewish study houses, and cemeteries which have formed the basis of my specific area of research over the past twenty years.

One of the most important insights I have gleaned through my work came from a business owner who allowed us to work inside his shop. When he asked me what I thought of it, I told him it looked quite nice; I added that I did not want to disturb anything, but rather allow him to learn more about his shop. He replied that this was acceptable, and then offered up a revealing piece of advice: "Someday someone will have an even better idea about how to find things, and they will have you to thank for not destroying them when you did your work." I have always remembered this. It keeps us humble in the field.

As a university professor of Judaic studies, I am committed to teaching about Jewish people using archaeology and geoscience for my Jewish and non-Jewish students, in the context of the departments of history and Judaism, but also in the university's multidisciplinary studies program that combines science and the humanities in a study-abroad context. I do think that everything an arts and sciences student can know about the world could be taught through Judaic studies. The Jews were living in their Diaspora for two thousand years or more, and through the lens of Jewish life, a student could come to know many other parts of the world. I also think that while students can learn about this in the classroom, most often today they study outside of it.

Why, you might ask, is the student interaction, study abroad, and field experience so important? To me, it's important to plant a seed for the future of this international perspective on fieldwork with a generation of students not necessarily committed to archaeology and geoscience, but who understand the value of technological innovation in unraveling historical mysteries. I find that it is a way of introducing millennials to a form of critical reasoning that involves technology, discovery, and experiential "hands-on" work; this piques many of their interests and talents, and involves students in a study-abroad "engaged" experience rather than a passive "touristic" experience. This is valuable not only for teaching geoscience and archaeology in and of themselves, but as a vehicle to teach about historical questions that cannot be resolved by literary and historical analysis in a traditional classroom. My colleagues and I have found that the international experience of students working together with local students on a project that involves serious interaction in the field suits this particular generation's learning models in unimagined ways. The written work and presentations that they make upon returning to campus have added immeasurably to the university's intellectual life. If field experience were the only goal, it would be enough to justify the enormous commitment that it takes to mount these expeditions every year.

WHY ARCHAEOLOGY IS ALWAYS ABOUT PEOPLE

I frequently emphasize my mantra—"Archaeology is always about people"—with my students and staff, as well as the local students and staff that I work with in areas associated with the Holocaust. I never want the students to forget that understanding the local population and the people that live—and lived—there is a significant part of the work. It was something that I learned early on in my studies at Bethsaida, Israel, when I interviewed a local Bedouin tribe leader (Talawiyah, "people of the tel") about what local indigenous people said about the site I was excavating. He launched into an unrehearsed, spontaneous, five-minute historical survey that covered almost three thousand years in the life of the site. His short survey included the ancient

Benjamin di Liscia; screenshot of his testimony given on the island of Rhodes, Greece, July 2014. (Courtesy of Richard Freund, the Avzaradel-Capuano Rhodes Excavations Project at the University of Hartford)

Israelites, the Greeks and Romans, the Christians, the Muslims, and ended with his own Bedouin group. His son, the researchers, and, I think, the TV crew which captured his interview, were all shocked to find that in the course of five minutes, this Bedouin leader had told us more about the site than any research study had ever provided. After the interview, the leader's son said, "Dad, you never told me any of this!" The leader then responded, as if to a joke: "You never asked!"

A short clip of the Bedouin leader's comments was included in UNO-TV's public television documentary, *The Lost City of Bethsaida*. It always reminds me of the importance of paying attention to the oral traditions of people from an archaeological site. Even when you are dealing with an ancient site, you should listen for clues from the locals as to what they think happened at one place or another.

One of the reasons I accept the challenge of working at a particular site, beyond being able to contribute scientifically to data collection, is to learn (and teach) something about people at the site. I am concerned with getting people, generally my own students and staff, to the field to work on solving many field-based mysteries using geoscience, but I am always trying to engage with the local population, and history. I want both my people and the locals to understand the history of the local Jews who lived in the place where I am working, and for locals to understand that this history of the Jews is worthy of study by non-Jews from a foreign country. I want them to see their land, its culture, its lives, its languages, as well as their literature, their buildings, and their artifacts as a real part of a living, breathing, larger definition of peoplehood. This can only be done with people who see each discovery of a dig site as a micro history. The coins from the mid-nineteenth century, the tiles on the walls and their decorations, the architecture of a room, the ritual baths and their placement, the column bases, the broken glass and cutlery—everything is part of a daily life that is no more. That, I think, has to be understood as a prerequisite of excavations.

I take photographs of each location from the air and compare them to photographs taken from before and during World War II. I look at architectural drawings of buildings of the area from the nineteenth, or even eighteenth, centuries. I read the literature of the people of an area for clues about who they were and what they saw when they looked at these buildings during their lifetimes.

I have developed two signature methods that I use with my group which are different from many other archaeological groups working on Holocaust projects. First, I start by assembling all of the available oral and written testimonies on the sites, and the historical literature—meaning everything from historical works associated with the origins, use, and reuse of a site, to illustrations, photographs, and maps. I start from the premise that I will take all of these sources seriously, and then I go one step further. My second method involves conducting my own interviews with any living witnesses to what happened there—"survivors," or often, the children of survivors. This kind of interview project means that I have the opportunity to ask simple questions about the life of the people before, during, and after the war. It serves to distinguish the kind of firsthand research of the survivors' memories, but also, what they told their children that often was of a more personal nature. It is an extraordinary asset, fast disappearing, to have access to living, firsthand witnesses of historical events. Archaeology of the Holocaust, like all archaeology, is, at the end of the day, all about people.

In 2014 and 2015, the Maurice Greenberg Center for Judaic Studies at the University of Hartford began conducting interviews with some of the survivors of Rhodes's and Vilna's Holocaust histories, both in the field and in the university studio. It also included the children of survivors. I hoped to gain information about the places and synagogues that was not included in books. One of the most compelling interviews I conducted on the island of Rhodes in 2014 was with Benjamin di Liscia, in an apartment directly adjacent to the Kahal Shalom Synagogue in Rhodes, near where he had lived as a child. Benjamin is a successful businessman who saw everything that happened in Rhodes on the fateful day when the Jews were rounded up, and rarely spoke about it, even to his own family. Mr. di Liscia and his wife Angele were visiting for the seventieth anniversary conference, where I was one of the participants, and he agreed to an interview, even though he emphasized: "I do not think of myself as a Holocaust survivor. I was saved from the terrible events of 1944 by my father, and I thank him and my mother every day for saving me."

His story captivated me, and gave me a sense of how complicated the Holocaust is when it includes the real stories of individuals who lived through it. Beni gave me much new information about the destruction of the synagogues of Rhodes, information that I could not find in any books. (Full disclosure: The di Liscias, and another family member, Benjamin Avzaradel, named the Rhodes project in honor of their ancestral connections in Rhodes and, among others, continue to support the work there.)

My colleague at the University of Hartford, Dr. Avinoam Patt, had earlier begun to gather testimonies from local survivors and their children and grandchildren, which included people from Vilna who now live in Greater Hartford. They form a group in the area called "Voices of Hope," and there is a "Hartford Remembers the Holocaust" permanent exhibition at the Museum of Jewish Civilization at the University of Hartford. The testimonies provided information on Vilna that was invaluable to my on-site research in Vilnius and Kaunas. The testimonies of the survivors and their children, and the research of the sites, reveals what life was like before the Holocaust; without this information, it would be difficult to grasp the scope of what was lost in the Holocaust.

In this book, I begin with the archaeology of the Jewish people in Rhodes and Vilna from its origins, and continue in different periods until the Holocaust, and even after the Holocaust. It is certainly not representative of the entire Holocaust in all countries, or the archaeology of the Holocaust in all of its myriad locations. By the end of the summer of 2018, my work encompassed twenty different sites in three countries (Poland, Greece, and Lithuania). The study of the Holocaust involves much more than these sites, and is made more meaningful when you can appreciate what was lost in these places rather than just mechanically sifting through the destruction of buildings and mass burial sites.

Rhodes and Vilna were unique centers of Jewish culture that were created and developed—and made a major impact—throughout the Jewish and non-Jewish worlds in which they existed for hundreds of years. In the case of Rhodes, the impact of the Jews went back thousands of years; in the case of Vilna, hundreds of years. These Jewish groups were defining religious and cultural traditions in these locations for very different types of Jews, but they both suffered nearly the same fate—near extinction. It is fortuitous that many Jews from Rhodes and Vilna left in the nineteenth and twentieth centuries; in their testimonies, many of them provide details of the life they heard about from their parents and grandparents.

The Jews of Rhodes and the surrounding area called Rhodes *La Chica Jerusalem* ("the little Jerusalem," in Ladino, a Jewish dialect derived from medieval Spanish), and Vilna was called the "Jerusalem of Lithuania" and the "Jerusalem of the North." These two cities were exemplars of two of the richest and most well-known Jewish groups: Sephardic and Ashkenazic Jewries. When researchers write about the Holocaust, they typically refer to the destruction of the Ashkenazic Jews of Europe; they do not generally include in their studies the destruction of Sephardic Jewry. One of the most poignant encounters that I have ever had on this issue came from one of the board members of my own University of Hartford Greenberg Center. The university sponsors an annual Holocaust Teachers' Workshop, and at one of the sessions I invited one of my board members, Mr. Henry Levy, a proud Sephardic Jew, to address the middle and high school teachers gathered for the workshop. Henry was a survivor of Auschwitz, and his story of survival is quite compelling. When he finished, we had a Q and A with the teachers. Usually the questions are about the survivor's details of internment, what they did at the camp, and about the daily life of the victims. In this case, one of the teachers raised his hand and asked, "What is a Sephardic Jew?" It was an important moment for me, as I saw for the first time how focused Holocaust studies had become.

Sephardic Jewry is usually associated with Spanish origins from the early Middle Ages onward, while Ashkenazic Jewry is usually associated with Central and Eastern European origins in the early Middle Ages. The Sephardic and Ashkenazic Jewries share the Jewish calendar, the use of the Hebrew Bible, and the reading of the Torah; they share the vast collection of early rabbinic literature, and have institutions that resemble one another, such as prayer books, synagogues, ritual baths (or *mikvaot*), study houses, and rabbinic authority. The way these manifestations are implemented are not exactly the same, but both are products of the locations where they were born and nurtured. The influences upon both were so dissimilar over such a long period of time that their architecture, clothes, food, and even languages became so different, they are rarely compared.

Both Jewries were destroyed in the space of only a few years during World War II. It is a tragedy, not only for Judaism, but also for the world at large. These two Jewries were repositories of world histories, languages, literature, art, and music; each represented a life that was unique. Though I did not start out to write a book about the cultures of two destroyed Jewries, it came naturally as I spent more and more time in Rhodes and Vilna. The loss of these Jewries matters, and the documentation of the pre-Holocaust and Holocaust era through texts, testimonies, and material culture is what this book is all about.

The idea of being able to compare institutions (buildings) of two major forms of Judaism in both their archaeology and Holocaust-period archaeology is important. Rhodes and Vilna were emblematic Sephardic and Ashkenazic cities, producing some of the greatest thinkers, authors, rabbis, poets, doctors, scientists, and politicians of the time. These cities fostered and developed two major Jewish languages—and cultures—associated with historical Sephardic Jewry and Eastern European Ashkenazic Jewry. Ladino, a Jewish language that emerged among Sephardic Jews, is based upon medieval Spanish. Yiddish, a Jewish language that emerged in Central and Eastern Europe, is based upon medieval German. Both languages are important parts of the life of Rhodes and Vilna in the periods right up until their destruction.

When I look at the cultures of the Jews in these places, often I am looking at multilingual groups that accepted varying amounts of cultural influence from the Greeks and the Lithuanians. When I find a ceramic tile in the bathhouse of the Great Synagogue of Vilna, it may look exactly like the tiles of the non-Jewish bathhouses of Vilnius, but when I find a poem uncovered from the ruins of the Vilna Ghetto, it will be written in Yiddish. By contrast, the remains of the wall dedications of the Kahal Shalom Synagogue of Rhodes will be written in Ladino.

It is important to know the culture of the Jews in each place before the Holocaust in order to understand the loss after the Holocaust. In both Rhodes and Vilna, 95 percent of the Jewries were wiped out in a relatively short period. In the case of Rhodes, what had taken thousands of years to create took less than two weeks to be destroyed. Archaeology can reveal what was lost during the few brief years of the Holocaust (1933–1945; although it can be argued that the devastation of the Holocaust in Rhodes and Vilna actually took place between 1941 and 1944).

WHY WE HAVE MULTIPLE "JERUSALEMS"

"Jerusalem" is the starting point for both Rhodes and Vilna. The fact that the local Jews called these places their "Jerusalem" was indeed a high compliment. It had little to do with the geography of either location. Rhodes is a Greek island in the Mediterranean, and Vilnius is a city in the middle of Lithuania, on flat ground. The physical placement of Jerusalem on a hill in central Israel as the biblical capital of the Israelites from the tenth century BCE onward is only one part of its legacy. It was apparently chosen as the capital in much the same way that many capitals are chosen; it was a compromise—a new city that would be like the Washington, DC, of the Israelites.

In antiquity, the Temple of Solomon, and the later Second Temple, rebuilt by King Herod, sat in Jerusalem's center as one of the largest religious institutions in the world. It was seen not only as a building among many buildings, but the place where the Divine resided. It was for the Jews the "gold standard" for ancient cities, not only because of its beauty, but because of what it represented. The people came on pilgrimage three times a year and offered sacrifices to the Divine. According to the Bible, Jerusalem was originally acquired by King David as his official capital in approximately 1000 BCE, and his son Solomon built the "Holy Temple" that stood at the heart of the city, near the king's palace. The Temple and Jerusalem were attacked and destroyed many times in the next three thousand years. The two most destructive periods were when the Temple was destroyed by the Babylonians in 586 BCE, and again in 70 CE by the Romans. Although a couple of attempts were made to rebuild "Jewish Temple Jerusalem," ultimately it was never rebuilt.

The Jews were exiled from Jerusalem, but they ended up creating mini versions of Jerusalem throughout the Diaspora. The mini versions of the Temple were often elaborate buildings or "synagogues" with decorations that resembled, but did not exactly copy, the ancient Temple. In place of sacrifices there were prayers that remembered the great Temple, and the people continued to search for the same level of cosmic interaction in their synagogues. The highest compliment one could bestow on one of these great cities and their synagogues was to call it a "Jerusalem." Though the Jews continued to pray for the restoration of Temple Judaism in Jerusalem three times a day at statutory prayer services, and at every meal and holiday, in general, their Jerusalem and their Temple were the place where they resided.

Both Rhodes and Vilna achieved this level of recognition as "Jerusalems" not only because of the beauty and unique architecture of their synagogues, but because of the level of religious and creative activity that the Jews achieved in these places. Usually the designation as a "Jerusalem" was meant to indicate a level of Jewish learning and engagement that was unparalleled. There were great rabbis and study houses in Rhodes and Vilna, but the pinnacles of their successes had to do with their unique cultures. Language, poetry, literature, song, food, dance, theater, daily life, and religious life all flourished. The lives of Jewish Rhodes and Vilna are revealed not only in their literary accounts—they are actually written into their material culture.

Although this book is about the uses of geoscience and archaeology in the period of the Holocaust, this is not how my research started out. I began working in the ancient period, and then was drawn to use the technologies and methodologies in researching Holocaust sites because they fulfilled some of the basic needs of Holocaust archaeology. Of the more than forty sites where I and my colleagues have used a combination of geoscience, archaeology, and history together, the oldest dates back to approximately 4000 BCE, while others date to the end of the medieval period (fifteenth century CE) and into the modern period. Most of the sites in Spain and Israel involved caves, cities, villages, synagogues, churches, and mosques that had been destroyed. In many ways, this early work prepared me for the work I am doing in Holocaust archaeology in ways that I never could have anticipated.

A SHORT INTRODUCTION TO THE HOLOCAUST

For the purposes of this book, the Holocaust refers to the period between 1933 and 1945, in which the Jews and other peoples deemed by the Nazis in Germany (and later, in the countries that the Nazis conquered) as undesirables (homosexuals, Roma, and Sinti, as well) were first disenfranchised of their legal and human rights; then dispossessed of all their businesses, trades, property, and assets; later interned in concentration camps and ghettos; and, finally, systematically exterminated in death camps and killing fields in Europe and North Africa.

In the case of many Eastern European countries to the east of Poland, the undesirables were exterminated by what I call the "Holocaust by bullets," where Jews were gunned down at mass killing sites established for that purpose. Some books on the Holocaust include entire chapters and sections on historical anti-Semitism in the nineteenth century as a root cause of the Holocaust; others include the centuries of anti-Judaism which preceded that as a root cause. I recommend that the reader seek out some of the books listed in the bibliography to learn more about these additional elements.[1]

Some historians wonder if, beginning in 1933, the Nazis actually *intended* to exterminate the undesirables and all of the Jews, or whether the Holocaust "just happened." The so-called "intentionalist" scholars,[2] such as Lucy Dawidowicz, for example, saw the idea of the Holocaust as part of a traceable trend that began way before Adolf Hitler's rise to power. The other group of Holocaust scholars tends to see what happened during the Holocaust as either an unexplained aberration that was not necessarily a natural progression of events, or a policy that just "went out of control," but was not really planned *ab initio*.[3] My view of history has taught me to be wary of chains of events that were not necessarily directly connected at the time, but, in retrospect, can be considered a continuous and connected pattern. It is rare to see so many factors line up to cause a single chain of events that causes such devastation. In particular, I have become aware of just how different the Holocaust was in places like Poland, Lithuania, and Greece.

I therefore would classify my own approach to the history of the Holocaust as "intentionalist-functionalist." The individual events and places need to speak for themselves. The events that occurred in Poland and Sobibor in 1942–1943, Rhodes in July 1944, and Vilna—and all over Lithuania—in 1941–1944 are not exactly the same. This does not mean there are not common catalysts or similarities in outcomes, but when studying the overall patterns, one can see that they are sufficiently different to warrant individual assessments. It is common intentionality of purpose, but not detailed intentionality. After viewing the documents for the planning of the Nazi death camps in Poland, and then seeing the work on the ground, for example, I am certain that they represent a clear intentionalist method from start to finish. On the other hand, the killing fields of Eastern Europe represent a functional approach that the Nazis utilized in their shared intentionality. All of this was part of a Nazi "Final Solution of the Jewish Problem" formulated by the Nazis in the early part of the 1940s, but which appears to have sprung from a prior motivation. It is hard not to trace the steps backward and see them as anything but calculated from an earlier period.

Consider the events surrounding the concept of the "Final Solution" doctrine that was "formulated" during a conference held at the large villa on 56–58 Wannsee Street, Berlin, Germany, on January 20, 1942. On this date, *SS-Obergruppenführer* (Senior Group Leader) Reinhard Heydrich, chief of the Reich Main Security Office (RSHA) and Himmler's second-in-command of the SS, convened the Wannsee Conference in Berlin with fifteen top Nazi bureaucrats. Their mission: to coordinate the Final Solution (German: *Endlösung*), in which the Nazis would attempt to exterminate the entire Jewish population of Europe, an estimated eleven million persons.

In fact, the idea of the Final Solution can be traced back much further in Nazi planning, demonstrated by the extermination pits that I investigated in the Ponar forest outside of Vilna. Starting in July 1941, six months before the SS came up with the plan for the death camps, a very systematic and organized mass execution was carried out in Ponar. I call this "Ground Zero" for the Final Solution, since it occurred before the Wannsee Conference, and was so calculated as to require extensive planning. When the Nazis were able to carry out mass executions of large groups of Jews in Lithuania on a daily basis, it was the "tipping point" for the possibility of doing it in German-occupied Poland. On July 31, 1941, Hermann Göring gave written authorization to Reinhard Heydrich to prepare and submit a plan for a "total solution of the Jewish question [read: destruction of the Jews]" in territories under German control, and to coordinate the participation of all involved governmental organizations. This is where the January meeting's agenda for involving all of the different state agencies in the Nazi government of these regions became so important.

Our Lithuanian archaeology of the Holocaust is very different from the Polish and Greek projects because of the different historical circumstances. The events of 1939–1941 in Lithuania were part of a larger Nazi plan to distract the Soviets from entering the war against them. Stalin and Hitler colluded through a secret agreement in August 1939 that created a nonaggression pact: In exchange for nonaggression during the coming war, the Nazis and Soviets divided "spheres of influence" in the areas of Poland, Lithuania, Latvia, Estonia, Finland, and Romania. The so-called "Molotov-Ribbentrop Pact," named for the ministers who created it—Vyacheslav Molotov for the Soviets and Joachim von Ribbentrop for the Nazis—produced an extremely dangerous situation for the Jews in Lithuania. First, they had to deal with the difficult norms of the Soviets (1940), and then with the breaking of the Soviet-Nazi pact, they faced the extreme measures of the Nazis (1941).

The pro-Soviet puppet government established in 1940 in Lithuania was controlled by Vladimir Dekanozov and Justas Paleckis, and a Sovietization program was launched immediately. Land, banks, and large businesses were nationalized. All religious, cultural, and political organizations were abolished during the occupation, which lasted just over a year. The short-lived Soviet regime endured through the early summer of 1941, when the German Army invaded Lithuania, on June 22, 1941, as part of a Nazi strategy known as "Operation Barbarossa." At first, the Lithuanian population considered the Nazis to be their liberators, saving them from Soviet excesses, and they were zealous participants in this new authority that looked like it was going to return Lithuanian sovereignty. The new pro-German Lithuanian government organized a Lithuanian militia, which then became Nazi manpower for rooting out Communist "sympathizers," and created an excuse for the local killing of Jews. The millions of Jews that the Nazis inherited by dislodging the Soviets from these countries in Eastern Europe created a new issue for their advance toward European domination. When the Nazis realized they would be unable to "export" all of the undesirables to another location, nor would they be able to have them killed through more-conventional means (starvation, deprivation, firing squads), they came up with the diabolical Final Solution that included many mass killing centers, whose only purpose was extermination, and later cremation, to make sure there was little or no physical evidence of their crimes.

Studying the Holocaust continues to be about finding and preserving physical evidence of crimes against humanity. One part of the reason why my geoscience and archaeology projects are different is because, almost from the start, I involve the testimonies of survivors. Unfortunately, fewer and fewer survivors remain to bear witness and join us in the field. I am forced to use only their words to direct me, and science must assume the heavy mantle of attempting to make determinations about what actually happened at a site.

AN INTRODUCTION TO THE TEACHING
OF THE HOLOCAUST AND ARCHAEOLOGY

The University of Hartford's Maurice Greenberg Center for Judaic Studies, which I direct and where I teach, has multiple courses on the Holocaust. Many are on the historical background of the Holocaust but also the ethical and theological implications of the Holocaust. We also house the HERO Center, which is devoted to Holocaust Education and Resource Outreach in the general community. The Center also stages major exhibitions in our museum on the Holocaust and holds multiple workshops so that middle and High school teachers can meet and share ideas about teaching the Holocaust. The Center gives area teachers and schools, both public and private, education grants and professional awards for innovative pedagogy of the Holocaust. I have learned a lot about how the Holocaust is taught in public and private schools from these teachers. For example, many schoolchildren are taught about the entire Holocaust through the lens of what happened at Auschwitz, or through the reading of *The Diary of Anne Frank*. Inevitably, with all of the other elements that have to be taught in the English, social studies, and sciences curriculum, it is difficult for these teachers to find a way to add a unit on the Holocaust, but, invariably, when they do, they include Auschwitz (often with an additional suggested reading of Elie Wiesel's *Night*) and *The Diary of Anne Frank*.

This may change in the future. The Connecticut state legislature voted in May 2018 to make Holocaust and genocide education mandatory, but the reality is that training a whole new generation of middle and high school teachers to teach about the complexities of the Holocaust is a long time away. The two elements for the most rudimentary understanding of the Holocaust—Auschwitz and Anne Frank—provide the bookends of the lessons of the Holocaust. They are both totally different facets. The first, Auschwitz (and Birkenau), was a death camp. It is a place that has become synonymous with death. Anne Frank provides the other end of the spectrum: hope.

Anne Frank was named by *Time* magazine as one of the one hundred most influential individuals of the twentieth century, and she will continue to be influential because of the way that her diary—and its stage and screen adaptations—have found a niche in the modern psyche. Why has this young Jewish woman come to symbolize the Holocaust? Is it because she revealed so much about her young life that she gave the general public a window into this horrific time, without the fully graphic details? She is clearly a humanizing element of the Holocaust. Anne Frank tells her story in her own words. Photos of her exist. She is about the same age as the middle and high school students who read her diary, so they can relate to her as a person rather than as an anonymous victim. Anne spent two years hiding in an attic in Amsterdam, from 1942, when she and her family went into hiding, until 1944, when she and her family were finally discovered and sent to Auschwitz. Unlike the stories of killings at Auschwitz, her message is the epitome of hope.

As I think about the work I have done in Poland, Greece, and Lithuania, I see that to understand the extent of the Holocaust, you must have a sense of the real depth of the loss, and the desire to continue to have hope despite the loss. The two are very stark, very clear and specific, and while Auschwitz is an anonymous story, Anne Frank's story contains very personal identities. We need both in understanding the archaeology of the Holocaust. I have tried throughout this book to show how intensely personal the study of the deaths of millions of people can be. I tell students in the field that in the end, the geoscience and archaeology that we are working on is always about people. It is a value that my colleagues and I have shared over the past quarter-century. I come from a humanities background, and they come from a science background, but we have met in the middle.

• 3 •

An Archaeological Discovery "Hidden" in Plain Sight

This book is filled with discoveries. In this chapter, I will introduce the discovery of the technology and methodology that I have used for the past twenty years in the field. I don't mean I will give you a history of the origins of the physics of subsurface imaging. Rather, I will show you what I learned, how I innovated, how I took a technology from physics and geoscience and adapted it to solve a puzzle in archaeology, and how, in the process, I pioneered a way to study the Holocaust that can be repeated in any location. I did none of these things alone, so I will give credit to each of my colleagues who contributed along the way.

The first time I encountered the full power of ground-penetrating radar (GPR) for large-scale archaeological projects in the field was on the northeast shore of the Sea of Galilee. I was working with Dr. Harry Jol of the University of Wisconsin–Eau Claire. Over the years, I had read a lot about how GPR worked, both the drawbacks and the benefits, but Harry Jol was the quintessential educator; not only did he educate me and my archaeology colleagues, but over the past twenty years, he has raised up a whole generation of students. They may not be geoscientists, but they will understand why geoscience can solve problems from many different fields. The question at the northeast shore of the Sea of Galilee was whether GPR could actually identify elements in the field that would normally take years of archaeological excavation to locate. In my case, standing on the plain in front of the Sea of Galilee in northern Israel, GPR showed a negative: There were no buildings, no systematic roads, no infrastructure for living in the plain. The plain was simply a marsh that had dried up; only much later did anyone build there.

I was a latecomer to GPR. It did not originate in the 1990s when I began using it. This technology started with the radar uses of World War

II. The machine blasts FM radio waves into the ground and the reflection that they create against massive materials below the earth indicates to the experienced operator the presence of buildings, burial sites, and other objects (such as hidden coastlines) that could not be discerned from above. It started in earnest in the 1970s, when the beginnings of personal computing allowed for a collection device that had a viewer to track the data in the field. The development of a mobile GPR unit that could be taken to the field with a small computer to guide the operator is just one step in its development.

I was trying to test the hypothesis that the coastline of the Sea of Galilee had changed. I had an idea that ended up saving thousands of hours in the field, hundreds of volunteers, and helped to solve a mystery that had been developing for fifteen hundred years. I also discovered that the technology was only as good as the operator. The technology was not an end in itself; it was a vehicle to a great end, but if and only if it was driven by a staff person who understood what she or he was looking at. Harry's previous ten years of work (which he continues today) was on coastlines and geomorphology (how they change). He did not know that the raging debate over the location of Bethsaida was one of the thorniest in what is called "sacred geography."

(Left to right) Professor Rami Arav, director of the Bethsaida Excavations Project; Professor John F. Shroder of the University of Nebraska at Omaha; and Professor Harry Jol of the University of Wisconsin–Eau Claire, at El Araj, a site on the present coastline of the Sea of Galilee, in the 1990s. (Courtesy of Richard Freund, on behalf of the Bethsaida Excavations Project at the University of Hartford)

This photograph shows how I began with GPR in the middle of the plain which sits just off of the present Sea of Galilee coastline, consisting of two miles of dry ground from the fishing village I was excavating. The photograph reminds me with every viewing how my own thinking developed. Harry, Jack Shroder (chief geologist), Phil Reeder (cartographer), and Dr. Rami Arav (chief archaeologist) of the Bethsaida project all met in the dry plain to determine whether there had ever been human settlement there, and if so, when. Normally, each of these different specialists would be asking different questions. The archaeologist wants to know about architecture and artifacts; the geologist wants to know about soils and rocks; the geoscientist wants to know what is below the surface; and the cartographer wants to put it all on a map. A map is a wonderful bookkeeping tool which records what was found, and where, thereby also serving as a guide for where to go next.

As I stood there, I realized this was the collaborative work that all archaeological projects needed. The week or so of the investigation covered miles of territory that would have simply been impossible to trench, sample, or excavate.[1] Harry finished, and simply said there were no building projects here, nor roads. "This looks like a sedimented plain after some form of catastrophic buildup," he said. "I would assume an earthquake, and the nearby Jordan River provided the sediments." Two different geoscientists coming to similar conclusions without having to destroy the fields or spend years trenching; it was, for me, the discovery of a process that changed forever the way I would approach my work.

It all began with a walk across campus.

In November of 1990, I had an appointment with one of my colleagues at the University of Nebraska at Omaha (UNO). I was a professor in the Department of Philosophy and Religion, and I was meeting with Dr. John (Jack) F. Shroder Jr., then the longtime chair of the Department of Geography and Geology at UNO. We were both professors in the College of Arts and Sciences, and I knew that Jack Shroder was one of the leading geologists in Afghanistan and Pakistan on projects related to the changing environments caused by geological forces. He tracked the caves, rivers, and other features of that region. I was at the same university teaching about the history of the Ancient Near East and Judaism, biblical archaeology, and the religions of the world. We were in the same university, in the same division, and yet we had never spoken.

My appointment with Jack Shroder was to inquire about how to solve a major mystery about the ancient coastline of the Sea of Galilee that affected my work on an archaeological site in Israel. Since he had never worked in Israel, I thought he would be able to give me an objective perspective. I was facing a very expensive, complicated, and labor-intensive phase in the excavation of a site identified as a fishing village by the presence of extensive fishing equipment (including massive stone boat anchors), almost two miles from the Sea of Galilee. My question was simple: "How could the Sea of Galilee have changed so dramatically more than two thousand years ago?" Was there a geoscientific explanation, and, if so, how could I prove it using geoscience methodology without engaging in a costly multiyear excavation of the entire two-mile plain in front of the site?

As I remember it, he regarded me with great skepticism even before I asked my question. He commented at the time that it was rare for someone from "that side of the campus" to have contact with anyone from "his" side (the science buildings were on the other side of the campus), even though we were both in the same College of Arts and Sciences. For non-university insiders, it is not self-evident that people in the same college division will ever talk to one another, attend public lectures in other divisions of the university, or even meet each other, except in rare administrative college meetings. The divide between the arts and the sciences is often so great that there would be little to talk about even if we did get together.

It is, in a sense, the way that compartmentalized, discipline-specialized, modern universities were constructed over the past one hundred years. I cannot imagine how the modern university would have developed if not for departments that grouped like specialties together, but today it creates a divide that often does not allow for interdisciplinary problem-solving. The Department of Geography and Geology at UNO was one of the strongest departments, with undergraduate and graduate programs that were the envy of the rest of the university, and with excellent students. I asked him in my naive way, "Jack, can a whole coastline move?" My untested hypothesis was that the coastline may have shifted over time, leaving the original fishing village now abandoned and isolated on a small hill. What I needed to know from Jack was whether conditions existed for testing the hypothesis of such a shift, and whether he would take up the challenge.

Jack rolled out maps on a long table in the geology lab that included the northeast shore of the Sea of Galilee, where I was working. He gazed at the maps, then gave me a short lecture on geological principles, many of which have stayed with me for the past twenty-eight years. "Things change over time," he said. "For things to have stayed the same in this area for the past two thousand years would be unusual." He states almost these exact words in three television documentaries in which we appeared together, and students to this day repeat those words in my own classes. I always remind them that he said it.

Jack Shroder agreed to send a team of his geologists and students to research the now-dry Bethsaida plain in front of the archaeological tel (mound) where I was working. I should add that the same study area was examined (after Jack and I published our results) by the Geological Survey of Israel, and they came to the same conclusions as Jack (although back in 1990, he was genuinely intrigued by the idea). It was a scientific question in and of itself. He was not as interested in the archaeological questions I was asking, although he was intrigued by the history of the earthquakes in the region, a record of which is preserved in ancient documents, including the Bible. He wanted to answer the "big" geological questions: Did the coastline of the Sea of Galilee change over time? If so, how did it change? What forces were involved? How much did it change, and over how much time? Neither of us wanted to excavate the entire coastal plain. We used geoscience to help answer the questions, but Jack also introduced a new methodology and mantra into my vocabulary. "Geoscience first; archaeology, if necessary, later."

This photo captures a seminal moment of when archaeology and geoscience combined to answer a big question without excavating. I convinced my colleague, Dr. Rami Arav, the chief archaeologist of the Bethsaida Excavations Project since 1987, to participate in the GPR study of the Bethsaida plain. Here, Jack Shroder, Rami Arav, and Harry Jol are setting up a GPR grid at El Araj, in the plain in front of Bethsaida, to see whether there were any structures located below the surface at the present coastline. Jack then did a follow-up to the trenching in the plain, and worked along the nearby Jordan River, which showed the ancient damming and extensive sedimentation pattern following the patterns of the ancient earthquakes.

Jack pronounced the big question "solved" by his research. The fishing village used to be along the ancient coastline of the Sea of Galilee. The site became slowly isolated over the past five thousand years following the regular pattern of earthquakes along the Syrian–African fault that runs right by Bethsaida, causing damming of the Jordan River, sedimentation following the breaking of the dams, uplift, and building out of the shoreline into the Sea of Galilee. We came to these conclusions in a matter of three short seasons of work in the field, with a minimum of staff, expense, and equipment, and all without major invasive (and destructive) excavations. I became a believer![2]

WHAT IS GEOSCIENCE?

Geoscience in this book refers to the use of a variety of techniques used in geology, geophysics, geochemistry, geography, geomorphology, and geographic information systems, among many other subspecialties, used together in the field study of a site. Most important, I use new technologies to evaluate earth science subsurface questions. The use of geoscience to evaluate archaeological sites is usually called *geo-archaeology*, but in this book I will refer to them separately, since the geoscience often became the end goal. The sites under investigation are not all archaeological sites, but they all present multiple strata, and although I may be interested in one stratum in particular—the Holocaust era, for example—I often need to gather as much information as possible about a site, above and below this stratum, as I would in a traditional archaeological site.

Once I identify the multiple periods present at a site—by examining the subsurface—and I determine whether archaeology can, or should, be done, I then generally ask my partners what they would like to do. When I am dealing with a specific historical context, such as the Holocaust or the Roman period, for example, the geoscience will often direct the archaeology. I prefer to think of my work as noninvasive, forensic geoscience in support of archaeology and history, defined by the technologies I use in the field. Traditional archaeo-logical excavations are sometimes recommended to my local hosts, and I will often continue as a consultant, but sometimes I just advocate for marking the site with a distinctive designation so that developers will be cautious—or forbidden to work—at the site. My group works with local archaeological authorities, and I am licensed by national archaeological authorities. The local authorities can determine what the next step should be at any site based upon their own priorities and practices. I may have recommendations, which are generally published or presented at conferences, but in the end, it is the local archaeologists who make the final call on whether to excavate or mark.

I have worked on sensitive sites inside of people's homes, businesses, religious institutions, cemeteries, and even parking lots. Some of these places would not be accessible to traditional archaeologists. For the most part, I am constantly testing new technologies to see whether they can solve more problems noninvasively. For the past twenty-five years, I have used both GPR and electrical resistivity tomography. ERT, quite different from GPR, is a geophysical technique used to image subsurface structures that measures the different resistances of subsurface materials. It can distinguish between stone, bone, metal, ceramic (fired and not), and glass. Gas and oil companies use ERT to identify gas and oil reserves below the surface and determine whether they can get to those reserves. The electricity from an electrical source—we use a car battery—is analyzed by specialized software, but it is collected by electrodes strategically placed in shallow boreholes, providing a very differ-ent form of imaging. GPR uses FM radio waves and ERT uses electricity. A related ERT method, induced polarization (which figures in our Ponar study of the Holocaust Escape Tunnel), has the added advantage of quite clearly

ERT and GPR lines laid out in grids at a mass burial site at Fort VII, one of nine nineteenth-century forts constructed to defend the city of Kaunas, and used as killing fields by the Nazis. Bones uncovered by the Fort VII administration were reburied and marked by a Star of David monument. (Courtesy of Harry Jol, University of Wisconsin–Eau Claire, on behalf of the Vilna Excavations Project at the University of Hartford)

identifying metal in the subsurface; this is because it stores electrical current even after the electricity source has been shut off!

I will briefly introduce the two technologies below, and then explain the different types of geoscience that these two technologies permit me to practice.

GROUND-PENETRATING RADAR (GPR)

I use GPR at a site much the same way a surgeon uses a preliminary X-ray, MRI, or CT scan before major surgery. I want to see what is below the surface before I decide to cut open the patient and root around underground. In the correct sedimentary context, the GPR technique can detail the location, extent, and character of subsurface features or artifacts by providing near-surface, high-resolution, and near-continuous profiles of the site being investigated.

The main issue is the near surface, since the FM radio waves, which are the light by which the GPR device sees, have a maximum penetration depth of twelve feet, and most of the time, less than that. Subsurface profiling with GPR is similar to seismic reflection, except it uses electromagnetic (EM) energy, not acoustic energy. A short pulse of high-frequency EM energy is transmitted into the ground, generating a wave front which moves downward in the soil. Due to a change in the subsurface materials and soils, some of the energy is reflected to the surface. At the surface, a receiver monitors the reflected energy. Fine-grained sediments such as silts and clays, which have high conductivities, cause significant signal attenuation of the radio frequency waves, and reduce the penetration to a few meters or less, while environments of low conductivity, such as sands, gravels, and limestone, allow for greater depth of penetration. Therefore, I have used GPR together with ERT to make sure that, whatever the sediments, I can collect data down to five or six meters (generally, fifteen to eighteen feet).

The idea of mixing two different geoscientific techniques was another innovation that began, originally, as an attempt to solve new and different problems, but also to have complementing sciences confirm one another. The students in the picture are working with GPR and ERT on one of the thorniest problems that I have ever been called upon to assess: mass burials. The ability to identify the actual substances above and below a mass burial site is crucial. I began using ERT to answer the question, since it can identify the different materials below the surface. (ERT is a complement to GPR, not just a way to confirm GPR results. I will discuss it in further detail in the next section.)

I started using GPR in the mid-1990s. Over the past thirty years, GPR has become important within archaeology as a way to locate graves without desecrating them. GPR has been successful in helping to locate shallow graves, tombs, buried walls, and tunnels and other voids, as well as mapping historic-period fortifications, defining the outlines of buried features such as buildings, and providing an immediate image of the site stratigraphy. Today, combining GPS mapping and GPR, archaeologists can prioritize excavation for "salvage" or "rescue," rather than just long-term excavation work.

Harry Jol of the University of Wisconsin–Eau Claire has operated the GPR device. He has also created a classroom in the field that has allowed scores of students to learn to collect GPR data. Students take notes on the work, do calculations, and illustrate and photograph locations. Ultimately, the scans that are processed become the daily discussion piece. Collecting GPR data is at least a two-person exercise, which makes it one of the best teaching tools that you can find. The GPR machine itself looks like a lawn mower, which is, in reality, shooting FM radio waves into the ground, then collecting the reflections, sending the information via fiber optics to the mini laptop, the brains of the device. The device is rolled in an ox-plow fashion along an imaginary grid superimposed on the site. One student can "mow" the site with the device while another controls the settings from the laptop. A faculty member can take notes on the settings or size of the grid, evaluate the data as it is collected, photograph the operation, or generally ensure the quality of the operation. The geoscientist must ensure that all of the pieces are functioning. Teaching students to troubleshoot in the field is one of the great lessons of the work, along with learning to create a data-gathering journal.

Harry's device (there are much newer and fancier devices, but his has its own advantages) was a field-portable, digital pulseEKKO 100 and 1000 GPR system. Harry and I have employed it for almost all of our projects since the late 1990s. It has the advantage of being lightweight and stable, but does have the disadvantage of needing a flat surface to map. While all of the raw data is collected right there, it is not as meaningful as the processed data. Today, Harry and I work with the Los Angeles–based GPR-SLICE, Dr. Dean Goodman's company, which takes our GPR data and processes it overnight. By the next morning, we have a clear sense of what we worked on the day before. This immediacy adds to operational expense, but I believe having a professionally processed data set the next day is crucial to making my work effective, all without excavating. If I decide to excavate, GPR-SLICE software can create 3-D models of the subsurface to tell me exactly where to dig.

Needing a flat surface has proven to be a major hurdle for my GPR work in some locations. In 2016, I used a so-called UltraGPR that is both flexible and lightweight, and enabled me to go into areas and up sides of walls that would simply have been impossible with more devices that have fixed and inflexible bases like the standard GPR. The basic GPR unit is one I have used for almost all of my work from 2008 through 2017, with small upgrades and different antennae. Harry's pulseEKKO GPR unit is a tool that lets archaeologists and geophysicists explore the subsurface without disturbing the land; no electrodes are needed, as is the case with ERT.

When searching for the parameters of archaeological sites, structures, and large anomalies, it is most effective in cemeteries that have been destroyed, individual graves that are not located in cemeteries, and mass burial sites. Based on data that is found from these results, GPS locations on sites can be pinpointed by the cartographer, and future investigations around an area of a building or a burial can be planned appropriately. This can save money, time, and manpower in modern archaeological digs, but, more important for my work in Holocaust sites, it can stop random desecrations at burial sites and ensure that any excavation at a grave with a significant find can proceed without disturbing the grave itself. Before GPR, archaeologists would excavate with little knowledge of what they might find under the surface. They had to dig first, and ask questions later.

A subsurface map can guide an excavation before digging actually begins. It can continue to guide the excavation well after commencement, as the anomalies on the map become physical objects in the ground. The GPR creates a form of stratigraphy that is helpful for archaeological work by building a 2-D and 3-D map of the subsurface. It gives me an accurate spatial picture of the area. After each day in the field, I receive processed data sets from GPR-SLICE that will direct the follow-up work I do the next day. The revolutionary aspect of the way my research team works is that there are scientists assisting us in different parts of the world during my fieldwork.

The GPR system first sends radio waves through the ground; then the reflections are transmitted via cables to the computer, which finally gives the operator an idea of what is going on below the surface. It is really an "echo" that is received at the computer from the transmission of these radio waves. It will build an image of the soil underneath, which contains patterns that are the result of what are usually natural events, or more-complex patterns that suggest a man-made structure may be present. My university does not have geoscientists, nor do we have this kind of equipment. This is why a collaborative model of research is so important. My students would never have the opportunity to learn about these geoscientific technologies if they did not go to the field and learn it with different teams and faculty. One of the most important things that the students have learned from working with Harry Jol is that generally, only humans make designs that have right angles. Nature does not generally create precise right angles, as humans do, so when I see these anomalies, I know that I have found a man-made configuration.

I typically study the historical maps and photographs of a site. When I work on that site the GPR can indicate the remains of a building, burial, structure, or installation that has absolutely no presence on the surface. Of course, it is not the technology alone that tells me what I want to know. The skills and experience of the scientist are vital to making the GPR reveal what lies unseen beneath my feet. In the twenty-five years that I have worked with Professor Jol on different sites around the world, I have learned that interpreting the GPR stratigraphy requires the depth of experience he has in the field, searching for buildings and burials. The GPR read-out can indicate past structures, even if they are no longer present, but only an experienced GPR technician can tell the difference between a large and a small building and a small burial and a mass grave. Every structure leaves a mark in the soil, and GPR allows archaeologists to determine where there may have been some sort of man-made structure in the past, indicating the depth at which it is located. Often when excavating a site, these telltale signs in the soil will not be perceptible, and thus, will be lost. GPR records this data in a computer so geophysicists and archaeologists can study the site even after leaving, and plan future work based upon information that has not yet been explored.

The radio waves produced by GPR are completely harmless to the environment, and it is the only effective and economical way in modern archaeology to perform a completely noninvasive sweep of an area to discover a foundation or structure underground. From these GPR scans, a 3-D (animated) map of the area can be created, which gives archaeologists a 360-degree view of anomalies in the subsurface.

ELECTRICAL RESISTIVITY TOMOGRAPHY (ERT)

Much like GPR, electrical resistivity tomography is another X-ray/MRI/CT scan type of device that creates an image of what lies below the surface. Instead of FM radio waves, however, ERT uses an electrical charge in the soil to determine what lies below. ERT is a surface geo-electrical technique for mapping the materials below the surface based upon their "resistance" or reaction to an electrical charge that is sent into the ground through an array of electrodes on the surface. The metal spikes or electrodes are usually pounded into the topsoil, connected with cables, and charged with a battery so that an electrical current flows through the array. In some cases, it is not necessary to plant the electrodes underground. For example, when working on the delicate floor in the Church of the Annunciation in Nazareth, the geophysicists used a conductive gel and metal mediator of the electricity (aluminum foil), and were able to achieve results without destroying the ancient marble.

Data are collected through a linear array of electrodes coupled to a DC source (we usually use a car battery), a resistivity transmitter/receiver, and an electronic switching box. The software of the data collection system on the laptop computers provide almost seamless processing of the work on the spot. WorleyParsons and the Advisian line also have a variety of data-processing people back in Calgary who provide another layer of processing in their lab.

The collection process is driven by a laptop computer that is also used for data recording, and the software can interpret the data to create an image that is meaningful both to the geophysicist and the public. In my work at Fort VII in Kaunas, I was able to trace the mass burial sites from the monument to the outer wall. The mass burials at the monument are only a few centimeters below the surface, while the burials near the outer wall are several meters belowground. According to the director of Fort VII, the materials on top of the mass burials by the outer wall came from trash that was placed there over the decades. Now with ERT studies, I can confirm and document the locations so no future development will desecrate the graves.

My team has worked in some of the most extreme conditions around the world. While GPR cannot function in the rain, or with extreme construction going on around the site of investigation, neither rain nor some types of construction affect ERT work; in fact, rain can actually enhance the electrical conductivity in the ground. Even with just a trace of soil moisture, ERT produces results, and I often bring water to the electrodes to enhance the signal. Even in places such as the Dead Sea Cave of Letters, or Qumran, for example, some of the driest places on Earth, the ERT surveys have been effective. In a place like Eastern Europe, especially in open areas, there is high soil moisture, which makes the work much easier.

The history of the physics of the ERT design goes back a century, but it has been the rapid development of technology in the past forty years that has allowed the field to develop. Once, calculations were done by hand with slide rules; today, calculations are computerized. All of this was made possible by the development of the portable switch box and laptop computer in the 1970s and 1980s.

My original connections with KOMEX, a company that became part of WorleyParsons, involved private industry gas and oil geophysicists who were encouraged to participate in my archaeological and historical projects, as part of their "public service" commitment. It was a huge advantage for my research group, since it is rare for a university to invest in technology such as ERT for researchers, let alone continue to update it. Paul Bauman has been my chief geophysicist since the late 1990s, and he introduced his colleagues from KOMEX, WorleyParsons, and now Advisian (another division of WorleyParsons), to my sites, and my work. For almost fifty years, the gas and oil industry has used noninvasive technologies to determine the presence of oil, gas, or precious metals below the surface before investing in the "excavating" to retrieve these natural resources.

The main difference between the technologies of GPR and ERT was developed as part of the "retrieval" process of the gas and oil industry. The industry wanted to systematize what had been a seemingly random selection process for drilling sites that often resulted in aborted efforts, as the drilling team was faced with materials below the surface that inhibited drilling, or the gas and oil available below the surface did not justify the investment for retrieval. The main advance in the past thirty years has been the ability to computerize the entire process of ERT. The ability to model the electrical responses, and to create a subsurface map of the data, has revolutionized the field. Now the captured data produces a rapid and reliable picture which can plot the "true" resistance and "true" depth of the natural resources in a matter of hours. For archaeology, this means that strata can be determined for excavation while the rest is left untouched.

One big development in the past decade has been so-called "induced polarity," which allows the technology to shut down the current, leaving the electrical charge in the ground, but only with certain "artifacts" that retain the electrical charge, such as metals. While the present version of ERT cannot give the type of vertical resolution that GPR enjoys, it can help direct an excavation because of the depth of the charge, which can reach 120 feet! I have committed most of my work to GPR and ERT, when possible. I have enjoyed working with the same experienced operators and staff for the past twenty-five years. I have tried "one-shot" operators with similar equipment, but have not enjoyed the same results. It is really about the experienced operators who work the equipment, compare the results, and solve problems in the field.

Professor Philip Reeder provided the maps for this book. The resolution and the materials can be precisely and confidently identified in the subsurface by creating a GPR grid on top of an ERT scan. The combination of the two technologies reveals much more information than a single technology could, alone.

GEOSCIENCE FOR THE SAKE OF GEOSCIENCE

Sometimes, I do research just to see whether the application has any use. Sometimes it is a hypothesis, but sometimes it is the moment of discovery. When I was asked back in 1997 why I wanted to bring all of the geoscience equipment into the Cave of Letters, I answered that it was to see whether or not it worked in a limestone cave. Other groups had brought heavy excavation equipment into this very-difficult-to-get-to cave. One group brought a jackhammer to clear out all of the roof fall and nearly asphyxiated everyone working in the cave. Others just haphazardly visited to see what they could see. My project was to see whether cave research in general would be aided by GPR, ERT, and fiber-optic cameras that could see below the roof fall. Most of the discoveries that had been made in the Dead Sea caves were made right at the surface, usually in corners or overhangs, where the materials were protected. My theory was simple: There were probably many more finds to be made in the thousands of caves along the fifty miles of the Dead Sea. The problem was how to identify them below the surface, and excavate the huge roof fall on top only in those areas where the geoscience identified something of interest. (The roof fall is thousands of pounds of limestone that has fallen after every shake in this earthquake-prone area.) I was told by good scientists that using GPR and ERT in these caves was impossible. They were wrong. The research revealed that these technologies were, in fact, quite effective. In a series of presentations and three books, I have demonstrated that this type of "geoscience for the sake of geoscience" allows for important discoveries.[3]

Some research is purely for the sake of research. When I did an X-ray fluorescence (XRF) analysis of more than two hundred pieces of pottery in the port of Rhodes, I was trying to establish a provenance for the pottery. XRF could identify the chemicals in each piece of pottery, and since I had pottery from different places, I could compare them and figure out where all of the unknown pieces came from, without destroying the pottery itself. A generation ago, I would have had to destroy a piece of the pottery in order to do an analysis. Today, I can evaluate noninvasively, and discover who was bringing what to Rhodes during a very specific time period.

My most significant early attempt to see how geoscience can be used for the sake of geoscience yielded a large amount of data, again without excavating. I was able to locate and record the depth and orientation of the 1,213 graves at Qumran on the Dead Sea.[4] This work led me to conclude that multiple generations of pilgrims and visitors used an easy-access cemetery for a variety of their needs. The various depths of the graves at the site, and their orientation, showed that different groups used the cemetery. It helped me to understand how graves in antiquity were built, and what might be inside a grave. It was geoscience in the service of geoscience, a tool to identify graves without having to excavate them. I would later use these technologies in other countries, especially in Holocaust archaeology.

The early 1990s research on the Sea of Galilee is what I classify as "geoscience for the sake of geoscience." From that initial conversation with Professor Shroder, I was introduced to a whole world of subspecialties that are rarely talked about in the world of archaeology or history, but which nevertheless significantly inform those fields. I came to know hydrologists, geomorphologists (coastline specialists), geographers and cartographers (who mapped the changing environments). I came to know cave and tunnel specialists, mountain and jungle experts, geochemists and geobiologists (who analyzed vegetation, soil, and rock), and GPR geoscientists and geophysicists.

I began to ask, Can I solve a purely geoscientific question that contributes to the archaeological question? I have discovered that my work was efficient, objective, economical, scientifically meaningful, and often an end in itself. The technology I used solved many different puzzles beyond that presented by the fishing village I was excavating two kilometers from the Sea of Galilee. It showed that the Sea of Galilee, the largest freshwater lake in the region, was shrinking because of geological forces that continued to exist. That was as important as the insights it gave to the archaeological question. I call this approach "geoscience for the sake of geoscience and archaeology." For Jack Shroder, the question was how the coastline changed, and why. It is a good earth science question; it has no purpose other than determining whether a principle of geoscience is at play in this location. I took his results and continued to work on the isolated and abandoned fishing site (Bethsaida), knowing that it had shifted because of geological forces that were understood and could be explained. The thousands of fishing artifacts that I discovered at Bethsaida, the houses that contained fishing-net lead weights, even a storage facility—all built on a mound that today sits two kilometers from the water, but in antiquity was right on a larger Sea of Galilee—everything was explained.

It was all hiding in plain sight.

GEOSCIENCE FOR MAPPING AND MARKING

Some of my Holocaust-era map projects have been meant to determine the specific location of human remains, marking them to prevent excavation or development (which would lead to desecration of graves). Certainly, that was the motivation when working with mass burial sites. The maps I produced in the Ponar forest outside of Vilnius, and the geoscience maps which I produced in the Kaunas area at Forts VII, IX, and the Jewish Cemetery of Kaunas, were all intended to mark a "no development zone" for the local municipality.

Other sites have already been disturbed. Just because the top layer has been destroyed does not mean that the area is no longer worthy of mapping. At some sites there is no local interest in traditional excavation, while at others there is considerable local interest. Sometimes, this interest may change, and a map will preserve information that might be significant later, when local interest is piqued. Of course, sometimes the map is the end goal. I know that my maps will not always be used for excavation or for marking the site on the surface, but I hope that at Holocaust sites, they ultimately will.

The good and the bad news about the "ghettoization" of the Jews is that their institutions are generally located in the same location for hundreds of years. This means that although the most recent building may have been destroyed, its location may preserve earlier iterations of Jewish institutions below it. Many sites in Europe and elsewhere—where Jewish institutions were originally located, but then destroyed during the Holocaust—may still hide an earlier destroyed institution of historical significance. In Rhodes, for example, my maps showed multiple layers of synagogues that had systematically been destroyed and reconstructed in the same location for hundreds of years. In this case, the mapping preserves the layers of features below for future excavations. Finding an "anomaly" means that further examination is necessary. It can be a wall, an artifact, a full layer, or just an area that does not fit the subsurface area around it. In a grave, an anomaly may mean that there is something buried with the individual that is worthy of a pinpoint excavation. I do not want to disturb the dead, but I do want to make sure that someone will not go looking for treasure there.

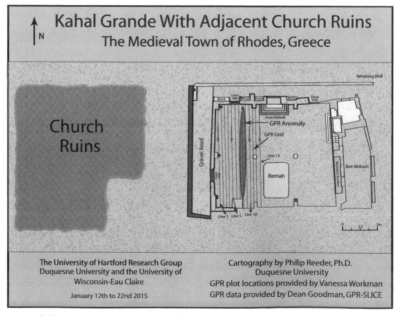

Map of the Great Synagogue of Rhodes with the GPR references indicating "anomalies," or, more probably, earlier substructures. (Courtesy of the Avzaradel-Capuano Rhodes Excavations Project at the University of Hartford)

The map is the guide, and often a geoscience, subsurface map of a synagogue will reveal an earlier level that, although destroyed, might still contain historically significant artifacts or data. A map like the one in the figure of the Kahal Grande in Rhodes also tells me about a lost social and religious history that needs to be more fully investigated. For example, when I compared the depth of the nearby church ruins with the GPR anomaly showing an earlier structure below the synagogue, I had possibly discovered that a Rhodes church and synagogue were located side by side in the fifteenth century. While it is impossible to know exactly what the relations between Jews and Christians were in the fifteenth century, the proximity of these structures is certainly suggestive of a positive relationship. Although one would not expect to gain information like this from geoscience, it often becomes crucial to the evaluation of the life of a site.

WHEN A MAP IS MORE THAN JUST A MAP: MOVING FROM A SITE TO TESTIMONY AND BACK AGAIN

The map created at the Star of David monument at Fort VII is a shared document for the local authorities and for the Jewish community of Lithuania, which was intensely interested in the size of the mass burial at Fort VII, and, more specifically, the exact location of the burials. The map was produced by geophysicists Paul Bauman and Alastair McClymont in the summer of 2017, and the result of many months of negotiations and discussions in Lithuania. Alastair McClymont had accompanied me for meetings in October 2016 in Kaunas, to discuss the site(s) we thought we could map in July 2017, with one or two days at each site. Fort VII was a particularly thorny issue for all concerned because, during a development project, a mass burial had been uncovered near the surface (and a monument or better burial marker was placed on the location). It showed just how important my type of work was for the area. The Fort VII area is now a museum, and its area has been subject to new projects that will continue to develop in the future. Mapping and marking the burial sites without disturbing them is an excellent use of the noninvasive combination of GPR and ERT. Lithuania is undergoing economic development at a very impressive pace, and the existence of many of these mass burials needs to be identified, so that they do not disappear under modern construction projects.

The events of 1941 at Fort VII are chronicled by different sources and testimonies, and this site holds a particular interest for me. Kaunas was one of the former capitals of Lithuania, and it was in Soviet hands in 1940. Jews have resided there since the sixteenth century. After the Nazis came there in

1941, the pace of the developing Holocaust in Lithuania increased quickly. By July of 1941, Jews were being dragged off to be killed at a series of enclosed structures, premodern forts which had been built in the nineteenth century to protect the city. Forts IV, VII, and IX were my projects in 2017, but Fort VII was different.

A personal testimony led me to this particular archaeological project.

WHY ARCHAEOLOGY IS REALLY ABOUT PEOPLE: FROM TESTIMONY TO ARCHAEOLOGY

When I was about to begin my work in Lithuania, I spoke to one of my neighbors in Connecticut for advice. I knew Florence (Newman) Post and her husband Philip from my local synagogue, and I had heard that she was a "hidden child" during the Holocaust. She was both articulate and had an excellent memory. After the war she and her family were reunited, and her father's story was about the Fort VII killings. She was responsible for naming the farmers who saved her as "Righteous Among the Nations," a category that recognizes the commitment and risk that non-Jews exercised during the war to ensure that a Jew would survive. I wanted her to take me to the farm, to help me speak to the children of those who saved her. She was skeptical at first. She wanted to see whether I could help her better understand the events surrounding the near death of her father, Itzhak. The more she told me about her father's experience at Fort VII, the more I understood that she was repeating important information about his escape, and that my work would involve Fort VII.

As I began my research, I came across Alex Faitelson's *The Truth and Nothing But the Truth: Jewish Resistance in Lithuania* (Jerusalem: Gefen, 2006, 91–94), in which there was a chapter entitled "The Fate of Itzhak Nemenchik." This short chapter made a huge impact on me. I was surprised as I read about his story, because it provided details that no other survivor testimony had. It was about what happened to him at Fort VII, and identified elements that I began to realize were unique. I had read other books and articles about the Fort VII site, but Florence's testimony provided a direct and personal connection unlike any I could find in other sources. She had had the opportunity to speak with her father before his death, and had made the story of being a "hidden child," and the story of her father's escaping the killing at Fort VII, a part of her own narrative.

I went to visit the site in the fall of 2016 with geophysicist Alastair McClymont to confirm that conditions would be favorable for the use of ERT and GPR. He and I spent the day with the director of what is now the

Photo taken in Bad Wörishofen, Germany, in a displaced persons camp, 1948. (Top row) Itzhak (Isaac) Nemenchik (Irving Newman). (Middle row) Fira Nemenchik (Florence Newman; married name, Post) and Dr. Lisa Nemenchik (Lea Newman). (Bottom row, left to right) Boris Nemenchik (William Newman); Ilana Ludwinovsky (Lana Newman), niece and adopted daughter. Itzhak survived the Fort VII, 1941, massacre, came home, and later placed his daughter Florence with non-Jewish farmers in central Lithuania. (Courtesy of the Post Family)

Fort VII museum. For Florence, Fort VII was a particularly grotesque place. Her father Itzhak had been taken there to be killed in the early months of the Holocaust in Kaunas. Thousands of Jews were murdered along the wall of Fort VII in a short period of time in 1941 (the wall is marked on the map on page 68). Thankfully, her father escaped Fort VII and returned to his family in the Kovno Ghetto. Nevertheless, Itzhak's testimony about what happened in the fort is still one of the most exacting descriptions of what I call the "Holocaust by bullets." I have listened to survivors speak about their parents, and I have discovered that although it is not "history," when a child repeats the story of a parent's escape, it is a form of historical memory that often preserves details that are not found in the official testimony of the older survivor. This Holocaust is not just the Holocaust of anonymous victims and survivors, or anonymous perpetrators that cannot be identified by their neighbors. The experience of listening to the testimony of a second generation, or child of a survivor, often provides insight which cannot be obtained any other way.

In the case of Itzhak, his story recalls the specific location of where gunmen stood on the hill above the wall where the Fort VII victims were shot. As I looked at the wall that I included in my geoscience survey, I could still see the bullet holes. The story of the Holocaust in Lithuania is not about anonymous people who pushed buttons in large death camps with gas chambers, but rather about neighbors shooting neighbors under the watchful eye of the Nazis, in smaller places like the forts around Kaunas. This experience is called to mind by the photograph of Florence's blended family, which includes Florence's cousins, who were adopted by William and Lea Newman into their new identities in the United States. To be able to uncover all of this information is a detective story within a detective story. These people left behind their names and their experiences in Europe to begin again in the United States—in this case, in Waterbury, Connecticut, where Florence graduated high school, became a teacher, and taught a generation of students.

Itzhak Nemenchik, Florence's father, survived the murder at Fort VII by hiding in the clefts in the walls of the dug burial pits, then escaping to the rambling hills surrounding the fort. He came home to his family and devised a plan that ultimately saved their lives during the Holocaust of 1941–1944 in Lithuania. He sent his children to be "hidden" with non-Jewish farmers far from Kaunas (these farmers were later awarded certificates as "Righteous Among the Nations" by Yad Vashem in Jerusalem in 2005), while the rest of the family hid elsewhere. Florence was only a young child at the time, and the trauma of having to leave her family, and to worry daily about whether she would be discovered and turned in to the authorities, made her life difficult. I have heard Florence tell students about these events, so deeply seared into her memory; she had the power to engage them. Florence (Newman) Post's entire testimony is archived at the University of Hartford's Museum of Jewish Civilization.

When I sat with Florence in West Hartford, she told me the details of what her father saw at Fort VII, and that she had always been haunted by this site. The events at Fort VII also haunted the Jewish community of Lithuania, and they were able to collaborate with the local municipality to arrange for me to do a proper mapping of the mass burial site at the fort in the summer of 2017. Thankfully, the local authorities, together with the museum of Fort VII, are working to make sure that this spot is properly marked, and that no development will take place there.

I was able to return to West Hartford in August 2017 and tell Florence personally what I had done. I feel that this provided a measure of closure for her, to know that the killing site where her father's life almost ended had been found. She expressed a measure of satisfaction, and I promised to get her a copy of the map. Sadly, Florence passed away in November 2017, never having seen the map. It was one of the many maps I produced of the site in my report to the government. When I look at this map I see the mass burial site of those who died, but I also see Itzhak Nemenchik, who lived. This is the moment when a map becomes something more than just a chart of a location; it is also the recognition of where a crime happened, which will not be easily forgotten.

GEOSCIENCE FOR MAPPING EXCAVATIONS

One of my geoscience innovations is to create a multilayered site map that contains every technological discovery layer and every anomaly that was encountered. This is one of often dozens of maps that are produced during a project. The first step is a GPR scan, followed by excavations, and then additional GPR and ERT scans, and then more excavations. Such a map is one of the great advantages of this system, but it requires that all of the collaborators agree to the different steps. Prioritizing the work on a map makes it much easier to think about what I will be doing from year to year.

I covered the site of the Great Synagogue excavations so the school atop the site could be used during the intervening months. This type of planning (mapping) is not the norm. It is time-consuming, but far less destructive than the traditional archaeological method. I did not know in many of the cases whether the entire site, or even part of the site that was digitally mapped (by multiple sources), would be excavated. The original work which I had done with Dr. Shroder at the University of Nebraska at

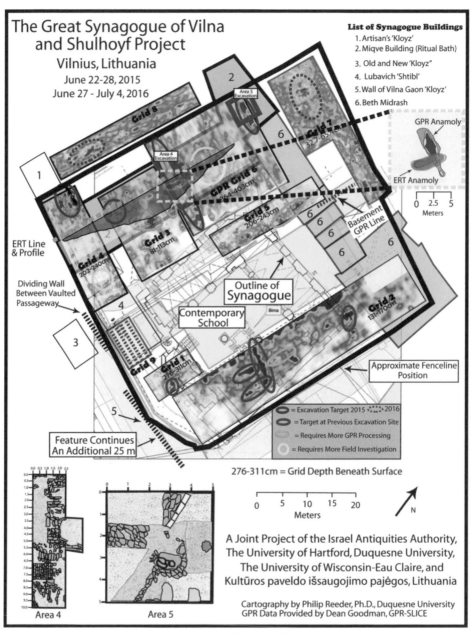

Map of the Great Synagogue of Vilna and Shulhoyf Project. (Courtesy of Philip Reeder, Duquesne University, on behalf of the Vilna Excavations Project at the University of Hartford)

Omaha (UNO) had started this pattern a quarter-century ago. Jack introduced me to his colleagues in the department of geology and geography, who added digital mapping to my work in the field.

In the 1990s, geographers were still making the transition from physically placing stencil-like letters on hand-drawn maps to making digital maps with computers. This transition point required working with computer-savvy geographers who wanted a chance to create a new archaeological and geological tool. Some of the younger professors in the geology and geography department were moving to replace the coordinates part of the map with a new global positioning system. Professor Philip Reeder, now dean of science at Duquesne University, was one of those faculty members I came to know at UNO (he arrived in the 1990s). I consulted him about the types of mapping done in the field, and what we could do to improve my model. He was at the time moving from the system of handmade mapping that I had been using in my excavations in Bethsaida, Israel, to a digital mapping program on his new Macintosh computer. The mapping programs alone seemed to justify working with computers. My first encounter with Jack Shroder, however, changed the way I conceived of archaeological work in so many different ways. Phil's idea was to have multiple layers on a map that would allow him to add finds from that particular layer at any level. This mapping strategy has served me well ever since. At sites in Israel, Spain, Greece, Poland, and Lithuania, this type of geoscience mapping can easily be understood by local authorities and researchers, and it also has the advantage of preserving the layers even as they are excavated.

GEOSCIENCE WHEN YOU CANNOT EXCAVATE

In traditional archaeology, you have only one opportunity to get an experiment right: the first time! Once you've excavated, the original conditions have been destroyed, and there is no repeat experiment. Even the most systematic archaeologists often find themselves reassessing a conclusion years later because of this method. With geoscience mapping, it is possible to at least assess a situation before doing any excavations. In the case of Holocaust-era archaeology, where there is a suspicion there might be mass burial sites, it means that an indignity will not be done to the dead—that the victims will not be victimized a second time.

Noninvasive archaeology has allowed me, over the years, to map the subsurface of entire cemeteries. It allowed me to evaluate 1,213 individual graves in the ancient Qumran (Dead Sea) area, and to identify what was in each grave without having to open every grave. In the 1950s and 1960s, other archaeologists had opened graves at Qumran in order to determine whether they were indeed burial sites, and what was inside.[5] At that time, this was the standard for anthropologists. They really could do very little but analyze the size, length, and density of bones, examine teeth, and discuss some forms of disease. This was what was done in Holocaust archaeology in the same period, and it was seen as insensitive, and particularly abusive for the Jews.

Using the technologies described earlier (GPR and ERT), I was able to identify all of the possible graves in a site where excavation was not an option. Qumran, the site where eleven caves that ring the ancient village contained more than nine hundred manuscripts, is an enigma, and every piece of evidence found can add to the body of knowledge of what happened there. The maps were produced in a relatively short excavation season, in 2001, and allowed the excavators to draw larger conclusions without desecrating the many burials there. I wanted to document these burials without disturbing the graves.

The Jewish concept of interment in the ground is meant to ensure that the body (or whatever remains of the body) would be available for the final physical "resurrection of the dead." Jews have believed in the concept of the "resurrection of the dead" as a principle of faith at least as far back as the Hellenistic and Roman periods. Unfortunately, Jews have known mass killings and undignified burials throughout the past two thousand years. There is a whole body of literature that has developed regarding the possible removal of a body from an undignified burial for its reinterment in a more-dignified burial place.

These examples all pale in the face of the Holocaust. Today, Jews are concerned about the millions of undignified mass burials during the Holocaust. The Jewish legal category is called *Kavod Hamet* in Hebrew (literally, the "dignity of the dead"), and it is a significant part of Jewish law. This value has always been a deeply rooted tradition within the Jewish people in almost every area of the world, but following the Holocaust, many religious and even nonreligious Jews have become very sensitive to the issue of burials. Therefore, when I began working in Poland, the first question the chief rabbi asked me about my work in a place like the extermination camp of Sobibor, Poland, was "Will the mass burials be disturbed?" Since the Holocaust includes Jewish mass burials, cremation ashes, and a whole variety of desecrated Jewish burials in cemeteries and in killing sites in locations throughout Europe, the use of the word *archaeology* often signals desecration to the religious. The fact that my work is noninvasive is the first lesson I teach students, and I explain why.

SPECIAL CASES: GEOSCIENCE IN SEARCH OF INDIVIDUALS

Throughout this book I introduce survivors of the Holocaust who have provided me with information that aided my investigations. I also include those subjects of my research who did not survive the war. Many write about the six million Jews who died as anonymous numbers, without names. To their families, they were more than just victims. They were people. I have the ability to search for individuals when I have good testimonies. Today, we are on the verge of a scientific revolution that might be able to put names to some of the previously unknown victims.

In the case of my work, I have often sought out individuals and their backstories as a part of the archaeology process. Archaeologists, in general, do not search for individuals, even those who might have been famous. Typically, all that can be done is to collect information on the area, the place, the city, or a specific site, but often this information is only an illustration or background to an individual's story. The ancient period is replete with individual "named" burials, better known as "relic" burials, to which people continue to make pilgrimage. My purpose is greater than just looking for individual named burials. When one reads an ancient text, and it says that someone was buried here or there in a certain place, it ultimately involves sacrosanct tradition which cannot easily be researched. When one seeks to find the "true" burial place of Jesus, Mary, King David, Goliath, John the Baptist, or any other figure from antiquity, it becomes more about the tradition than it is about the science.

In Vilna, I went in search of the HKP 562 labor camp (which you will read about later), where Major Karl Plagge, an altruistic Nazi engineer, worked. I went in search of the place where Itzhak Nemenchik was almost killed at Fort VII to understand the conditions of the killing field there. I searched for the mass burials located at Forts IX, VII, IV, because I have testimonies that tell me what happened there. I try to transform the anonymous people of these killing fields back into people. Remarkably, the names of the people who lived and died at HKP 562 are known. I did not really search for Major Plagge's body (he died in Darmstadt, Germany in 1957), but I did go in search of the places where he worked, to ensure that the testimonies are matched to physical locations.

The search for individual burials is inherently different from the search for mass burials, but often, there are special cases where it is possible to find individuals in the midst of the masses of dead. When there are a number of good literary or oral accounts, I can pursue the search with a good scientific perspective. Searching for the famed burial site of Genghis Khan in Mongolia is a real quest among archaeologists. Searching for the burial site of Alexander the Great, certain pharaohs, and even the daughter of the last czar of Russia, are real quests that have occupied serious scholars. It requires serious science, and with the advent of DNA sampling and comparison, the idea of finding a body to sample and the possibility of comparing it to a known relative is seriously compelling.

In 2008, I worked at a small village called Otwock, located outside of Warsaw. Instead of 250,000 people, I was looking for a family. The eyewitnesses had localized the work for me, pinpointing a field behind a series of homes that are still lived in. I did the project for two reasons: First, there was a personal petition from the chief rabbi; second, he had provided trustworthy testimonies to direct my work. Three elements became my guides for all future work on individual graves: a clear area which I would be licensed to survey; a personal petition from a credible source; and testimonies which gave me direction. Geophysicist Paul Bauman gave the final okay in this situation, since it was really more than I had originally planned to do that summer.

It is important to point out here that this was part of the mystery of what still lies buried in Holocaust-era sites. Rabbi Schudrich—the chief rabbi of Poland, who had worked with me on the Sobibor and Luta projects—had made a personal petition for me to use GPR to help find the missing burial sites of a family that had been shot in the middle of the war. The suspected area was forested, with bungalows lining the muddy roads that led through the forest. My team arrived, and I began the work by listening to the testimony of the family who knew the story of the killings. They indicated where the graves were thought to be.

On the day I arrived, Rabbi Schudrich had brought someone from the burial society of Poland, as well as a rabbi who specialized in burials in Israel, an expert on the questions of location and disinterment. This rabbi was involved with a group that handles the reinterment of bodies in Israel with meticulous care, interviewing the family to determine whether there is a very specific reason why a person should be disinterred and then reinterred in a more-dignified place, such as a formal cemetery, or a cemetery in Israel. Moving a body from an undignified place of burial qualifies as a reason for disinterring, but first, one must know where to look. The testimonies are key to the enterprise.

The rabbi from Israel brought his divining (or dowsing) rods. The image of the rabbi and the geophysicist working together captures two technologies used to search for bodies, one ancient and one modern. When I asked how the dowsing rods work, the rabbi explained that it is based upon the ability to understand and read the energy present at the site. Some people continue to use these rods to search for water, and they claim to have the ability to sense,

The rabbi and the geophysicist (Paul Bauman) at the Otwock site outside of Warsaw, Poland. (Courtesy of the Sobibor Documentation Project at the University of Hartford)

on almost a biological level, the energy displacement where water molecules and regular oxygen molecules collide in the field. I brought my technology; he brought his technology. The rabbi went over the spots where the testimonies indicated the remains of the family could be found. I went over the same area with my equipment. It was a case where faith and science met. The dowsing rods and the magnetometer eventually provided a clear indication of where they were buried. At the end of the day, I said my good-byes to the rabbis at Otwock, gave them digital copies of the research to study and act upon, packed up, and went to the airport.

NAMING NAMES: GENS, GOL, DUGIN, ZAIDEL, WALKER, NIES, TEAL, NEMENCHIK, PLAGGE, AND OLKIN

The search for individuals using geoscience and archaeology is not always about finding remains, but has everything to do with tracing the physical evidence of the lives and deaths of these individuals. I think that the archaeology of the Holocaust should personalize at least some of the research goals. In 2007, when I spoke to Yoram Haimi for the first time about his desire to excavate Sobibor, it was because he had lost family members in that camp. When I spoke to Jon Seligman about what motivated him to go to work on the Great Synagogue, it was because he too had lost family members in Lithuania. When I spoke to Benjamin di Liscia about his desire for me to go back to Rhodes and figure out what happened there, it was because he was hoping to find out more information about his grandmother. His earliest memories are of being a part of a loving Jewish community in Rhodes, and although he was lucky enough to be saved by his father's status as an Italian citizen and military officer, he vividly remembers the roundup of Jews, watching as family and friends were taken to the port for their long journey to Auschwitz.

I cannot avoid making the archaeology of the Holocaust personal. I include information on some of the individual cases on which I worked as examples. Most of what I have done is thanks to both the technology and the testimonies. Part of the reason for my work is to restore the names of people who died during this era. The more I can associate the Holocaust era with individuals, the better.

Almost ten years after Otwock, in Vilna, Paul Bauman and I had a similar conversation about looking for the burial site of Jacob Gens, in Rasu Prison, at the outskirts of downtown Vilnius. There would be no dowsing rods, but after we had been convinced by the testimonies that there was good reason to believe Jacob Gens was buried there, we did use GPR and ERT. There are inevitably many projects like this that we would like to do, but only some fit our time constraints for the equipment and staff when we are in-country.

In 2015 in Lithuania, my group finished the GPR survey of the Great Synagogue in a week, and came home to process the data. It was clear that the Great Synagogue had many new "discoveries" for excavations, and my Lithuanian partners were happy to collaborate for 2016. I was committed to working with the Vilna Gaon Jewish State Museum's Ponar site, in search of mass burials and a mysterious "escape" tunnel. The search for individuals once again motivated my work. The Ponar museum had materials from the testimonies of the eleven Jews who had survived the tunnel escape, and the accounts of a non-Jewish newspaper reporter who lived outside the killing fields.

After the discovery of the Great Synagogue's subsurface in areas around the elementary school, the news was featured in many media outlets worldwide. Often, I receive letters from people who have read these stories and then write to offer a new site, an idea, or assistance. In the case of the original 2015 stories, I received a number of letters suggesting possible sites for future research. One, in particular, was very moving:

September 2, 2015

Dear Dr. Freund,

By way of introduction, I am the granddaughter of Jacob Gens, Ghetto Representative of the Vilna Ghetto, until he was executed by Obersturmführer Neuegebauer, Sipo Commander in Vilnius, on September 14, 1943. He was allegedly executed at a small jail on Rossa Street in Vilnius and buried in a grave there that had already been prepared for him in the courtyard of the prison. I've read with great interest about the "The Great Synagogue and Shulhoyf of Vilna" project which you will be heading, and the use by your archaeological team of innovative ground-penetrating imaging technologies. I am writing you to discuss the possibility of working out some sort of an arrangement with your team to use your technologies to search for his body in the courtyard at this site when your team is working in Vilnius, and was wondering if you would be willing to discuss this possibility with either myself or my mother, Mrs. Ada Ustjanauskas (neé Gensaitė). As it happens, my mother lives in West Hartford, not far from U of H [University of Hartford].

Sincerely,

Irene Bernhard

Irene Bernhard and Ada Ustjanauskas are my neighbors here in West Hartford, Connecticut. They live not far from where I live, teach, and shop. I have for the past eighteen years gone to their small supermarket here in town. While it is rare to have a personal connection with excavations, it's wonderful when it happens. I have always insisted that archaeology is always about people.

WHO IS JACOB GENS, AND WHY
SHOULD I SEARCH FOR HIM?

In a world of limited resources and opportunities, why should I look for one individual or group over another? The reason is not, as you might think, just whether that person is famous. It is usually a combination of timing, connections, a specific set of circumstances, availability of funding, and the level of documentation that exists for the project. The case of Jacob Gens was one of those stories. I learned much about Gens from his family. His daughter Ada, granddaughter Irene, and the rest of his family provided the most compelling and specific details of his life, most of which were never part of the official record.

On September 17, 2015, when Ada and Irene came to the university to tell their stories of their father and grandfather, Jacob Gens, I filmed it in the university studios. I thought about how difficult it is to find an individual from the Holocaust. To search for a single person among the millions of Jews who were killed is fraught with so many problems, but in this case, I had the elements I needed. Irene and Ada gave specific testimonies, and personally made a petition, which gave the work meaning. I received the licenses to work for two days during my hectic schedule in Lithuania. There was one other motivating factor, which only became apparent as I started to evaluate the testimonies. Gens was not just any Jew who died during the Holocaust; he was the director of the Jewish Council (Judenrat) of the Vilna Ghetto, which oversaw the daily supervision of the daily goings-on there. Unlike many of the others I have searched for in Lithuania and Poland, Gens was a controversial leader, and his role is important to the history of the Holocaust in Lithuania. All of these reasons convinced me that I should look for his grave.

Jacob Gens was born on April 1, 1903, within the Siauliai district of Lithuania. He was not born and raised in Vilnius. Gens was the son of a middle-class Jewish merchant, Elias Emanuel Gens, the eldest of four children. He was born in a time in Jewish history when Jews had become integrated in many parts of Lithuania. They lived in more than two hundred villages and cities in the country, and made up a sizable part of the population. Unlike in most other countries, Jews in Lithuania did not live only in Jewish quarters. Jews were found in almost every aspect of the cultural life in the country, serving as lawyers, bankers, theater directors, authors, composers, and musicians of note.

By the end of the nineteenth century, the so-called "Pale of Settlement" was not really one big "ghetto," but an enormous multistate area in Eastern Europe where the vast majority of Jewish communities extended through the Baltics to Poland in the west, and throughout what we call Ukraine and Belarus. Millions of Jews enjoyed religious, cultural, and educational opportunities, and even within their diversity were united by their ancient faith and their shared Yiddish language.

This was the result of a process which today is called the Jewish Enlightenment, which paralleled the European movement of the same name. Although these Jews lived as part of Lithuanian, Slavic, and Baltic cultures, they had two degrees of separation from the local populations. Beyond their separation by the local governments, the Jews separated themselves into groups of common religious and cultural interests. Because they had to learn to take care of their own poor, young, old, and sick, and develop their own guilds, businesses, and sports and educational institutions (they were not allowed to access the services of non-Jewish society), they developed organizations in the Jewish community that cemented their reputation as "a people of organizations."[6] As was the case with Jacob Gens, most Jews spoke Russian, Lithuanian, Latvian, German, and Yiddish, and could attend some public and some non-Jewish private schools, attend universities, serve in the military, vote, and participate in the building of the state where they lived. Perhaps they were not absolutely "full" citizens of the state, but they were a step beyond how Jews had lived in the medieval cities and ghettos of previous centuries.

In the early part of his life, Jacob Gens, like any other Jew of the early twentieth century in Eastern Europe, was unaware of the tumultuous and tragic events that would soon descend upon his country during the onslaught of World War I, and then, later, in World War II. Although Gens could not have anticipated the ferocity of World War II, he was no stranger to military life and service, having served as a military officer in World War I, and in the fight for a free and independent Lithuania that followed. Gens was recruited in 1919 to fight in the Lithuanian War of Independence. As his military career steadily progressed, he married in 1922, and they welcomed their only daughter, Ada, in 1926.

Two years earlier, his active service in the Lithuanian army ended, Gens began a career teaching the Lithuanian language and physical education at a number of Jewish schools in the nearby city of Kaunas. (I will use the Lithuanian "Kaunas" interchangeably with the Yiddish "Kovno." Kovno was the "second" city of medieval Lithuania, but in this period it was part of an independent Lithuania, and quite different from the Vilnius/Vilna that at the time was a part of greater Poland.) Gens represented the thoroughly modern Jew: He was a member of the Revisionist branch of Zionism founded by Vladimir Jabotinsky, which emphasized the military aspects of the struggle in Palestine; he spoke Yiddish, and was a part of the Jewish community of Kovno. At the same time, he was also married to a Catholic Lithuanian, and embraced his Lithuanian identity and citizenship.

In 1927, Gens was hired as an accountant for the Ministry of Justice in Kaunas. After finishing a law degree in 1935, he was hired by the Shell Oil Company, followed by the Lietukis Company. The transition during the "Soviet" period changed life for Jews all over the country. Gens left his job with the Lietukis Company and moved to Vilnius. As an outspoken Zionist who was actively engaged with the Revisionist movement, Gens had every right to fear for his safety. In addition to seeking refuge from persecution, Gens's relocation was motivated by his mother, who lived in Vilna.

Gens was also the quintessential "outsider" in Vilna's Jewish community. He was married to a Catholic, had a young non-Jewish daughter, and had remained a part of the Lithuanian army reserve. His military service made him part of a call-up in 1938, and, thanks to his military school background and service, he rose to the rank of captain just when the Nazis came to Lithuania in 1941. When the Nazis occupied Vilnius in 1941, the former captain was appointed director of the Jewish hospital, due to important connections he had made during his other previous jobs. Gens's career would change yet again after a police force and an overseeing directorate (the Judenrat) was established in the ghetto in September of 1941. Following the reconstitution of the Judenrat in July of 1942, Gens became the director of the Vilna Ghetto. This Nazi appointment would affect Gens's reputation, ultimately leading to his execution in Rasu Prison on September 14, 1943. The entire tenure of his directorship spans just over thirteen months.

I have heard Jacob Gens' entire life story multiple times now, during lunches and dinners with Ada and Irene, in Lithuania and the United States, and I have spent countless hours reading about his decision-making, visiting the places where he and his family lived, walking the places he walked. My work in Rasu Prison is a study in what I can learn about the Holocaust from researching one person's history.

FINDING JACOB GENS IN EYEWITNESS TESTIMONIES

I have become very aware of the importance of oral and literary accounts as basic parts of archaeological research, from the ancient period to the modern period. At Sobibor, I spoke to many individuals who had escaped, and they provided me with some of the best insights into my work. I also read their testimonies. For both antiquity and the modern period, I follow a single rule about oral and written accounts: I take these accounts seriously, but I do not take them literally. This means that often when I read different versions of an event, I can see similar lines of evidence that seem to converge. To understand Gens's life, I had to look for the same types of evidence. I listened to Ada speak about her Jewish father as if she were still living on Geliu Street (where she and her non-Jewish mother lived during Ada's youth), outside of the Vilna Ghetto, visiting him in his office every day. She was a precocious sixteen-year-old, and decades later, she remembered details about his life and the life of the ghetto that only an outsider could see. She knew his life from before the ghetto in Kovno, and, in Vilna, before the Nazis arrived, and she remembered the day of his death, and her escape from Vilnius, as if it had all happened yesterday.

Among the many testimonies and sources that the family had gathered, there was one that stood out. It was the testimony of Ona Simaite, who died in 1970. She was one of the most famous non-Jewish "Righteous Gentiles" of the Holocaust in Vilnius. In her role as a non-Jewish librarian at Vilnius University, she had regular contact with the ghetto. She was involved in the dangerous and successful rescue of many of the significant books from the ghetto, and used her position to aid and rescue many Jews, as she was allowed to enter and leave. Her testimony was a credible description of what she saw in the Vilna Ghetto.

After the Nazi invasion and the creation of the Vilna Ghetto in 1941, Ona began entering the ghetto under the pretext of recovering library books from Jewish university students. She must have maintained continuous contact with Jacob Gens during this period. The famed book rescue assumes her reliability as a source, and no one questions her motives. During the course of three years (1941–1944), Ona smuggled in food, small arms, and other provisions; hid Jews in the library; smuggled out some of the most important literary and historical documents of the Jews; and served as a mail courier for the ghetto inhabitants, connecting them with the news of the outside world. Her actions were "sanctioned" or "recognized" by the head of the Judenrat, Jacob Gens, and made the Jews feel they had some measure of control in the midst of the massacres.

Ona also found people who would forge documents for Jews, offered her home as a temporary refuge, and smuggled Jewish children out of the ghetto to families she found who agreed to hide them. In April 1944, the Gestapo arrested and tortured Ona Simaite. A ransom for her release was paid by the rector of the university, and she was deported to the Dachau concentration camp, and later transferred to Ludelange internment camp in France. Following liberation by the Allies, Simaite remained in France, working as a librarian, except for a period from 1953 to 1956, which she spent in Israel. In March of 1966, Yad Vashem gave Simaite the highest honor for those who saved or helped Jews in the Holocaust: "A Righteous Among the Nations." In 2015, a street sign honoring her was erected in Vilnius.

All of this background is necessary to establish the importance of a piece of information Simaite provided for finding Jacob Gens's burial place, key to my decision to search where I did. Her testimony concerning the burial of Gens states:

> Whatever Gens wrote, all that is hidden in a box in his grave. There are three gardens there. The garden which contains the grave borders Sub-aciaus Street. Right next to the wall there is a grave of an executed Polish national; at his feet is the grave of executed Gens; at Gens's feet there is a grave of an executed Lithuanian. In order to identify Gens's grave, Chasia Vigdorcik placed a broken plate inside his grave.

I did ERT and GPR research in the garden, and located a potential grave site. I spent a year in meetings to obtain licenses and sponsorships, seeking permission for an actual excavation, after searching for and deciding on the location that best fit all of the characteristics of the prison gardens. I pored over testimonies and writings in five languages, with the help of Ada's daughter, Irene, master of the list of sources. It is clear from a comparison of all of the sources that there were multiple graves in the garden. I made my case—with the help of these testimonies—to the cultural ministry and the prison authority (it is still a prison today), and received permission to do a detailed GPR and ERT study, followed by a single excavation at one of the sites identified in the gardens of the prison.

The burial site which matched the most geoscience markers was excavated on October 26, 2016. A single burial under Soviet debris was found at 1.9 meters. Two samples for DNA testing were collected from the incomplete remains in the grave. (I found the head; there was more to be excavated, but my restricted license did not allow us to excavate beyond the edge of the prescribed site.) Samples from Ada and the buried male remains were compared. The DNA of the remains I found was significantly degraded, but the comparison showed a close relationship between Ada and the unidentified male. It was not, however, close enough to call a perfect match, and carbon 14 tests did not place it in the right period. Without more conclusive information, I could not continue the work.

Nevertheless, for Ada, who stood by the excavation site as I uncovered the skull, and her family, it seemed to be enough. She told me that she felt, at least for one moment, that the seventy-three years of waiting had been worth it. It was a measure of closure for her and her family, even though I could not definitively claim the remains to be those of Jacob Gens.

· 4 ·

The Significance of Tunnels:
Geoscience and Archaeology from
the Ancient World to the Holocaust

$\mathcal{J}$ust when I think that I have discovered the best way to uncover subsurface mysteries, I am introduced to a new technology that increases the potential for discovery. Even as I am doing cutting-edge work in the field, I am constantly thinking about how to do it better. Of course, I am not alone; all good scientists do this. I like to keep abreast of developments in related fields, and mine them for use in archaeology. I am happy that I work with some of the best geoscience people in the world who share my passion for innovation.

In order to gain a clear perspective on a site, I started out by using cameras and photographers hanging from tall ladders; then I used cameras attached to kites and weather balloons; and today, I have been introduced to cameras and magnetometers attached to drones that soon will be flown from remote access areas. I use these to evaluate a space completely in a short period of time. I have the facilities of two companies who evaluate data from the field, GPR-SLICE in Los Angeles and WorleyParsons in Calgary, Alberta, Canada. In addition, the best and the brightest geophysicists volunteer their time to make my work more seamless in the field.

In 2016, Dr. Alastair McClymont introduced a new technology (according to him, "still in development") called UltraGPR, certain to become a future standard. This hypersensitive, very flexible, "jump-rope-like" device will allow me to gather much more data at sites that my current GPR equipment cannot easily access. Moreover, this nimble device will allow me to work more or less unobtrusively without removing the large plants, trees, and obstacles that make GPR collection slightly invasive (ideally needs relatively flat surfaces) and without attracting the attention of the many bystanders often present at sites.

This use of noninvasive technology to collect data is not only ideal for Holocaust sites; it can be helpful when used at all kinds of sensitive sites.

My noninvasive work in the archaeology of the Holocaust is meant to ensure that victims are not victimized again, especially at burial sites, but it is also important to consider the sensitivities of the survivors and their families. The new frontier in this evolving technology is to make it possible to do noninvasive work at extremely sensitive sites, where religious, ethnic, and political sensitivities are significant. Even when I have a permit to survey a site noninvasively, and respectfully, and I am accompanied by area staff, some locals may still find it offensive. The new technology is both less-invasive and less obvious than it was a generation ago. Nonetheless, in many Holocaust-era sites in countries like Lithuania and Poland, locals suspect their own properties may be surveyed next. This has created a sense of anxiety for many of neighbors, who regularly ask me what I am "up to."

I have been asked why every archaeological team is not using noninvasive technology if it is so groundbreaking and successful. The technology itself is not a single tool, but multiple pieces of equipment that are ever-changing, even as I write this. I mentioned ERT and GPR technology in chapter 3. Few universities or excavation teams could afford the equipment and upgrades and backup staff that I have had access to in the past twenty years. No university or institute could easily afford what private industry uses in the field to find gas and oil for profit. Even if they could, they would likely not have the incentive to create new and more-effective devices like the UltraGPR, which can take hundreds of readings just by dragging it along the ground. A generation ago—and without this technology—people just excavated to see what was there.

The Holocaust-era sites that I investigate are often overgrown, filled with decades' worth of debris, and inaccessible today. Certainly, that was the case in the Ponar forest, but the UltraGPR proved to be one of the invaluable tools that led to a remarkable discovery as I searched for the parameters of the missing burial pits: the entrance to the Holocaust Escape Tunnel. This location was first examined in 2004 by V. Urbanivicius on behalf of the Vilna Gaon Jewish State Museum. I have been asked why this archaeologist did not discover the tunnel entrance at the time. The answer is simple: It would have been a near impossibility, given what we know about the depth of the tunnel, the state of disrepair of the wood shorings which would have held up the roof in 1944, and, most important—he would have had to destroy it to excavate it! We are in fact indebted to V. Urbanivicius for his restraint in 2004, which allowed us to have a clear geophysical survey field to work with, and the insight of where to begin.

Another innovative technology I have used is lidar (light detection and ranging), which has many applications in the field of archaeology, including aiding in the planning of field campaigns, mapping features beneath forest canopy, and providing an overview of broad, continuous features that may be indistinguishable on the ground. It can be employed from the ground, with millions of images stitched together, or from an aerial platform, which provides a grand panoramic view. Lidar can also create high-resolution digital elevation models (DEMs) of archaeological sites that can reveal microtopography (tiny changes in elevation) that indicate a buried structure, or other elements, that would otherwise be hidden by vegetation or a canopy of trees.

This was exactly the case in Ponar. Lidar was used there before I arrived, so I was able to use those scans to compare to the 1944 historical flyover photos of the site that I found at the US Naval Archives. Elevation mapping is invaluable in searching for building, caves, and hidden features that you simply cannot see when you are walking around the site. Lidar-derived products can be easily integrated into a geographic information system (GIS) for analysis and interpretation. It is a wonderfully complementary technology to GPR and ERT. Unfortunately, lidar without a follow-up project on the ground, such as ERT or GPR, provides maps that cannot easily be truth-tested.

I know the value of noninvasive technology, and I use it as often as I can. I am also interested in trying to work at as many sites, with as many students and different local archaeologists, as possible, to drive home the significance of noninvasive work. Since my methods are quick, I am not usually the one applying for the long-term excavation licenses at these sites. Using geoscience, I can repeat my work multiple times to determine the exact nature of a discovery below the surface without damaging it. This means that I would like to come back to a site year after year to see what has been done, and to suggest new work to the local archaeologists. In medicine, thanks to multiple imaging techniques in radiology, before a surgery, a surgeon knows what he or she will find when the patient is actually under the knife. Medical imaging technology allows surgeons to do as little damage as possible to surrounding organs, thanks to this pre-surgery imaging. After surgery, more imaging ensures that the actual invasive process was successful.

I recommend this methodology at every archaeological site, before it is excavated and at stages after the excavation has progressed. An archaeologist is much like a surgeon, also in need of guidance as the excavation progresses. I use multiple technologies to collect subsurface images from multiple perspectives before I recommend any excavating. I know with reasonable accuracy where and what should be excavated, and because I realize that sometimes it will not all be excavated in one year, I recommend what I call periodic "checkups." Some of these subsurface mapping technologies have been part of my excavations in Israel for a quarter-century. Now, in Greece and Lithuania, those sites are the beneficiaries of this experience in the field.

I have used ERT and GPR in my work at the Cave of Letters and at Qumran, the site near the caves where the Dead Sea Scrolls were found. I discovered a buried cave at Qumran, which I theorized might be under the dump site used for the original excavations (chronicled in my book, *Digging through History* [Rowman & Littlefield, 2012]). My own interest in tunnels and caves was fueled by the sense that they were good targets for testing the geoscience equipment. I was originally told that ERT and GPR would not work in caves (some geoscientists insisted that the FM radio waves of GPR, and the electrical signals of ERT, would just have a "belling effect," and be reflected haphazardly off of the cave surfaces to the receivers; they were wrong). Nevertheless, I persisted. Fortunately, I was working with geoscientists who shared my confidence. Since that initial work, I have moved from one site to another, testing the limits of the technology in different environments, all the time sharing the technology and the expertise of the geoscientists with local archaeologists and museums, when working with the equipment in-country. Some were skeptical about being directed by geoscientists; others were not. Those who accepted the mapping technology seemed to be more successful in their digs because they had these helpful "subsurface" guides.

My work with geology and geoscience subsurface mapping began over twenty-five years ago in a search for the original Bethsaida in Galilee, Israel. I needed to know why an ancient tiny fishing village was so far from the sea. The geoscience team concluded that the port and low-lying marsh had been overwhelmed by sedimentation after a series of historical earthquakes caused damming and even uplift. It was subsequently redone by the Geological Survey of Israel who came up with the same results. Then, as now, I worked in teams that included geomorphologists, hydrologists, GPR, and geologists. Each one of the innovations I pioneered was "tried out" at Bethsaida. Using ERT and GPR, we "found" what looked like a "tunnel" from an Iron Age palace near the outer wall at Bethsaida. It appeared to begin at the main Iron Age palace complex, and it ran toward the outside double wall of the city. There are such "escape" tunnels mentioned in the Bible and ancient Near Eastern literature.

I was lucky to have a volunteer architect, Ken Bensimon, who wanted to pursue the tunnel project. Ken had worked on prison architecture (as he tells it, "to keep prisoners from being able to escape and tunnel out!"), and had a sense about how tunnel building was done. He was instrumental in the efforts to dig the tunnel. This tunnel in or by the city wall was reminiscent of the biblical story of Joshua's spies that were sent to determine the situation in the city (book of Joshua, chapter 2). In the biblical story, the "spies" ended up being able to get out of the city through what appears to be a tunnel in the city wall. Reading this story really does inform my work. It is possible to understand how and why people built these tunnels. The idea of escape was not unique to the ancient Israelites, or even the Ancient Near East. Many kings and leaders knew that it was important to have an escape plan that included a tunnel. Tunnels served as important escape routes from Mesopotamia to Egypt, and throughout all ancient civilizations. When I decided to look for the tunnel of the Jewish prisoners at Ponar, I brought architect Ken Bensimon to Lithuania to help me locate it.

TUNNELS AS "JEWISH" ARCHAEOLOGICAL ETHNIC MARKERS

I have been asked whether the search for tunnels used by Jews to escape from the Holocaust was an extraordinary event. In fact, it appears that tunnels (and cave and hideaways in general) had a variety of strategic uses among Jews for thousands of years and figure in biblical and rabbinic lore. Tunnels, caves, and hideaways served as architectural features in building (perhaps used for storage) but also both for refuge, tactical advantage, and rescue. One might say that this feature was embedded in Jewish survival tactics dictated by circumstances beyond their control. It became, we think, a traceable characteristic of Jewish life.

Archaeologists have always asked themselves if there were easy ways of identifying the areas they excavate before or early on in their investigations so they could properly compare the site with other similar sites. Developing an anthropological "ethnic" marker for a people sounds a little far-fetched, but it allows archaeologists to have a series of ready tools in the field to help assign a site to a certain group, and can help direct the work. I first heard about this from Dr. Mordechai Aviam, and I am indebted to him for the insight.[1]

Archaeologists have a difficult time in the field when it comes to establishing the types of ethnic markers that allow them to identify who lived at a site in antiquity. The Jews are indeed a unique people because they have developed a whole series of characteristic artifacts that they alone use. They can be tracked and distinguished by these artifacts, symbols, and architecturally unique structures. Even when the Jews are using a common artifact (like a ceramic or glass vessel or coin), often the Jews developed their own manifestation (with a specific decoration or other marking) of the coin, metal, seal, glass, or ceramic vessel. The refuse piles present at Jewish sites are different from those at non-Jewish sites, because animal bones that would be present at a Jewish site will be different from what will be present at a non-Jewish site—for example, few if any pig bones compared to a larger amount of kosher animal bones. It is hard to think about archaeological ethnic markers as innovations that characterize a certain people in a certain time period, but archaeology has taken to this idea to help direct some of their studies as they look at new and unknown sites. The Jews in ancient Israel might have ethnic markers in their literature for what constitute kosher animals, and the absence or presence of pig bones could be a comparison of non-Jews and Jews at a single site. The use of certain symbols over others might be another marker. There is, indeed, a type of Jewish pottery from the Roman period in ancient Israel that allows us to assign not only its pottery form, but today—thanks to meticulous studies of the clay—we can say with confidence that they were made at a specific area, where the clays contain certain chemical signatures. All of these things help us to understand how the Jews of antiquity lived.

Hidden or dug tunnels and hideaways may not be the first ethnic marker one would associate with Jews, but they, along with refuge caves, found their way into the landscape of Israel and the Diaspora.[2] Perhaps because of their minority status in the Greco-Roman period, Jews probably dug tunnels and created hideaways and refuge caves to hide from their enemies in troubled times. One could say that an escape tunnel allowed for a measure of freedom while living among a hostile population, and the Jews became well acquainted with the use of secret hideaways, caves, and tunnels at sites from the north and south of Israel. "Jewish" tunnels were not only used defensively, for hiding, but also offensively, as a base from which to attack. The tunnels and caves used by the Bar Kokhba fighters at Herodium, Israel, for example, served them well in the early years of the Second Rebellion against the Romans. They were used for guerrilla warfare and to escape from overwhelming forces. Jews utilized tunnels as did other people in the ancient Near East. The Israelites and later Jews may have built tunnels as a way of ensuring easy "secret" exits just as the Egyptians did after they built their tombs.

The engineering of tunnels, from Greek theaters to ancient water tunnels, to the great Herodian Second Temple tunnels of Jerusalem, show us their many uses. The tunnels were not only used for escape or during wartime. The Coliseum of Rome—and, indeed, most of the great amphitheaters of the Roman Empire—included tunnels in order to create their great staged dramas, moving actors, slaves, animals, and monarchs from full view, and for enhancing a story line. The tunnel was a transnational idea. The idea of a strategic military tunnel was not invented by the Jews nor the Egyptians, Greeks, or Romans. There have been caves and tunnels in ancient China and along the Silk Road for more than two thousand years.

Many Israeli archaeologists realized early on that noninvasive techniques might be of use in looking for subsurface structures like tunnels in and around the Temple Mount area. Tunnels at or near the Temple Mount near the Western Wall is the exact type of project that geoscience devices were made for. Early archaeologists conducted work by digging shafts and tunnels through the subsurface. Over twenty years ago, while working at the northern end of the Western Wall, archaeologists discovered an area of massive tunnels under the Temple Mount. It resulted in riots and ill feelings about the intent of the excavators, but revealed an enormous system of tunnels from the Second Temple building project of King Herod. The outer Western Wall my

Searching for tunnels behind the Western Wall in Jerusalem using GPR technology. (Courtesy of Paul Bauman, WorleyParsons, Inc., on behalf of the Yavne Excavations Project at the University of Hartford)

colleagues were with archaeologist Dan Bahat is still a very sensitive area for both Jews and Muslims alike. I uncovered what I think were infill vacuums, tunnel-like areas behind the large Western Wall limestone blocks. There were no riots while I was there, and I collected unique data about the Wall that may be useful for future excavators in the area.

Tunnel use was not restricted to the ancient period of the Jews in Israel. While working in Burgos, Spain, in 2005, I discovered tunnels that apparently led from a feudal fortress through to a Jewish cemetery in medieval Spain (chronicled in my book, *Digging through History*). Other groups developed systems of tunnels in the medieval period, including during the Crusades. Tunnels were built in many monasteries and nunneries during this period to allow for escape and easy transfer of materials, and people. Maya, Aztec, and Inca escape tunnels in Latin and South America tell a similar story. The monarchies of Europe continued to build and use escape tunnels right up until the modern period, and in the famed American Underground Railroad movement of slaves in the nineteenth century, carefully dug and strategically placed tunnels became a part of the transfers. Tunnels for the legendary prison escapes of Union soldiers from prisons in the South are described during the Civil War, and in East Asia, tunnels were used by the local populations for escape and strategic attacks right through the modern period.

The history of tunnel building during the twentieth century is found in literary and cinematic presentations. Tunnels present dramatic escape routes. Trench warfare during World War I is famous. Perhaps not so famous is the fact that the knowledge and technology of tunnel building aided some of the most famous escapes from prisoner-of-war camps in World War I and II. Tunnels have provided a means of escape from persecution and oppression in recent history, like those found under the Berlin Wall during the Cold War period. Tunnels offer tactical advantages even in our modern world of Google Earth and satellite photography. Most recently, news reports have focused on the negative uses of tunnels by drug lords, terrorists, and human smugglers, from Colombia to the US border. All of this attention on tunnels has convinced me that people around the world could readily understand the complexities and the significance of the discovery of a Holocaust-era escape tunnel in Lithuania.

TRACKING ESCAPES FROM THE HOLOCAUST: RETURN TO SOBIBOR

In *Digging through History*, I devoted an entire chapter to "The Hidden Holocaust" (*Digging through History*, 179–238). I wrote about the escape from Sobibor in 1943, which I think changed how Jews viewed the possibility of Holocaust escapes. Tunnels were used by Jews to escape from ghettos, death camps, and concentration and labor camps, as well as for hiding, attacking, and taking refuge. This is not typically included in a student's education about the Holocaust. It is part of the larger topic of Jewish resistance during the Holocaust that is not as well-known as the story of the extermination of the Jews. Many of my own students did not know that Jews have been known for their resistance movements from antiquity to World War II. This could be an important new field of research for those studying the archaeology of the Holocaust. How did Jews build these tunnels? Tunnels are also excellent archaeological time capsules, since they exist belowground, and often do not suffer the same fate of Holocaust-era buildings aboveground. Most of the tunnels found after the war were not part of the main death and concentration camps that were either burned by retreating Nazis, or by the Allies (to stop the outbreak of disease from decaying bodies). Tunnels were not of much interest when there were millions of dead, as well as displaced persons, taking priority. Technology was also a factor.

So significant were hiding places to the Jews during the Holocaust that they coined a word for them: *malines*—Yiddish slang for created hiding spaces used during the Holocaust all over Europe, many of which may still lie hidden below the surface or behind a wall. It became a quest to find these *malines* using my geoscience technologies. I do have testimonies from some survivors who were old enough to recognize the tunnels. Often, they just need to be asked specifically about hiding places or tunnels, and it jogs their memories and new information emerges.

The number of escapes by Jews escalated in 1943, mostly due to the presence of Soviet Jewish soldiers who were added to the ranks of the camps. Unlike the many Jews in ghettos, death camps, and concentration camps, these captured Soviet Jewish soldiers were also physically able to plan and execute some of these tunnels, and subsequent escapes. On August 2, 1943, at Treblinka, a group of prisoners seized weapons from the SS storeroom, attacked the German and Ukrainian guards, and ultimately broke through the barbed wire and escaped. Of an estimated three hundred inmates who escaped from Treblinka that day, about one hundred survived the massive SS manhunt.

These escapes often slowed the killing, so why weren't there more attempts? It is important to study each escape to understand just how difficult it was in each location. The death camp system ensured it would not be easy for prisoners to be able to rebel. Because of poor diet, grueling work, sporadic checks, and violence, it was hard for the Jews to figure out how they could disrupt the system and thereby stop the killing. The Nazi guards were also counting on the fact that the Jews who were interned in the death camps would not have the time, experience, or knowledge to escape. Cumulatively, the story of these escapes reveals something quite different from most people's understanding of the Holocaust.

Treblinka, in German-occupied Poland, was one of the planned "Final Solution" death camps built solely for extermination. Approximately 900,000 Jews were murdered there in just fifteen months. In the summer of 1943, the tide of World War II had begun to turn against Nazi Germany, and the Soviet advance was clear. The Soviet POWs inevitably included Soviet Jewish soldiers. They were the "tipping point" for the escape movements in Eastern Europe. Losses in North Africa and the massive defeat of the Germans at Stalingrad introduced a new "X factor," as the captured Soviet Jewish soldiers were first interned in POW camps, and later, turned in by their fellow soldiers. They were transferred to death camps, and their introduction to the Jewish death camp population added well-trained Jewish soldiers to the mix, who were trained to escape.

1943: ESCAPE TUNNELS FROM THE HOLOCAUST

My geoscience work at Sobibor, Poland, in 2008, revealed a lot about the underground work done to prepare for the escape that changed the way I think about the Holocaust. It is important to note that the way the post–World War II Sobibor park was configured for visitors (the walkways and the monument, for example) looks nothing like the original camp. Although it had the same basic structure as Treblinka, Sobibor did not have crematoria, as Auschwitz did. The Germans usually stationed minimal troops in this far-flung location, ensuring the camp was secure without being a drain on the war effort. They counted on having a local non-Jewish population to oversee the camp.

On October 14, 1943, there was a successful rebellion at Sobibor. This uprising, in combination with the one at Treblinka in August, caused fear to engulf the Nazi officials. They were afraid that other camps would rebel and chaos would break out, disrupting the well-oiled machine that was the Final Solution.

Sobibor is an excellent example of how tunnels were unreliable methods of escape in some regions. When I worked at Sobibor, the first question I asked was, why October of 1943? The Sobibor rebellion really began on September 23, 1943, when two thousand Jews from Minsk arrived at Sobibor. They were not just Jews from Polish villages; they included newly captured Soviet Jewish prisoners of war, among them an officer named Alexander Pechersky. In the film *Sobibor* (2018), Russian movie star and director Konstantin Khabensky, who plays Pechersky, makes him the almost legendary hero of the film. The three hundred people who ended up escaping from Sobibor were emboldened by the presence of these Soviet Jews, who had the skill set necessary to plan an escape.

According to the testimonies of Sobibor escape survivors, Pechersky and Leon Feldhendler met on September 29, 1943, and immediately began planning an escape that would take place two weeks later. According to some, Pechersky's first plan involved a tunnel. They planned it with the staff of the escape committee, which included a whole group of people who were excellent tunnel builders. Boris Tsibulsky, a miner from Donbas at the carpentry shop, became a key player, according to some of the testimonies.

The plan for the escape tunnel was to place its entrance in the shop closest to the barracks, and it would run under fences and minefields for thirty-five meters. The number of people who might be able to exit undetected was minimal, but it would allow those who made it out to foment a major rebellion. The tunnel they were digging was seventy-five centimeters by seventy-five centimeters, and only eighty centimeters below the surface. They constantly worried about the water table, which was very high at Sobibor. They worked on the tunnel for two weeks.

Unfortunately, according to those testimonies that mention a tunnel, in early October 1943, there were major rainstorms at the camp. On October 8 and 9, a deluge of water flooded the tunnel, causing the prisoners to abandon it as a means of escape. The prisoners may have worried that their tunnel would be discovered, after which the whole enterprise would be quashed. Instead, they carried out their Plan B on October 14, when 650 inmates stole weapons, killed SS guards, and made a break for it; perhaps as many as 300 made it out. Although it appeared to be audacious and spontaneous, it was not.

It is not so much that tunnel making was specifically a Jewish mode of escape; I think it was something Jews could use for escape when conditions were right. I have always wondered whether the idea of an escape tunnel was a military option taught to Soviet soldiers as part of their training. It may just be that this is the key to understanding its use during the Holocaust.

In October 2016, an escape tunnel was unearthed during ongoing excavations at Sobibor, but it was not the same one initiated by Pechersky.[3] It is thought to have been an unfinished Sonderkommando tunnel, probably built to give them an escape route as the extermination machine of Sobibor tapered down in the fall of 1943. This was the signal for others to create an escape plan, as well. Sonderkommandos were "special units" at death camps made up of Jews who performed a variety of tasks for the Nazis. They enjoyed some benefits, but in the end knew that they, too, were expendable.

I have every reason to assume there were multiple escape tunnels at Sobibor, and therefore, suspect that other tunnels existed at other camps and ghettos. Perhaps the designers of these tunnels may not have lived to tell where they were located. In fact, there had been many successful small rebellions and individual escapes, both at Sobibor and other camps, but nothing matched the scope of Sobibor's October 1943 rebellion. Up until that time, it is estimated that 250,000 Jews had been transferred to and killed at Sobibor. The rebellion is important because survivors told their stories after the war, giving the kind of details about life and death at the camp that has informed modern understanding of how an extermination camp worked.

Only about half of the six hundred prisoners present in the camp on the day of the rebellion escaped. Some died in the minefields, and some perished in the following weeks and months. Only fifty to seventy of those escapees survived the war, but their testimonies are significant. They are firsthand accounts of life at the camps built on the original model formulated by Eichmann in the Wannsee Conference proposals. Most important, Sobibor was closed almost immediately after the rebellion, and not totally destroyed by the Nazis or the Allies, as in the case of other death camps. This had the effect of preserving Sobibor at a moment in history, for modern study. In turn, the camp can serve as a model for reexamining (especially using geoscience) other death camps that were totally transformed at the end of the war.

After the Sobibor rebellion, the Nazis made every attempt to cover up what had happened there, and between October and December 1943, search parties rounded up as many rebels as they could and shot them in the forests. They closed and exterminated the labor camp at Luta, Poland (near Sobibor), and, unfortunately, even Polish resistance fighters who were fighting the Nazis turned in some of the Jewish rebels. Within ten weeks of the Sobibor rebellion, the Nazis began the great deception of hiding Sobibor from the Poles, the rest of the Nazi hierarchy, and from other extermination camps, by burying the camp. The great irony, of course, is that in the hurried Nazi attempt to cover up the camp in the middle of the war, they preserved the evidence. Many camps at the end of World War II were thoroughly destroyed, dismantled, or burned, out of fear of being discovered by Allied forces. As the Russians overran the camps in 1944–1945, many of the camps in their sector were reused, when possible, for housing political prisoners.

Sobibor, however, was not reused. It lay covered with dirt in the middle of a dense forest on the border of what is today the Ukraine. In the case of many other death camps, all that remains are the memories of survivors, and whatever physical evidence can be found at the site. In the case of Sobibor, there is an abundance of information, both from the memories of the survivors, and at the physical site itself. In the Sobibor documentation project, I used both.

FINISHED AND UNFINISHED TUNNELS

Holocaust scholars have researched attempts to dig escape tunnels in many places. The tunnel as an escape route was not just an invention of the Soviets, but must have been a well-known method among resistance fighters elsewhere. World War I provided some of the most dramatic examples of escape through tunnels, but even before that, tunnels for escape have been part of the strategy of kings, armies, refugees, and prisoners throughout history.

Not all of the tunnels planned and dug as a method of escape during the Holocaust were unsuccessful. In August of 1941, the French police conducted raids in Paris, arresting more than 4,000 Jews. They interned the Jews in the area of Drancy, created an enclosed barracks with a courtyard and a barbed-wire fence, and provided guards. By 1942, after the beginning of Operation Reinhard (in Named for Reinhard Heydrich) for the building of the Nazi extermination camps in Poland, many from Drancy ended up in Auschwitz and Sobibor: one convoy, number 73, was sent to Fort IX in Kaunas, Lithuania, for extermination. The Drancy concentration camp was under the control of French police until the beginning of July 1943, when the Nazis took over full control. Designed to hold 700 people, at its peak Drancy held more than 7,000. Of the 75,000 Jews deported from France by French and German authorities, over 65,000 were sent directly from Drancy to Auschwitz. Only 2,000 survived their captivity.

The total number of tunnels dug by Jews during the Holocaust will never be known. Many of these tunnels, like the unfinished one at the concentration camp in Drancy, France, were discovered before they were finished. The Drancy tunnel was a very unique form of resistance, given the circumstances. In 1943, some Resistance members at Drancy dug an escape tunnel that extended 115 feet; it was apparently just 1.5 meters from completion when the Nazis uncovered the plot. They tortured one of the diggers, who gave up the names of the other diggers. One of the only reasons we know about this tunnel in Darcy is because some of these Resistance fighters escaped from a train that was transporting them to the death camps in the east. The testimonies of these Jews tell a terrifying tale of how they attempted to build a tunnel that could take all of the people in the Drancy camp out. The size and length of this type of tunnel proved to be one of the most difficult parts; working inside of a camp was different than working in a remote forest site or from a ghetto location.

NOWOGRODEK (POLAND/SOVIET UNION/BELARUS) TUNNEL ESCAPE

The city of Nowogrodek in Poland had 6,500 Jews in 1938. It was absorbed into the Soviet Union as part of the Molotov–Ribbentrop Pact, after the German invasion of Poland. In December 1941, a Jewish ghetto was established by the Nazis, and by May of 1943, only 500 Jews remained in the city. The slow process of liquidating the ghetto began, and the Jews decided to tunnel underneath the walls of the ghetto to a field and the woods beyond. The starting place from a local barn in the ghetto allowed their clandestine work to continue without discovery, well into September 1943. It was a long tunnel involving teams of people, and they even took a final vote on whether the tunnel should be used. Again, as in other locations like Sobibor, where the water table was high, actually building the tunnel became the single greatest detriment to the success of the endeavor. In the area where the ghetto was located, the high water table made it dangerous to dig too deep; the tunnel was built just six feet below the surface, in the range of two feet by two feet in height and depth in many areas. It was similar to the Ponar tunnel: just big enough for an emaciated person to slink through. Also, as in Ponar, they needed to provide electric lights to ensure that the workers could see what they were doing, as candles or lamps absorbed too much precious oxygen.

On the night of September 26, 1943, one of the largest and most successful tunnel escapes of the Holocaust took place: 170 people survived the escape and the subsequent Nazi manhunt, until they were able to link up with partisans. The original plan was to stage a Treblinka/Sobibor-esque frontal attack, but the prisoners decided in the end to build a 750-foot-long tunnel (estimated; survivors differ in their testimonies on the actual length), leading into a field and forest next to the ghetto.

In many ways, this is the most complex engineering achievement of all of the tunnels I have researched, helped by the fact that the ghetto and its substructure allowed for the creation of a small underground light rail line for bringing dirt in and out as it reached its full length. As with Sobibor (after the rebellion), following this successful tunnel escape, the Nazis abandoned this site, as well. It was only a decade ago that the site was rediscovered and excavated.

This type of massive engineering effort was quite different from the next example, which essentially used an existing tunnel. They all represent the same audacious form of resistance, however. Escaping safely through a tunnel was only one of the challenges; another danger was making sure that the undernourished and overworked people who knew about the plan kept it secret.

CHRISTMAS DAY 1943 TUNNEL ESCAPE FROM FORT IX, KAUNAS, LITHUANIA

On the wall outside one of the cells where the members of the "Burning Brigade" of Fort IX were held during 1943 is a statement made by survivor and escapee, Alex Faitelson: "I do not know whether Jesus was really born on Christmas, but we, the corpse burners, did indeed come to life on that night. Christmas night marked the birth of Christianity; we created the legend of the rebellion." Alex Faitelson's book, *The Truth and Nothing But the Truth: Jewish Resistance in Lithuania* (Gefen Publishing, 2006), was my introduction to the story of the escape from Fort IX. My neighbor in West Hartford, Connecticut, Florence Post, loaned me her autographed copy of Faitelson's 2006 book, insistent that I take good care of it, since her father was featured in the book. I carried the book in my backpack as we worked at Fort IX, VII ,and IV in 2017 and regularly consulted it for clues.

When I first was brought to Fort IX in October of 2016 to evaluate what we would do there, I was surprised at the size of the campus. It was an open space on the outskirts of Kaunas, with a small amount of foliage, a large museum complex, and a massive memorial. There were both rolling hills and

The escape tunnel from Fort IX. Sign above the tunnel door reads: "64 prisoners escaped through this [tunnel] door on December 25, 1943 [Christmas Day]," Fort IX, Kaunas, Lithuania. (Courtesy of Richard Freund, the Vilna Excavations Project at the University of Hartford)

unusually flat areas that I knew were hiding the remains of the masses of Jews who were killed and then burned there between 1941 and 1944. My research in Ponar brought me to Kaunas (Kovno, in Yiddish) in 2017, where I was invited to investigate what is probably one of the catalysts for the escape from Ponar. Kaunas is located ninety miles north of Ponar, and in the nineteenth century, a series of protective forts was built around the city. These forts are amazing structures, positioned throughout the city in such a way as to make them desirable as public parks—except for the fact that some of them were used as killing fields during the period of 1941–1944.

The forts were originally built to protect the city from invasion. Although ineffective as defensive structures, they proved to be effective sites for the Nazis, who used their high walls and locations as places to carry out their deadly work in Kovno. Fort IX, the most infamous and expansive World War I fort, was used by the Nazis as a mass killing field: 50,000 people, including 30,000 Jews, were exterminated there. Unlike Ponar, Fort IX was equipped with prison cells, guard towers, wells, and a large infrastructure. The fort suited the Nazi extermination model because it was closest to the Kovno Ghetto, where Jews were brought in 1941. It was located just four kilometers from the famous Kovno Jewish community, and the Jews from the ghetto were marched to the site and killed there.

The Jewish community of Kovno was legendary for its great scholars, *yeshivot*, and Jewish life. Today, the site of Fort IX houses a museum with one of the most extensive collections of artifacts and presentations of the Holocaust in Lithuania. On October 28 and 29, 1941, the "Great *Aktion*"—a roundup that resulted in the movement of thousands of Jews to the Fort IX site for killing—took place. It is believed to be the single most destructive day for Lithuanian Jewish life: 9,200 Jews were killed on those two days at Fort IX. By 1943, nearly 30,000 Jews had been killed there.

Fort IX also includes an example of the so-called Burning Brigade. Starting as early as late 1942, the Nazis issued the order, codenamed "*Aktion 1005*," to burn the bodies of the victims at mass burial sites in eastern locations, where there were no extermination camps. Thus was born the burning brigade at Fort IX and Ponar, in 1943.

The escape from Fort IX was not through a dug tunnel, but rather through an already-constructed cement tunnel used for materials storage. Members of the burning brigade at Fort IX systematically drilled holes in the locked metal door that separated this cement "escape" tunnel from the cells. Their final escape was readied for Christmas Day, 1943, a day when they thought supervision would be lax at the fort. They basically left through the tunnel and climbed over a wall. All of the participants were able to escape.[4]

This still represented an audacious plan, and there is every reason to suspect that the December 1943 escape inspired the Ponar tunnel escape that began over a month later. The Ponar escape by comparison was far more complicated and horrific. The Ponar tunnel, built by the prisoners, resulted in only a small group of escapees, but nonetheless became a story that inspired the world.

· 5 ·

Why I Came to Rhodes

I never planned to work on the island of Rhodes. Although it is a place I had heard about for most of my life, I thought that my Rhodian experience would simply involve working on the large amount of Rhodian pottery that we found in our Israeli excavations. But in the end, I went to Rhodes to uncover evidence of what happened to their synagogues before, during, and after the Holocaust, and in the process recovering much about who these Jews were.

In order to understand the archaeology of the Holocaust in Rhodes, I had to know what the Jews of Rhodes, and their unique Jewish culture and religion, were like before the Holocaust. I had to contrast the peaceful lives these people led on this Mediterranean island for nearly 2,300 years with one horrible day in 1944.

The photo in the (overleaf) is of Nissim and Rachel Cohen, grandparents of author and researcher, Esther Fintz Menascé,[1] who helped to arrange my own exhibition at the University of Hartford with some of her own photographs of her family and the island. Rachel Cohen (born Tarica, in 1846, to Rafael Yehuda Tarica) was already long past the age of sixty when this photo was taken. She is wearing a typical Sephardic Jewish married woman's head covering that would have fit in equally well in Rhodes among Ottoman Muslims. This is a studio shot, of course—she probably would not have dressed this way in her daily life—but it is an indicator of what was being worn by women within her lifetime, and tells much about the multiculturalism of Rhodes at the beginning of the twentieth century. Her long dress and embroidered jacket were typical for the era, befitting the "dignified" definition of a Rhodesli Jewish matron. (*Rhodesli* is the designation used by Rhodes Jews for themselves.)

Rachel married Nissim Cohen probably in the 1860s, when Jewish Rhodes was quite successful, and Jewish institutions of the era were all

97

"It Was Paradise: Jewish Rhodes" exhibition poster at the University of Hartford. (Courtesy of the Avzaradel-Capuano Rhodes Excavations Project at the University of Hartford)

intact. Rachel passed away in 1940, before the changes of the Nazi government were implemented, but she would have been aware of the changes on the island in the late 1930s, as the new Mussolini leadership passively began the anti-Jewish laws of the Third Reich. Nissim was born in 1839 on Rhodes. One immediately notices Nissim's head covering as an Ottoman-style fez, as well as his striped *jalabiyah*-like robe that would have been part of Ottoman finery, as well.

Nissim and Rachel had six children, among them Rebecca Cohen Fintz and Harry Asher Cohen. It is key to note that this is the way the Rhodesli lived, up to the twentieth century, and that they employed the modern technology of studio photography to preserve their images, which they seemed to sense was significant. In addition, these images reveal how much they looked like the rest of the Ottomans living on the island of Rhodes in this period—an important fact. When the Italians took over the island in 1912, it changed a dynamic that had been in place for almost five hundred years of Ottoman rule. It was a period of calm before the storm. For the Jews on the island, especially the Old Town Jews, Rhodes, at the time, was a form of "paradise," where in one period there were as many as six synagogues which served as many as five thousand Jews as places of learning and integration, as well as overnight visitors from around the Mediterranean. Rachel and Nissim lived quite differently than Jews in many other parts of the world at that time. Jewish businesses were integral to the local economy, comprising as much as 40 percent of local businesses in the Old Town of Rhodes, and they had good relations with the Ottomans. It seemed like the Italian occupation was going to continue this cultural integration that the Jews of Rhodes embraced, with new educational and religious institutions—until it all changed.

These maps tell a whole story by themselves: the location of Rhodes, an island, in a specific area of the Mediterranean Sea, and an important part of the Greek economy there; the location of the famed deepwater port of Rhodes, and the development of the city; and finally, the location of the walled city of the Old Town, including the four sites where I worked. This is the single image of the entire area which I used in my university exhibition to tell the story of my work in Rhodes, and the central place of the synagogues in that story.

Rhodes is one of many islands in the Greek archipelago. It is associated with the Dodecanese island chain (literally, "twelve islands"), but is part of a much larger group of 15 large islands and 150 smaller islands in the southeastern Aegean Sea. This island group generally defines the eastern limit of the Sea of Crete. The proximity to Turkey is important, but the location of Rhodes as a protected deepwater port, starting in antiquity, made it a primary destination for ships traveling to other harbors in the Mediterranean. In some

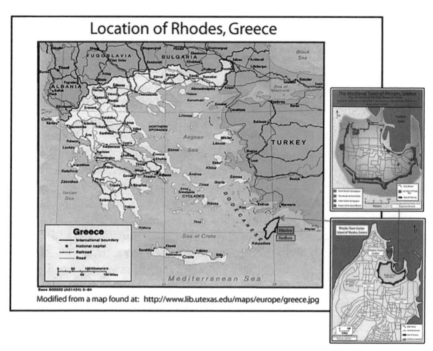

Maps of Rhodes and the Mediterranean, the island of Rhodes, and the four projects in the Old Town. (Courtesy of Philip Reeder, Duquesne University, on behalf of the Avzaradel-Capuano Rhodes Excavations Project at the University of Hartford)

ways Rhodes was the "Hartford, Connecticut, USA," or "Bristol, UK," of its day, as a port that led to much larger markets. I also include a map showing the location of the port itself in Rhodes, and my own work sites. A phenomenon of a protected deepwater port on an island was not easily created in antiquity. Rhodes had a naturally protected harbor, and the slope from the Acropolis to the main city, where the Rhodes culture developed, was inside a curtain wall that protected the goods and the peoples who arrived there.

The Old Town, or the walled city—presumably where most of the Jews arrived, near the port of Rhodes some 2,300 years ago—is where we assume they were first allowed to settle. The Jewish presence in Rhodes and in the entire Mediterranean was enhanced by commercial ventures that started in the time of Alexander the Great, and then continued in the Seleucid and Ptolemian kingdoms, and especially in the time of the Maccabees, in the second and first centuries BCE. The Jews who arrived in Rhodes 2,300 years ago were interested in creating international relations between Judea, and later, Galilee, from the ports that ran up and down the coast, and the ports of Greece, North Africa, and Europe. The Jews were allowed to establish themselves probably first at the port, and then later, inside the walled city.

The map in this figure features the three synagogue sites that we investigated. There were a total of four sites that I was brought in to research, including the Ottoman Classical School site, where the old Byzantine, and even the Hellenistic walls of the city, lay buried below the ground; the Kahal Shalom Synagogue (originally built in the sixteenth century); the Kahal Grande Synagogue (the so-called "Great Synagogue," also built in the sixteenth century); and the site called "the Church of the Victory," built on what might have been the area where the first synagogue of the Jews was located, at the wall nearest the port and adjacent to the original cemetery of the Jews.

I started with one mystery at the Kahal Shalom Synagogue, and my work uncovered other mysteries that constitute my major discoveries in Rhodes. My work was not only about the archaeology of the Holocaust in Rhodes. The Kahal Shalom mystery is only indirectly related to the Holocaust, since the site was damaged during the Holocaust, but reconstructed in the last twenty years. I also explored the Kahal Grande (Great Synagogue), which was not reconstructed. When my research group brings very expensive technology into a country such as Greece, Spain, Israel, Poland, or Lithuania, I offer this technology to other archaeological projects nearby. That is how I ended up with four projects.

The first mystery was the one I saw in the photos of the two arks. The search for the first synagogue at the port, and the Great Synagogue, were the next projects I added, and finally, I added the project of looking for the ancient walls of the city that were originally different from the placement of the present walls. I was invited to Rhodes to solve an archaeological mystery in the Kahal Shalom Synagogue in 2013, and over the past five years I have conducted interviews with survivors and immigrants to ascertain what traditions, photographs, and memories of the synagogues of Rhodes were retained by Rhodesli worldwide, including those from Argentina, South Africa, Congo, Israel, multiple sites in the United States, France, Greece, and Italy. In almost the same way that Lithuanian Jews found a unique designation outside of the country (in South Africa, Argentina, Israel, and many sites in the United States), using the designation of "Litvaks" rather than just "Lithuanian Jews" for their identity, the "Rhodesli" also found a new designation that was convenient both in Greece, and then later in the Diaspora, which identified them to their compatriots.

The ancient archaeology of Rhodes is still being written, and the archaeology of the Holocaust era in Rhodes is the second part of my work. The original archaeological mystery I set out to solve involved the two arks, and a central door between them, found in the main prayer hall of the Kahal Shalom Synagogue. A rabbi attending one of my lectures in the United Kingdom in 2012 had asked me about this configuration, and I had been stumped. "Why," he asked, "would any congregation build a synagogue with a door in between the arks?" He provided me with contacts in Rhodes, and I was able to begin discussions with the Kahal Shalom Synagogue's administrator, Carmen Cohen, obtaining materials for research, and setting up a preliminary "look-see" of the site. I realized very early on in this project that this would involve not just the archaeological mystery of the Kahal Shalom, but also trying to understand the destruction of what had been as many as six synagogues in the Rhodes Old Town before the Holocaust.

This ark arrangement became emblematic of our work. My research group is committed to resolving questions at a site that cannot easily be resolved by using traditional excavation. The Kahal Shalom Synagogue had been reconstructed some twenty years ago; we did not intend to excavate, but rather to see what earlier incarnations of the synagogue might lie beneath the sixteenth-century synagogue. The island of Rhodes is earthquake-prone, and we know that well-documented historical earthquakes probably destroyed the earlier synagogues. We were on a hunt to find evidence of earlier synagogues, especially in a unique eastern wall configuration.

We want to learn about all of the different lives of various features, and that required permits from the archaeological authorities of Greece. I will be using the aediculae designation to describe a standard architectural feature: a beautiful accent above a door-like structure for the housing or protecting of holy artifacts—in short, a Torah ark. This small shrine-like mini closet with the accent on top is standard in many ancient and modern religious sites. The difference with the Kahal Shalom synagogue is that it had two of these arks on two sides of the eastern wall, with a door in the center of the two arks. In most synagogues, both in the Diaspora and in Israel, there is a single, central ark in the middle of the wall facing Jerusalem (so worshippers will be facing toward Jerusalem, generally to the east). Even in Greece evidence shows that there is usually only one ark in the center of the eastern wall. While some synagogues have multiple arks, the element that does not fit with the Kahal Shalom synagogue is the door in between. This seemed like a recipe for unnecessary interruption from the plaza beyond during the solemn prayer services of the synagogue. For this reason, I felt the door must have some other function. I could find no other precedents in either historical Sephardic or Ashkenazic synagogue architecture, so it was a mystery. This type of architectural choice is unusual, ritually almost untenable, and unique to the styles of historical synagogues which appear throughout the world. A door in the middle of the line of sight of the congregation facing east, toward the arks that contain the Torah, might mean that a child or an adult could come into the middle of the service and totally disrupt it. If anything, it is a distraction.

The two arks are serviceable—Jews could read as many as three Torah scrolls for a holiday or Sabbath, and the arks could easily accommodate multiple scrolls—but require that the leader know exactly which ark contains the appropriate Torah scroll to be read in what order at the service. The symmetry of placing a door in front of the viewing public synagogue certainly was not traditional, usual, functional, or religiously ordained, and invites all types of logistical problems. It is, as one Rhodesli told me, "an additional exit, just in case!"—implying that the Jews did indeed think about security, even during earlier periods. Although the additional ark might solve other ritual problems, such as storage and disposal of additional materials (e.g., nonusable scrolls, prayer books, prayer shawls, etc.), I did want to find other historical precedents to see whether there was a traditional or symbolic meaning hidden in this arrangement. Our work there led me down a rabbit hole that took me back to the very origins of synagogue life.

This picture shows the inside of the synagogue, in the direction of the prayer (to the east), and the door leads out to a patio. Why this was so was the mystery I had been asked to solve. I started looking for comparisons or precedents, which meant a thorough search—not only of modern synagogues,

The two arks with the door in between, east wall of the Kahal Shalom Synagogue in Rhodes, facing Jerusalem. (Courtesy of the Avzaradel-Capuano Rhodes Excavations Project at the University of Hartford)

but also of ancient and medieval synagogues throughout the world. It meant looking at illustrations, archaeological reports, and, most important, works that had been written on the Greek synagogues in the Sephardic tradition that might have influenced the specific creation of this particular configuration here. Synagogues, like churches and mosques, usually have a "line of sight" design relatively consistent throughout the ages that helps to direct most archaeological research of synagogues. There is a focus on the central shrine—in this case, the ark with the Torah scrolls inside—as is found in some of the other synagogues of Greece (e.g., in Corfu and Salonika). While architects were artists with their own ideas about what might be inviting to the worshipper, there were standards that gave the worshipper a sense of the history of the location, the "gravitas." Furthermore, the logistics of worship necessitated a certain flow in the building, and I could not imagine how this design fulfilled either the architectural or the religious objectives.

I set off to look for designs in archaeological archives, and in the meantime I was invited to a conference in Rhodes in July 2014, sponsored by the Rhodes synagogue. Since my group has specialized in subsurface mapping of archaeological sites, I assumed that the first problem I would try to solve was whether this feature of two arks and a door in between was just part of the last incarnation of the synagogue (which, according to the foundation stone, was built in 1577), or whether this feature had also been part of the earlier synagogues, which had probably shared the exact same location. While for my group this was an excellent "living" problem that geoscience could help investigate and resolve, it was cast in the midst of the archaeology of the Holocaust.

There are only about ten Jews living on the island of Rhodes today. The Holocaust decimated this "paradise" on a single day in 1944.

WEDNESDAY, JULY 23, 2014

The memorial in this picture commemorates the end of Rhodes Jewry, which took place on July 23, 1944. This is the date on which most of the island's Jews were rounded up and sent on boats to Athens, enduring the longest journey of any group in the history of the Holocaust—three weeks to get to Auschwitz—where most of them were killed during their first days in the camp.

The design and placement of this memorial were not without controversy. It sits in the midst of the Jewish Quarter, the historical site of most of the Jewish businesses and institutions on the island. There are no Jewish businesses, or Jews, in the area now, save for the Rhodes Jewish Museum, housed in the Kahal Shalom Synagogue. On June 23, 2002, Rhodes's Jews

The Holocaust Memorial Stone in the Juderia (Jewish Quarter) of Rhodes, Greece. (Courtesy Harry Jol, University of Wisconsin-Eau Claire on behalf of the Avzaradel-Capuano Rhodes Excavations Project at the University of Hartford)

from all over the world gathered at the square now known as *Plateia Martyron Evreion*—the Square of the Jewish Martyrs (of the Holocaust)—in advance of the coming anniversary of the roundup of the Jews of Rhodes on July 23, 1944. The street of the Old Town traveling west from the square had been the Jewish commercial zone of the Old Town's Jewish quarter for the past one thousand years. The Rhodesli had gathered to commemorate the unveiling of a six-sided-column Holocaust memorial translated into the six languages spoken by the Rhodes Jews. The inscription reads: NEVER FORGET. IN ETERNAL MEMORY OF THE 1,604 JEWISH MARTYRS OF RHODES AND COS,[2] WHO WERE MURDERED IN NAZI DEATH CAMPS, JULY 23, 1944. Atop each inscription is a Jewish symbol, and on the base, beneath the column, the six-pointed star.

When I arrived in Rhodes in July of 2014 for the seventieth anniversary commemoration conference, I realized that I was part of a special gathering dedicated to the Holocaust, rather than the historical research I had come to conduct on the synagogues and the Jewish community. Most of the conference was focused on the history of the most recent chapter of the Jews of Rhodes: the roundup, and the destruction of Rhodes Jewry. The lecture I had prepared was about the archaeology of synagogues, and the beginnings of understanding the synagogues of Rhodes. I had come with a film crew headed by Ari Jacobson, and his presence gave us invaluable information, in addition to the testimonies of the families he was able to film.

Many elements of the synagogue had been destroyed after July 23, 1944, when the Jews of Rhodes were rounded up by the Nazis and transported on boats (with a stop on the island of Kos to round up the Jews there) to the port in Athens, where they were transferred to trains that took them to Auschwitz. The damage had been wrought not only by the Allied bombing of the island, but, according to those who were on Rhodes after July 23, by the neighbors of the Jews who ransacked the synagogues in search of treasures. The Jews who left could not take their possessions with them, so it was assumed they had somehow hidden their treasures in order to retrieve them later. It was, by all accounts, from start to finish, the "longest journey" of any Jewry in the Holocaust.

My own talk on July 23, 2014, was devoted to sharing some of the data I had collected on the three synagogues I would be researching, comparing the Kahal Shalom (the "Peace" synagogue); the Kahal Grande (the "Great" Synagogue); and the proposed "original" location of a synagogue (the so-called "Church of the Victory," discussed below) located closer to the port of Rhodes, where local archaeologists believe the Jewish community was based in earlier periods. My goal was not necessarily to see what was destroyed in the Holocaust era, but rather, to see what might still be left following earlier destructions.

THE PRINCIPLES OF SUPERIMPOSITION
AND CULTURAL MICRO-SUPERIMPOSITION

One of the most important innovations I have introduced over the years is a way to understand local Jewish history from earlier periods without excavating, but rather using noninvasive technology to gather information of what still lies below the surface, and then to do pinpoint archaeology on that precise site. On Rhodes, I used extensive textual traditions about the island to help me understand what had happened in a single location, and then, based upon the destruction on the island in general, I assumed that I might find an earlier structure below the present structure. This idea is not new; it is one of the founding principles of archaeology, and, originally, in geology: superimposition, or superposition. The principle of *superimposition* dictates that the most ancient layer is below the most recent layer of construction. This theory first emerged in the writings of Danish scientist Nicolas Steno in the seventeenth century, and, then, later in the eighteenth and nineteenth centuries, became a standard part of geology.

Steno observed that the oldest layers of rock were on the bottom of a formation, and the youngest layers were on top. In the study of archaeology, this principle is used to identify the strata, especially as excavators go through horizontal layers of detritus. What I do with culturally significant locations like synagogues, churches, and mosques (which often cannot be traditionally excavated), for example, is use GPR and ERT to identify these destroyed floors below the top layer, to see how many iterations of the building may have existed in the same location (sometimes, if possible, sampling those layers), and determining at what depths these more-ancient floors and debris occur. Then I sync that information with the local written records of building and destruction at the site.

I have slightly modified the principle of superimposition to help my students understand a principle of archaeology that is extremely well founded in the excavations of Jewish sites, especially synagogues. I call this *cultural micro-superimposition*, since I am looking for small areas of layers that suggest earlier floors and debris of earlier Jewish institutions under the present floors of synagogues. I use geoscience—especially at synagogues like the Kahal Shalom (KS) and the Kahal Grande (KG) of Rhodes—not so much to see the present debris from the Holocaust era that is usually right below the surface, but rather to see how the earlier layers of the synagogues were constructed, and to see where there are earlier strata that preserve artifacts in their original locations. These earlier layers may preserve much more about the history of the Jews of Rhodes than any other location since. In general, people in earlier periods did not have access to heavy equipment, and were forced to build right on top of the debris piles from earlier destructions.

During much of the past two thousand years, the Jews of the Diaspora were allocated a specific "site" where they were allowed to live and build their institutions; they were not free to build at any location. It was not always the best area of a village/city. Usually they were allowed to build only with wood (less permanent), and then later, they would be allowed to build with stone and brick. It was a pattern that makes archaeological stratigraphy much easier to track than in areas where people were free to abandon a site and start up someplace else. Thus, when one of the Jewish institutions—for example, a synagogue, study house, or ritual bath—was destroyed by either natural or human disasters, they inevitably had to rebuild in the same location. Hence, cultural micro-superimposition means that if we know the Jews were located in a place in a city, all other things being equal, it is pretty much a given that this was the location they had been allocated at an earlier time. If there is a synagogue in a certain location into the pre-modern and modern periods, it was probably there before that period as well.

Records indicate that the present KS and KG buildings may have been built in the sixteenth century, but they were repaired in the eighteenth and nineteenth centuries, after minor seismic activity. More important for my work is that in the centuries prior to the sixteenth century, these same structures may have been totally reconstructed after major earthquakes. When I am asked what I am looking for at the KS and KG buildings, it is not necessarily damage from the Holocaust, but rather the remains of the medieval synagogues in the same place. These earlier layers in KS and KG are like time capsules that tell more about the material culture and customs of the people inside of the synagogue than the upper layers ever can. This form of cultural micro-superimposition means that in a particular setting, I will usually find one era of Jewish life built on top of an earlier era, more often than not preserving more at the bottom than at the top because of two other principles: the principle of scarce resources, and the principle of secondary use of sacred spaces. These are relevant not only when considering the archaeology of Rhodes, but for most Jewish communities.

The destruction of a holy space did not mean that you threw out all of the columns, architecture, and design materials from the old structure; instead, they would be incorporated into the new structure. (It was also easier than digging them out and disposing of them.) In fact, every ancient or medieval synagogue is a mini time capsule when it comes to archaeology. In other places and among other peoples, if a building was destroyed, people could (and often would) abandon that original location and rebuild elsewhere.

In the case of the Jews on the island of Rhodes, we have a combination of factors that contributed to the locations of KS and KG.

The third Rhodes "synagogue" site we worked on for more than two seasons is the so-called "Church of the Victory," by the Gate of St. Catherine. This site, which may still lie buried underneath the church, was accessible to our research group since it too was destroyed. Dr. George Dellas, chief architect of Rhodes, was the proponent of this work, which required another permit from the Ephorate. The Church of the Victory is a more-complex cultural micro-superimposition site than the other two synagogues in Rhodes.

Before the Jews took up residence in the area where the present-day Juderia is located, they were probably located closer to the port. The area of the church is directly adjacent to the old Jewish cemetery (which was moved in the Italian period), and the church architecture suggests that there were multiple buildings located at the site. The Jews presumably moved their KS and KG synagogues to their present locations after the Crusades, so when we see multiple strata in the KS and KG, we assume that they may preserve what was left of the buildings after the earthquake in Rhodes of 1481.

The original Church of the Victory, built during the Crusades, may preserve the earliest remnants of Jewish life on the island. This was not the first time that we were looking for remnants of Jewish life under a church. Back in 2005 I was invited to do similar GPR scans for a Crusades-era synagogue in Burgos, in northern Spain.[3] This church had also been destroyed (in the Napoleonic period) by the time we got there, so once again, we had a clear field on which to work. (Today it is a park very close to the entrance of the famed Castillo.) Our work at the Iglesia de la Blanca in Burgos, Spain, revealed the synagogue beneath. This is what we are working on at this third "synagogue" of Rhodes. While not necessarily connected with the archaeology of the Holocaust, it is very instructive about the history of the Jews in Rhodes.

When considering the archaeology of the Holocaust, it is important to bear in mind that although a synagogue, bathhouse, ritual bath, or study house may have been destroyed in the Holocaust, what's underneath may be a preserved ruin of an earlier structure, and may contribute to our understanding of the roots of Jewish life. Part of my work is to understand and preserve the earlier history of the Jews in the area. The archaeology of the Jewish experience in history provides me with a barometer by which to measure the culture which has been lost and a series of principles that help us find what we are looking for.

This is not only about the ghettoization of the Jews. Historically in the Diaspora, and even in post-biblical Israel, Jews were restricted to very specific areas of a village or city. Some of this had to do with access to cemeteries, but sometimes it had to do with meeting the simplest of daily needs, such as water and bathing. These areas included not only ghettos, a term which conjures up walls of enclosure, but often even separate parts of a town or village. In the case of Rhodes, it involved a Jewish quarter to the walled Old Town. Jews could not build anywhere they wished, could not generally purchase or own or have title to land acquisitions anywhere, so the idea of looking at synagogues built upon synagogues upon synagogues is a form of cultural micro-superimposition that is aided by Jewish isolation. The ruins are specific to Jewish buildings like synagogues, bathhouses and ritual baths, and study houses, for example.

I also used this principle of cultural micro-superimposition at the Vilna Great Synagogue and Shulhoyf in Vilnius. Although the synagogue and bathhouse had been destroyed in the Holocaust, it had been rebuilt and renovated after fires in the eighteenth and nineteenth centuries. Part of my research was to find the earliest foundations (in the same area) in downtown Vilnius. I have found this same form of cultural superimposition in ancient churches, such as the Greek Orthodox Church of the Annunciation in Nazareth, Israel, where I have been working for fifteen years. Often, an event is so important to the reason for the establishment of the church that even when it is destroyed (for natural or man-made reasons), it is rebuilt in almost the same location, reusing materials without excavating down to the foundations, just capping the debris and building right on top of it.

The particulars of the Holocaust in Rhodes are well documented.[4] Italy took over the administration of Rhodes from the Ottomans in 1912. The Jews and the Italian administrators enjoyed a cordial relationship with the Jewish community of Rhodes, and the teaching and study of Italian by the Jews there increased. In the Rhodes Jewish community, a yeshiva was developed, followed by a modern rabbinical college. The Jewish community created modern Jewish educational facilities, added synagogues, and increased economic ties with the Italian colonies. In general, this was part of the two-thousand-year development period of the Jews of Rhodes.

As Nazism grew in Germany, and Fascism, in Italy, Hitler and Mussolini developed many of the same major ideas about ethnic and racial laws, although they differed on their implementation, beginning in 1935 (the year of the Nuremberg Laws in Germany). The anti-Jewish (racial) laws that restricted much of Jewish life in Nazi Germany, and later Austria, were not as intense in the Italian sectors. Tensions on Rhodes had been building since the beginning of Fascism in Italy, in Mussolini's administration. A dramatic change in the ratio of men to women caused many women to become engaged via mail before joining their husbands overseas.

In 1928, the Fascist Italian governor of Rhodes, Cesare Maria De Vecchi, closed a recently opened yeshiva. Many new Jewish immigrants were expelled, and the community faced discriminatory laws. One of the issues that I have been examining in my archaeological work is the account that the governor used Jewish tombstones to build his own house. More important, the ancient Jewish cemetery of Rhodes, located by the walls of the Old Town, was turned into a park, and although many of the Jews were able to move their family tombstones to a new location outside of town, most were not financially able to do this. (Part of an archaeological research project on the Avzaradel-Capuano family that I've undertaken at the University of Hartford has included work in both the ancient and modern cemeteries in Rhodes, as well as excavations of the synagogues.)

The implementation of these "orders" by the Italian governor caused great alarm and hardship to the Jewish community, although it was nothing like what had already taken place in Germany. It resulted in a swift exodus of more than 2,000 Jews from Rhodes, which, prior to then, had had a population of 4,500. It is this exodus that provided an important resource for my work in Rhodes. The rest of the Jews felt they were relatively protected because they lived on an island, disconnected from the rest of Europe. They were wrong. If anything, the fact that Rhodes was an island made it an easy target for the Nazis' *Judenrein* ("devoid of Jews") policy. By the end of the war, it seemed that the extermination of the Jews was one of the few goals the Nazis still seemed to be interested in achieving.

THE HOLOCAUST IN GREECE

I will not be writing an entire Holocaust history of the Jews of the Sephardic world, nor about the Sephardic losses in the Holocaust.[5] So many different countries would be involved, from Holland, France, and Morocco, to all around the Mediterranean and Turkey. I want to emphasize that what happened to the Rhodesli was not inevitable. In some parts of the Sephardic world, integration with their neighbors served to save some Jews. This book is focused on the Holocaust in Greece. While most of the 6 million Jews killed in the Holocaust were European Ashkenazic Jews, hunted down in as many as twenty countries, 67,000 Greek Jews were also included in this number.

I have talked with survivors about the experience of Sephardic Jews at Auschwitz, including Henry Levy. One of the board members of the Greenberg Center at the University of Hartford, Henry was a Ladino-speaking Jew from Thessaloniki when he arrived in Auschwitz, where he encountered many fellow Jews who spoke Yiddish, German, Polish, Lithuanian, Romanian, Hungarian, and other European languages. They had a hard time accepting Henry as their "brother" because of the language difference. It was not only about language; it was a cultural divide. Although it may seem irrelevant today, in the period of the Holocaust, all Jews were under threat, whether North African, Mediterranean, Eastern or Western European. The Jews in the death camps always suspected that infiltrators were being placed in the camps to gather intel. Nazi camp staff also struggled to understand Henry. Greek and Ladino were the two languages that he knew well, and neither one helped to establish him in the camp.

While this may seem like a minor point, it is important when it comes to the overall understanding of Holocaust archaeology done in Europe during the past couple of decades. It was part of the postwar legal battles, but not part of the investigations conducted by communities where Sephardim lived. While European Jewish claims against the European governments that appropriated their properties were careful to use the court systems and establish protocols, in many places in the Mediterranean Jewish communities (who suffered equally the appropriation of their properties), their governments were slow to attend to this issue after the war. This makes my work in Rhodes both groundbreaking and a crucial part of the larger archaeology of the Holocaust.

The mainland of Greece and a few key cities and islands (Corfu, Crete, and Rhodes, along with Kos) define the borders of the Greek Jewish world. There were approximately 75,000 Jews in all of Greece before the Holocaust. The end of the "Golden Age of Rhodes Jewry," 1522–1840, under the Ottomans, actually began in the Italian period. Jews started immigrating in the 1880s, and part of the migration was the result of the infamous Rhodes Blood Libel of 1840. The "blood libel," used in Europe for centuries at Passover and Easter as a canard of anti-Judaism, has many earlier incarnations. It refers to the unfounded contention that Jews needed "Christian blood" for the making of their Passover matzah.

In 1840, there was a blood libel in Damascus and Rhodes that brought to the forefront the new alliances of Europeans in the Middle East and the Mediterranean. The story served Christian Europe as part of the other anti-Jewish measures in many communities. While it had no founding in Islamic traditions, the local authorities nonetheless arrested some Jews, interrogating the chief rabbi of Rhodes intensely about the blood libel. Ultimately, the sultan in Constantinople denounced the blood libel charge as false, and the incident was checked, but the damage had been done. If not for the intervention of Sir Moses Montefiore in London, and Baron Rothschild in Vienna, this might have ended Rhodes's Jewry even earlier. Anti-Judaism that had not really been a major part of the story of the Sephardic, highly Ottoman Jews of Rhodes suddenly was brought from other areas of Europe in new and virulent ways. After the Balkan Wars (1912), the Italians ruled the island, and many in the Jewish community moved to Africa and began the trek to the Americas.

For Greece, Hitler's war started in October 1940, when Italy invaded those parts of Greece on behalf of the new Axis alliance. Germany had to come to the aid of Italy in the conquest of Greece, which was divided into German and Bulgarian zones, with 62,000 Jews, and an Italian zone, with 15,000 Jews. In the winter of 1941–1942, refugees from Thrace, eastern Macedonia, and the Bulgarian territory fled to Thessaloniki and Athens. The food supplies of Thessaloniki gave out and starvation and typhus were rampant. The Nazis conducted summary arrests and executions. Approximately 60 Jews died each day. On December 6, the Jewish cemeteries of Thessaloniki were confiscated and pillaged. The largest group of Jews (2,800) was rounded up by the occupying German forces on March 15, 1943. In the next three months, 45,649 Jews were sent from Thessaloniki to Auschwitz. Only a handful survived. The Jews of Rhodes were rounded up only in July of 1944. By August 1943, 46,091 Jews had been deported to Auschwitz. Of those, 1,950 survived. Fewer than 5,000 of the 80,000 Jews living in Greece survived. The majority, after returning from the camps, emigrated to Israel. While the 2,300-year history of the Jews in Greece had not ended, it was devastated. Perhaps 10 Jews live permanently on the island of Rhodes today.

Italy, as an ally of Germany during World War II, allowed the Germans to share control over the island of Rhodes from 1941 to 1943. In September 1943, with the fall of Mussolini and the Italian military surrender, full control of Rhodes was ceded to the Germans. The Jews of Rhodes had no way of leaving the island in an organized way. But for the efforts of a lone Turkish diplomat in the wake of the first roundups in July 1944, none might have survived. Selahattin Ulkumen, a thirty-year-old Muslim consul in Rhodes, saved approximately fifty Jews with visas that he issued to those Jews with Turkish citizenship. In 1989, Israel recognized him as one of the "Righteous Among the Nations," and listed his name at Yad Vashem. Bernard Turiel and his brother Elliot were two of those saved by the consul. Bernard is one of my interview subjects in the University of Hartford project. I was able to interview him in his summer home in Massachusetts. His stories about his life—and his final days—in Rhodes provided me with important information on the atmosphere in the area where the synagogue was located.

The way the roundups unfolded had many twists and turns for the Jews in July of 1944. On July 18, 1944, the male Jews of Rhodes, age sixteen and older, were ordered by the German military commanders to appear the following morning with their identity cards and work permits at the Air Force Command Center. The tactic of requiring the work permits was, of course, a deception. The Jews were fooled into thinking they were being summoned to be sent to a work camp. The next morning, after the Jewish men were assembled, they were brutalized and threatened by the Nazi soldiers, who proceeded to take away their identity cards and work permits, and herded the Jews into the basement of the building.

On July 20, an unusual news broadcast from Europe reported an attempt on Hitler's life, which raised the hopes of many Jews that the war would be over and their perilous state ended. But on July 23, 1944, the 1,673 Jews of Rhodes were ordered to march to the port, where they boarded three crowded boats. On that single day, a 2,300-year-old Jewish community ceased to exist. The crossing from Rhodes to the mainland of Greece lasted eight days and was horrendous. Seven people died during the trip. They stopped once at the island of Leros, where they were joined by another small cargo boat carrying about a hundred Jews from the island of Kos. Like the people from Rhodes, they had also been herded onto the boat after being stripped of all their valuables and identity papers. After landing in Piraeus (Athens), and staying at the Haidari concentration camp, they were forced onto trains to Auschwitz, where most of them were murdered. There were just 151 survivors.

WHAT WAS LOST: THE ROMANIOTE AND SEPHARDIC LEGACIES OF GREECE

Most of what has been written focuses on the loss of the distinctive Sephardic traditions of Greece and especially Rhodes during the Holocaust. In fact two different traditions were lost. The Romaniotes, an early Jewish group that populated the area of Greece, spoke a Jewish dialect of Greek that mixed Hebrew, Aramaic, and Arabic. The ancient Jewish Greek speaking Inhabitants lived for almost 2000 years in Greece before the arrival of the Sephardim. The Sephardic traditions that were so well known in Rhodes before the Holocaust were a result of large migrations of ex-pats from Spain after the Jewish expulsion in 1492. The "new" Sephardic tradition absorbed many but not all of the Romaniote traditions, and the Ladino was now laced with Turkish and the older Jewish Greek remnants.

In the history of archaeology and the Holocaust there is a special category for those Jewish peoples who did not fit into the "natural" definitions of the Nuremberg Laws. The Sephardic Jewish peoples, who had spread originally in the post-1492 expulsion period from the Iberian Peninsula to many of the ports of Europe, continued to spread in the fifteenth and sixteenth centuries across the islands of the Mediterranean to the ports of Turkey, the Middle East, India, and even to the coast of China. The Sephardic peoples were linked by their original ancestry in Spain, but the Jews were ethnically linked with many different peoples of the Mediterranean and Asia.

It might seem that this group of Jews should be immune to the Holocaust because of their inherent connections to the local communities who were themselves non-Aryans, and because of the distance from the center of the Third Reich. They were not saved. The two most important Sephardic communities of the twentieth century in Greece, the Jewish communities of Thessaloniki and Rhodes, were both rounded up and sent to Auschwitz, despite having survived until July of 1944, unscathed. This chapter is about the archaeology of the Jewish community of Rhodes, and the archaeology of the Holocaust in Rhodes—two seemingly different projects, but interrelated because they reveal an aspect of the Holocaust which will be contrasted with the more-well-known Eastern European Holocaust characterized by my work in Lithuania.

I cannot emphasize enough just how important it is to combine geoscience with traditional archaeological methodology. I must investigate the testimonies of the people who lived in the very places I am working; then we do the geoscience and archaeology, sometimes returning to the testimonies multiple times. I am sure I'm not the first person to ask questions about the sites the people lived in. I also know that we do not want to seem like "cultural interlopers" who come to a place just to excavate and send back reports on our findings. We want our students to meet and work with locals—to feel like they are good citizens who truly want to know the people. The places can only mean something when we have documented information from the survivors and observers. When I say to locals and ex-patriot Rhodesli that "Archaeology is really about people," they understand that I am doing this work so we can all preserve what is still left of a destroyed ancient community. Since there are so few survivors to speak about the structures I am investigating, it is very important to go to Rhodesli worldwide to provide documentation about their venerated traditions, and for me to tell them what we discover about them.

Most of my interviews can be viewed on the University of Hartford Maurice Greenberg Center for Judaic Studies website (www.hartford.edu/greenberg). The interviews were conducted over the past four years, many in 2014 at the gathering in Rhodes, and on the island of Kos, which I visited as well. My interviews continued over the next two years, to include Rhodesli in the United States, especially in Los Angeles and my own area, but also in Buenos Aires, Argentina.

I wanted to add an anecdote here about the interview process. In searching out Rhodesli who had stories that they wished to tell, I was drawn to the story of one of my geoscientists, whose family was, remarkably, from Rhodes. On November 24, 2014, I sat in the home of Dr. Dean Goodman in Woodland Hills, California. Dr. Goodman is the director of GPR-SLICE, one of the principal inventors and proprietors of data processing for GPR, whose company I have been using for years. His work is quite well-known. When he found out I would be sending him data from Rhodes, he volunteered his own background, so I arranged for an interview of Rhodesli from the Los Angeles area to come and give their testimonies.

During this research trip I had lunch with Dean Goodman's mother, Rachel (Israel) Goodman, as well as Selma (Franco) Jeffrey, and Arthur Beneveniste. Rachel's parents were born in Rhodes, and while Selma and Arthur were both born on the island of Rhodes, they grew up and live in Los Angeles in a community that has existed for most of the twentieth century. They use Ladino nomenclature, calling their original synagogue (founded in 1917) a "Comunidad." The lunch was filled with tidbits of information about the life of Rhodes, and especially their recollections about the two synagogues that existed there a generation before the Holocaust. When we finished eating our meal, one of the participants said, "Let's thank God for such a good meal."

They were not really calling for the official rabbinic "Grace after Meals," but it was a moment where I looked around at the three eighty-plus-year-olds—who were all still connected with the traditions of their ancestors from Rhodes, even though they had not lived there for most of their lives—and I spontaneously broke into a rendition of the shortened "Grace after Meals" in Ladino. I thought they might recognize the "Blessed Are We" (known as *Bendigamos* in Ladino), which follows some of the traditional themes of the longer rabbinic form. *Bendigamos* is thought to have emerged from the lives and archives of the exiles from Spain. I had studied it and other Ladino documents and knew it by heart.

> *Bendigamos al altisimo por el Senhor que nos creo*
> *demosle agradicimiento por los bienes que nos dio.*
>
> (Blessed is the Lord most High who created us
> and to whom we give thanks for what it is that he has given us.)

Most think that this prayer could be five hundred years old or more, composed by a Sephardic exile of Spain. The words would have been a good "cover" for a *marrano* or *converso* (a convert to Christianity) who perhaps no longer knew the official rabbinic Hebrew version of the "Grace after Meals" prayer. It is thought to have been passed down generation after generation to exiles in their new locations to remember where they came from. Ladino is a Spanish dialect that is not unlike the Spanish of today, but is really a time capsule of a life and times that no longer exist.

The Jews of Rhodes also knew and used this version, and Rhodesli I have met have mentioned it to me. After 1492, many exiles from Spain ended up in Rhodes in the sixteenth century, just about the time that the synagogues I was investigating in Rhodes were being built. This "Grace after Meals" was probably being recited at that time.

Rachel, Selma, and Arthur were a little shocked that I knew this song they had grown up with, but they all started to sing along with me in Ladino. For that moment, an Ashkenazic (Vilna Jew) archaeologist connected them with the Sephardic past of Rhodes in a Los Angeles living room. It was quite mystical.

I purposely conducted these interviews not in a studio, but on locations in Rhodes and Kos—most in an apartment near the Kahal Shalom Synagogue, some in the new Jewish cemetery of Rhodes, and one in the excavations of the ancient city of Kos, which is in close proximity to the synagogue of Kos. Since the lives of the Jews of Rhodes and Kos are intertwined from antiquity to the Holocaust because of proximity (there is no established group of Jews on the island of Kos, but there are caretakers), and because of the roundups in July of 1944, it is only fitting that I conducted this latter interview there. An important synagogue was originally built on the island of Kos, also in the sixteenth century, and there are Jewish cemeteries there that will need to be fully surveyed, more than likely a future project.

I want to mention a few aspects about the interviews and how they contributed to the archaeological work. Some of the interviews were filled with information about the survival of relatives from Auschwitz or Bergen-Belsen after the war, and the survivors' words are spoken by their relatives, often cousins, nieces and nephews, children and grandchildren, who as children heard about the life of their beloved Rhodesli, and what it was like after the roundup. Others told me about the use of the *mikveh* in the synagogue and the local Turkish *hamam* (the bathhouse) of Rhodes. The interviews centered on their memories of the synagogue arks, and what they remembered is what they were told by their parents and grandparents. It is through these interviews that I answered a significant archaeological question about the size and use of the *mikveh* that is located in a small area of the KS synagogue. The *mikveh* is small, although sufficient for Jewish legal purposes, and its location, though secluded, suggests that it was more honorific than functional. When we examined it we found that it did not seem to be easily accessible. When I spoke to the women in Los Angeles about the use of the *mikveh*, they clued me in to the fact that there was apparently a kosher *mikveh* arrangement at the local *hamam*. It is this type of firsthand information that makes our work more meaningful.

The most interesting experience involved the interview with Dr. Giuseppe Mallel, a young millennial who himself is now religious. He is from Italy, and we conducted our interview on the island of Kos in the middle of the archaeological ruins of the island. Dr. Mallel and the others all attended the conference. I was visiting with the film crew to capture the interviews and the information on the synagogues in 2014, and many of the interviews were

Professor Richard Freund interviewing Dr. Giuseppe Mallel of Italy on the island of Kos in the archaeological ruins. (Courtesy of the Avzaradel-Capuano Rhodes Excavations Project at the University of Hartford)

conducted in and around the synagogue in Rhodes and the new cemetery of Rhodes, all of which were locations of the conference. Intimate details of how these people's families have preserved the memory of the synagogues and Jewish life in the Diaspora of the Rhodesli provided my archaeological staff with a clear understanding of why this work matters.

Aron Hasson, a Los Angeles attorney who had four Rhodesli grandparents, is an excellent example of how the interviews provide helpful archaeological information. In the course of the interview, he told me about the initial efforts to preserve what was left of the synagogues, and the synagogue restoration, and then gave me photos of the locations before they were touched. The sites were in an especially poor condition when he established the foundation in 1997, which is the current vehicle for preservation. His photographs revealed columns from earlier iterations of the KG synagogue holding up later walls, and medieval paths that were only a few feet from a large medieval (now destroyed) church next door. I realized that the juxtaposition of the Great Synagogue of Rhodes next to a major church complex spoke volumes about the relations between the Jews and Christians on the island during this period. It really was because of Aron's interview that I started the process of formulating my own archaeological projects at the places that they, and their Rhodesli loved ones, had known well. This is invaluable material for me and for the community of Rhodesli worldwide. It is why archaeology is always about people.

· *6* ·

The Secret of Jewish Rhodes

*W*hile I came to Rhodes to investigate the archaeology of Jewish culture—the destroyed buildings and mysteries of the architecture, from before the Holocaust era to the present day—I also came to Rhodes because there were so many different possible projects I could do with geoscience, and so many good colleagues with whom to collaborate. Furthermore, I had a lingering archaeological question that I wanted to solve from my work in Israel.

It may seem strange, but one thing that made me very curious to visit Rhodes was the ceramic pots. The amphora pictured on the next page, from the excavations of Bethsaida, was discovered in the 1990s and has always been a favorite of mine. Bethsaida is where I have spent my summers for most of the past thirty years. We found hundreds of fragments of Rhodian amphorae, but this amphora became the symbol of our work because we were able to take the many pieces and put it together and get a sense of its grandeur. We used it as a symbol on our own Bethsaida wine, which was produced in Israel during the excavations, and it graced the cover of the third volume of our investigations, titled *Bethsaida: A City by the North Shore of the Sea of Galilee,*[1] which I co-edited in 2004 with Dr. Rami Arav. When reconstructed, this Rhodian amphora truly reveals that it was unlike any other pottery vessels found in the excavation—a "Cadillac" of pots that could hold as much as one hundred pounds of liquid or grain. Some amphorae were five feet tall. Our Rhodian amphorae were not the largest or the smallest; they seem to have been the right size to travel over the seas and land to arrive at a site far from the coast.

An amphora is a large pot with slim handles precariously placed on both sides and a pointy bottom that does not sit flat anywhere. I assumed that the ancient travelers who came to Bethsaida bearing these amphorae had specially built racks for keeping them upright in a bullock cart, either

A Rhodian amphora from Bethsaida, Israel. (Courtesy of the Bethsaida Excavations Project at the University of Hartford)

with notches drilled in wood for the pointy bottoms, or berths of sand to adapt to the shape.

My students always marveled at the reconstructed Rhodian amphora that we had at our exhibitions. It is not just the design of the Rhodian amphorae that were found at Bethsaida that makes them special; it is also the seals on the handles, which tell me the date they were shipped from Rhodes, and even the names of those who shipped them. Dedicated researchers like Donald Ariel—of the Antiquities Authority of Israel, who wrote the chapter in volume four of our study of the site—chronicled the seals and imprints on the handles of the amphorae. Adding individual names to a discovery always enhances its significance.[2] This reconstructed Rhodian amphora fascinated me, my colleagues, and the students—so much so that it was featured at the center of the Bethsaida exhibitions. It demonstrated that Bethsaida was not just a village in the wilds of the Galilee and Golan, but an international trade center.

Remarkably, the village that today is located scores of miles from the coast of Israel was, in antiquity, on a main road to the port of Akko, and a destination spot. That one clay pot and its shipping seal was evidence of a whole group of middlemen and merchants that made their living by transporting these vessels all over the ancient world. The large amphorae with their delicate and ornate arms required an entire mechanism for their transport, not to mention the production of whatever goods they contained. They first had to be loaded into a cart specially configured with wood cutouts to accommodate the size and shape of the vessel. Then these amphorae were transported to the port of Rhodes to a waiting ship also built to accommodate the oddly shaped pots. They had to survive the journey to the next port. From the moment they arrived at the port in ancient Israel, they required the same specially designed carts with cutouts to accommodate the shape of the long pointy bottom, in order to deliver them safely to different locations. All of this was dependent upon the existence of roads that led from Mediterranean ports through Galilee to inland locations. That road had to be able to accommodate a transport vehicle loaded with fragile amphorae that led to a location like Bethsaida, which today is quite isolated.

The presence of these amphorae speaks volumes—not only about the vessels themselves, but about the sites where they were found. Although it was an arduous journey, it must have been lucrative enough to make it worthwhile for the many people in between. The existence of these many intermediaries—presumably both Jewish and non-Jewish purveyors, who had to know the roads, the clientele, and even the products, both in Bethsaida and in Rhodes—encouraged me to think that the populations of Bethsaida and

Rhodes must have been connected, even in this early period (the second and third centuries BCE).

Over the period of a decade, fourteen stamped handles from amphorae were found at Bethsaida, which were shipped from Rhodes to Bethsaida in the second century BCE. This does not include the hundreds of other pieces of amphorae discovered at the site that did not have Rhodian seals informing us of when, what, and by whom. To my mind, this is where one sees the relationship between the material culture and the people. The people of Bethsaida and the people of Rhodes were connected in a very real way by their commerce. Presumably, the amphorae were all shipped in a small window of time from the island of Rhodes to this fishing village, and probably contained either olive oil or Rhodes's famed wine. It is also not clear whether they were from "kosher" dealers in Rhodes, or just for general consumption, since it appears that in the second century BCE, Bethsaida had a Greek military outpost. I will not debate here whether all Jews used only Jewish products in all times, or whether Bethsaida was Jewish during every period of occupation. It is possible that this Bethsaida was a Greek Seleucid outpost, where the soldiers ordered up a taste of home, but it is equally possible that there were Jews involved in the mechanism of transport and processing of the products for export from Rhodes to ancient Galilee. It is a piece of the puzzle that makes archaeology a study of peoples and their movements over time.

Hundreds of stamped handles with the "Rose of Rhodes" symbol have been found throughout the Galilee and Jerusalem from the same time period, and to me it personalizes the connection between my archaeological interventions in ancient Israel and Rhodes. It is impossible to say whether all of the shipments were only for non-Jews, but it is reasonable to assume that some of the purveyors, transporters, consumers, sellers, and their agents were Jews, leading me back to my first question: Was there a Jewish presence in Rhodes during the Greco-Roman period? My first interest in working in Rhodes was to look for the same elements that I had found in Israel. I am interested in the relationship between the lands of Israel and Rhodes in the Hellenistic period, because that is what the literary evidence points to, and the recent discovery of a third-century-BCE olive press in Rhodes marked with a menorah may actually confirm that some of those amphorae may have been coming from supervised "kosher," or Jewish, olive oil makers in Rhodes.

The island of Rhodes has a very long and well-documented ancient archaeological record, significantly augmented by reconstructions at the ancient port of Rhodes even after having suffered during World War II. It was one of the most important of the many islands of ancient Greece, and renowned for its bronze, and its deepwater ports. Judging from the numbers of finds on the island, these ports served the entire North Africa coast and the Mediterranean, and resulted in Rhodes having one of the leading economies of ancient Greece from the classical period to the Roman period.

In antiquity, Rhodes was an island dedicated to the god of the sun, Helios. Because it was a transit point between the Middle East, Asia, and Europe, its traditions were known from even before the Greek period, and possibly, by biblical writers. Archaeologists confirm that the island has been inhabited and culturally significant since the New Minoan age (1700–1400 BCE), and that the area south of the present Rhodes Old Town has been inhabited since the Mycenaean period (1600–1200 BCE). Rhodes had protected bays, natural clay soil that was advantageous for ceramic production, the raw materials for bronze production in a later period, the possibility of trade with the most distant settlements to the east on the Silk Road, and easy access to the north to what is today Turkey. Rhodes must have been a part of the regular Phoenician visits from the Middle East to Spain and North Africa, from the earliest periods of commerce. It was, in short, a cultural Mecca of antiquity.

The search for *La Chica Jerusalem*—how and why Jewish Rhodes became a "little Jerusalem"—may not only be from the history of the Jews in the medieval and premodern period, but also from antiquity. It may have originated as an economic connection between the island port of Rhodes and the ancient land of Israel, even while the Temple of Jerusalem was still standing, and perhaps that connection was preserved in their artifactual history. I think this connection in no small measure preserved a part of that Jerusalem, both in lore and in material culture, of the Jews there. The cover of this book, the Kahal Shalom Synagogue with the menorah on the beam, is in fact an updated version of the menorah that is preserved on the Arch of Titus in Rome. It was, I think, decorated with a variety of symbols, and the original menorot (in the Temple of Solomon there were eleven menorot, and I can only assume a similar number stood in the Herodian Temple) stood in the main hall of the Temple of Jerusalem to light the enclosed room. The Kahal Shalom had this modern reminder of the Temple, but was, I think, one of a style of synagogues that actually mirrored some of the features of the Temple of Jerusalem.

A LITERARY AND MATERIAL CULTURE HISTORY OF RHODES

Literary sources, such as the noncanonical book of I Maccabees—written in Greek about the time of the Jewish leader, Simon the Hasmonean, in 138

BCE—confirm that there were agreements established between Rhodes and Judea. In I Maccabees 15:15–22, there is a very important indication that the Jews were well aware of the Seleucid and Ptolemian Greek tensions, and had, by the Hasmonean period, learned to court both Greek groups equally (Rhodes is specifically included as a signatory of the agreements between the Maccabees and the Greeks in the book of Maccabees):

> Meanwhile, Numenius and those with him arrived in Jerusalem from Rome with the following letter addressed to various kings and countries: From Lucius, consul of the Romans, to King Ptolemy, greetings. A delegation from our friends and allies the Jews has come to us to renew the earlier treaty of friendship and alliance. They were sent by the High Priest Simon and the Jewish people, and they have brought as a gift a gold shield weighing half a ton. So we have decided to write to various kings and countries urging them not to harm the Jews, their towns, or their country in any way. They must not make war against the Jews or give support to those who attack them. We have decided to accept the shield and grant them protection. Therefore if any traitors escape from Judea and seek refuge in your land, hand them over to Simon the High Priest, so that he may punish them according to Jewish law. Lucius wrote the same letter to King Demetrius [the Seleucid king] to Attalus, Ariarathes, and Arsaces, and to all the following countries: Sampsames, Sparta, Delos, Myndos, Sicyon, Caria, Samos, Pamphylia, Lycia, Halicarnassus, Rhodes, Phaselis, Kos, Side, Aradus, Gortyna, Cnidus, Cyprus, and Cyrene. A copy of the letter was also sent to Simon the High Priest.

It is difficult to say whether this literary reference is a complete fiction, a partial fiction, or a representation of the actual state of affairs of the relationship between the Jews of the second century BCE, but the fact that Delos is listed here, and that there was a synagogue on the island of Delos in this time period, leads historians to assume that there were some Jews who had established themselves on a series of islands, including Rhodes, perhaps as a result of the Hasmonean independent Jewish movement in Judea, or simply because Jews were trading partners from even earlier periods. Understanding the situation on Rhodes is dependent upon learning more about the material culture found there, and its comparison to other literary evidence.

When I put the literary and material culture discoveries together, it appears that the Hasmoneans, and later the Herodians, maintained a close relationship with Rhodes throughout the first century BCE, according to Josephus Flavius, the first-century Jewish historian. By the first century CE (New Testament), the voyage of Paul to Rhodes may be understood as an indication that there was a Jewish community for him to preach to in Rhodes.

THE BIBLE AND RHODES

How long had the relationship between the Jews and the Greeks been going on? It appears that it started in the classical biblical period, before the rise of Alexander the Great, but it was certainly enhanced by Alexander's conquests, including routes that led from the Mediterranean ports to the east. My question was whether the relationship was a development of the Greco-Roman period only, or was it seen by the ancient Israelites and Judeans as part of a longer, more-ancient relationship between the peoples of the Mediterranean in the time of the writing of the Hebrew Bible? The Hebrew Bible is not a geography text, nor is it a newspaper. The question of the written origins of the Hebrew Bible has occupied scholars for the past two centuries, and they have developed a series of conclusions that help direct my own inquiry.[3] In the Hebrew Bible, the people who occupied the islands of Greece were known to the ancient Israelites as "the sons of Javan." The book of Genesis, which was written in the tenth century BCE, lists the peoples of the Mediterranean simply as "Elishah, and Tarshish, Kittim, and Dodanim" (Genesis 10:4). The "-im" endings in Hebrew indicate that they are a plural of some sort. "Kittim and Dodanim" identifies these as a group of peoples (or a place with multiple locations), as opposed to the names "Elishah and Tarshish," which are singular names or individuals (or a specific place), and therefore do not seem to be a group of peoples.

This section of Genesis, which is attributed (by those who ascribe to the Documentary Hypothesis about the writing of the Hebrew Bible) to the Priestly [P] writer, and these traditions, would have been written down in the seventh to the sixth centuries BCE, a time just before the historian Herodotus was writing his own history for the Greeks. The names, although they are supposed to be proper names, may represent the ancient peoples or places of antiquity that were known in the period of the writer. Moving from east to west, Bible scholars have identified the "Elishah" as the island of Cyprus, and Tarshish as the farthest island of the Mediterranean Sea.

The interesting part of the designation "Dodanim" is how unprecedented it is, with no known literary parallel. Bible scholars recognize that a slight change in the curvature of the Hebrew letter "D" would make it an "R," and suddenly the unknown **D**odanim becomes the well-known ancient Rhodians. In the Greek translation of the Hebrew Bible, called the Septuagint (finished in the third century BCE), the name is in fact written "Rodioi," meaning, the people of Rhodes (indicating that the Greek translator was probably working from a Hebrew text that had corrected the "D" to the "R"). Elsewhere in the Bible, it is cited incorrectly.

In the sixth-century biblical book of Ezekiel 27:15, there appears to be the same scribal error, where the prophet Ezekiel writes of an unknown people, the "**D**edenim" (literally, "the children of Dedan"), who enjoy a close relationship with the ancient Israelites. Both Israelites and Rhodians were probably in contact for hundreds of years with people in the Middle East, even before the Greek conquest in the period of Alexander the Great, in the fourth century BCE. The correct reading actually would tell us just how familiar the ancient prophets of the Hebrew Bible were with the island of Rhodes. The corrected text of Ezekiel would read: "The children of Rhodes were your merchants and from the islands they multiplied your merchandise." It was a positive and perhaps lucrative relationship for both the ancient Israelites and the Rhodians.

TRACKING THE JEWS: THE MENORAH AND THE STAR OF DAVID ON THE ISLAND OF RHODES

The menorah, a seven-branched candelabrum, is one of the two main symbols of Judaism from antiquity. The other symbol is the six- (and sometimes) five-pointed star, which is either called the "Star of David" or the "Star of Solomon." These stars are perhaps examples of totally aniconic/nonrepresentational symbols that became important for some Jews, who felt that the Ten Commandments prohibited any representation "in the heavens above; the earth beneath." Jewish artistic expression was limited by a variety of factors, not least of which was their attempt to create their own identity in these symbols. In the period before, and then especially after the destruction of the Temple of Jerusalem, in the year 70 CE, the Jewish Diaspora of the exiles from ancient Judea used a variety of decorations that connected them to a now-destroyed institution.

The star is found on almost everything, including ceramics, memorial stones, glass, and metals in antiquity. The seven-branched menorah, which was itself thought to have been derived from the image of a sacred tree, is a symbol of the Temple of Jerusalem, and originally part of the Tabernacle of the ancient Israelites in the desert. The seven-branched menorah is a representation of a holy artifact used in the rituals of the Jews, and seems not to have been universally accepted. Perhaps because it was a "holy object," its representation offended some who held that Jews should not make representational art of items that existed in the Temple, or as elements in the world.

The Star of David, however, is an aniconic representation that had no equivalent in the actual rituals of Judaism, nor represented anything in this world. The six-pointed star was not a part of the ancient Israelite or Judean worship ceremonies, and its configuration of two interlocking triangles was, I think, an attempt to do something totally different. *Aniconic* representation—what I would call a wholly symbolic or even abstract representation as a designation for a group or people—is not unprecedented. There are other groups around the world which have chosen symbolic representations, rather than a literal artistic rendering or likeness, in their temples and religious institutions. Aniconic representation is not only a Jewish idea, but it became an art form early on in ancient Israel.

The six- and five-pointed star is a geometric series of lines found on Iron Age pottery. Although it may have begun as a potter's mark, easy to incise by using a sharp-edged object, it ultimately became something more. The menorah had a storied use in Jewish life, since it was found in synagogue floors, walls, memorial stones, lintels, and doors of synagogues of ancient Israel and the Diaspora from the Greco-Roman through the Byzantine periods. The 1990s discovery on the island of Rhodes—part of an olive press with a menorah etched in marble, over an early Hellenistic inscription—is the earliest piece of material culture that indicates Jews were on the island of Rhodes. This apparently shows it was either made for, or by, Jews; it might even be seen as a "kosher" object for Jewish distribution of olive oil.

The original oil press itself was of an early design that used weights, not the screw-press design commonly used in Rhodes from the fifth century BCE.[4] Whether Jews should be using Diaspora olive oil (not only in the Diaspora, but in export to the Land of Israel) was argued among the rabbis, who lived in a war-ravaged time. Kosher bread, wine, milk, oil, and other local goods formed the basis of a heated debate among the rabbis, as the local Roman economy in the Land of Israel struggled to survive after two major wars and the onslaught of cheaper imports from the islands. Even Rabbi Judah the Prince in the Mishnah (third century CE), editor of this earliest rabbinic collection, weighed in on the issue. The Rhodes archaeologist of record for the discovery of the menorah on the olive oil press writes that the dating of the secondary use of the altar as a counterweight olive press, and the engraving of the menorah, places it in the Hellenistic period, and even cited the rabbinic debate over the issue as a *terminus ad quem*. The idea that it was in secondary use in the third century BCE implies, I think, that the etching of the menorah was meant to ensure this particular oil press would be used for Jewish oil. The menorah of Rhodes was apparently an important symbol for synagogue and industry alike. It is interesting that the other symbol of ancient Israel became the more prominent on the memorial stones for Jews, often along with the "Rose of Rhodes" to signify their deep love for the island that they called home.

The stars on the memorial stone in the new Jewish Cemetery of Rhodes. (Courtesy of the Avzaradel-Capuano Rhodes Excavations Project at the University of Hartford)

MORE LITERARY EVIDENCE:
JEWS IN FIRST-CENTURY RHODES

A number of first-century-BCE literary sources indicate that the Jews had not only taken up residence in Rhodes, but that they had also been noticed by their pagan Greek neighbors.

Tracking the pre-classical rabbinic traditions of Judaism is difficult. Most ancient sources rarely mention the different traditions of other religions unless it affected them. A series of noticeably different Jewish traditions are mentioned by others on Rhodes. The first-century-BCE Greek writer, Apollonius Molon, who took up residence in Rhodes, is the second writer (after the fourth-century-BCE Greek writer, Hecataeus) to mention the Jews. Apollonius may have gained his knowledge from firsthand contact with a Jewish community in Rhodes (he might have had contact in his travels, as well), but his information is distinctive. Josephus considered him one of two sources (the other being Posidonius) for the anti-Jewish rants of Apion (Josephus, *Against Apion* 2:79–96). There is evidence that by the second century BCE, a synagogue life existed in the Mediterranean Diaspora, including the Greek island of Delos. If synagogues did indeed exist that early on islands like Delos, it is quite possible there was a "synagogue-like" institution on the island of Rhodes that attracted Apollonius's attention.

The idea that the Jews had grown beyond a very random grouping and had a real synagogue is not yet supported by archaeology, but Greco-Roman literature suggests that some of these sources knew a very institutionalized Jewish community by the first century CE. The first- and early-second-century-CE Roman writer Suetonius has the first piece of specific information of Jews gathering on Rhodes on the Sabbath and listening to a *grammaticus* (possibly a Latin substitution for "rabbi/teacher"). Suetonius, in his writing "On Tiberius," 32:2, writes of one Diogenes, who spoke regularly on the Sabbath during Tiberius's stay in Rhodes (6 BCE–2 CE), and who turned him away. There is even inscription evidence that there was a community in Rhodes which may have included "god-fearers," in the first century CE. It was perhaps this community that Paul turned to in his visit there (Acts 21:1–2), as part of his mission to the Jews, and perhaps these types of "god-fearers."

This kind of literary evidence—about a first-century-CE settlement of Jews who practiced the Sabbath, which caught the attention of Greek and Roman writers—may mean there is more archaeological evidence to look for on the island.

FROM JUDEA TO RHODES AND BACK

The most famous connections between Judea and Rhodes were the frequent trips and benefit projects of Herod the Great in the first century BCE in Rhodes. Herod's first visit was in 40 BCE when, having set sail for Pamphylia on his way to Rome, he was nearly shipwrecked, making his way with difficulty to Rhodes. There, according to Josephus's account (*Antiquities of the Jews*, 14:377–78, and *Wars of the Jews*, 1:280), he found the city devastated by the war against Cassius, and "did not hesitate to help it even though he was in need of funds, but actually exceeded his means in restoring it."

Herod the Great had a love–hate relationship with Rhodes, and he visited many times. It was in the spring of 30 BCE that Herod the aspiring king experienced one of the most important events of his life, in the main reception hall of Rhodes: He begged the emperor of Rome, Octavian, to let him keep his job, with the title *rex socius et amicus populi Romani* ("King [of Judea] and a friend of Rome"). When Herod showed up that spring, the authority of Rome had passed to Octavian after the Battle of Actium in September, 31 BCE, where Herod's friend and ally, Marc Antony, had been defeated.

The year 31 BCE had not been a good one for the empire. In addition to the war which drained the realm of its talent and divided its resources, the earthquake of 31 BCE had damaged many important sources of revenue, including Judea. That earthquake and the defeat of Marc Antony made Herod sorely afraid that the people would rise up against him. He would create palaces in the desert to ensure that he could escape from the Jews of Judea. Only seven years into his rule, he had not yet begun his marvelous run of building. The shoring up of his authority was first, and creating places of refuge for himself and some of his family to safeguard his ruling power was second. After his return to Judea in 30 BCE, Herod launched a campaign in Judea, dedicating himself to building the country into something worthy of Octavian's support.

If anyone had asked me a few years ago to name the crowning achievement of Herod's massive building projects, I think I would have said the Temple of Jerusalem, or even the monumental port city of Caesarea Maritima. I was surprised when a colleague in Greece pointed out to me that Herod's crowning architectural achievement, according to the writings of Josephus, was not the Jewish Temple of Jerusalem in ancient Judea, but the Temple of Apollo in ancient Rhodes. In fact, this may provide the clue to understanding the Jewish archaeology of Rhodes and ancient Israel. Josephus writes, "[B]ut the greatest and most illustrious of all his [Herod's] works he erected at Apollo's Temple at Rhodes, at a great expense, and gave them a great number of talents of silver to rebuild their fleet" (Josephus Flavius, *Antiquities of the Jews*, 16:5.3). According to Josephus, this reconstruction of the Temple of Apollo happened in the twenty-eighth year of Herod's reign, or around the year 10 BCE, about a decade into the reconstruction project of the Temple of Jerusalem. What this means is that there might have been some connection between the work that Herod was doing in Rhodes and in Jerusalem. The elements which he may have seen in his many visits to Rhodes may have affected his building project in Jerusalem; but perhaps Jerusalem, and Herod's many other projects in Israel, may have affected his projects in Rhodes.

Herod the Great was the King of Judea from approximately 37 BCE until 4 BCE. Known for his ruthless behavior designed to acquire and maintain his power in Judea, he played a key role in creating the most famous architecture of first-century BCE Israel. His port city at Caesarea Maritima, the palaces at Masada and Herodion, and especially the Temple of Jerusalem, are very distinctive, and easily compared to the work at the Temple of Apollo in Rhodes. The Acropolis of Rhodes still overlooks the ancient harbor, and my archaeological group has had many different opportunities to observe and analyze the archaeology there. The Italians who reconstructed the site in the 1920s show an Acropolis dating from the Classical Greek period (fifth–third century BCE), two miles from the center of Rhodes, with multiple layers of work that date all the way up to the first century. The Acropolis is occupied by the ruins of a temple from the Hellenistic period, and a destroyed area of undetermined use to the north. Local geologists have researched a long and very clear earthquake history. In the third century BCE there was a famous earthquake that destroyed the famed "Colossus of Rhodes," and in the second century BCE, another earthquake followed that would have devastating consequences for parts of the island not yet rebuilt. An earthquake devastated ancient Israel in 31 BCE, followed by Herod's visit in 30 BCE. The Temple of Apollo on the Acropolis of Rhodes was, therefore, restored at just about the same time as the Temple of Herod of Jerusalem.

Earthquakes are one of the main indicators for archaeological strata, because rebuilding rarely meant moving from one's traditional locations. Without heavy equipment, it would have been extremely unusual to try to build a new foundation for a ruined building. The work was one additional layer on top of the existing structures, often using the same materials on-site to rebuild. Earthquakes have been carefully tracked, and a pattern of destruction emerged on the islands of Rhodes, Kos, and other nearby islands, of whatever structures the Jews may have created by the port, or in what is now the Jewish quarter. The famous earthquake that destroyed the Colossus statue in 227/6 BCE, and a follow-up earthquake in 199–198 BCE, in Rhodes, may have been the back-to-back disasters that put an end to the rebuilding of the Colossus on the island. (The Oracle at Delphi is blamed for not allowing the Rhodians to rebuild, but it may be that the earthquakes were simply spaced so closely together that rebuilding seemed impractical.)

The next two thousand years of earthquakes, and what were probably tsunamis, changed the fortunes of Rhodes, and were recorded in the literature. In 148 CE, the rebuilt Rhodes was hit by a major earthquake and tsunami. Antonius Pius, emperor of Rome, helped to rebuild, and was mentioned in the Roman writings of Pausanias. In the Byzantine era, but before the first Islamic conquest there, when it is assumed that the Jews had a community in Rhodes, there were earthquakes in 344 and 515 CE. Strabo writes that although King Ptolemy III offered to pay for the reconstruction of the Colossus, the Oracle at Delphi prophesied that the people had offended Helios, and therefore should leave the statue in place, in pieces. Both Pliny the Elder and Strabo state that the statue lay in ruins, and continued to attract travelers for the next few centuries. According to the early medieval Chronicle of Theophanes the Confessor, when the Muslims arrived on the island under the Umayyad leader, Muawiyah I, in 653, he found the broken statue still sitting in place. He asked that the bronze of the statue be collected and shipped off by Jewish merchants, who carried the bronze on nine hundred camels to the city of Emessa (modern Homs, Syria), a major city of the

Umayyads at the time. The fact that the Jews are specifically mentioned as the agents for disposing of the material of the Colossus bronze is unusual, and a detail which may actually point to ancient tradition with great authenticity.

The earthquakes are good indicators of the changes on the island. Five hundred years later, an earthquake of 1303 may have been the catalyst for the Templars being able to conquer the island. This 1303 earthquake was one of the largest earthquakes and tsunamis ever reported in the Mediterranean Sea. It has been documented in a large number of Latin, Arabic, and Byzantine literary sources. The Templars arrived in 1308–1309, and they encountered a Jewish community. It is in this period that the Church of the Victory was built and the Jews were moved to the area where the synagogues reside today. In 1481–1482, there were a series of earthquakes that struck Rhodes that would have destroyed the synagogues, and would have called for a major rebuilding project. After an epidemic of plague in 1498–1500, the Templars expelled Jews who would not be baptized, but in the period following this event, through the mid-sixteenth century, the Templars brought Jews from around the Mediterranean as slave laborers. It is probably during this last period that the Jews began the rebuilding of the Kahal Shalom and Kahal Grande synagogues that had been transferred there earlier. It is also in this period that the Jewish refugees from the expulsion from Spain in 1492 began arriving in Rhodes, putting their stamp on the language and culture of the Greek Jews who were already living there. It was not the first time that the influences of the Jews of Rhodes came from within and without.

Returning to the ancient "Herodian" connections, it is clear that the stones on the Acropolis of Rhodes and the Jerusalem Herodian stones are similar in style and design. The stones located on the area of the raised platform for the Temple of Apollo at the Acropolis have, all around the outside of the construction, drafted margins. These drafted margin stones were used throughout the Greek period by a number of builders. If this is indeed the Temple of Apollo that Herod the Great rebuilt, to ingratiate himself with Rome, the stones may provide a connection between Rhodes and Jerusalem from two thousand years ago. It may be a coincidence, but in Israel, many of the building projects that are directly linked with King Herod have these drafted margins, including the most famous one, the Temple of Jerusalem. Did King Herod bring the building style of the drafted margins to ancient Israel from Rhodes? Probably not; it was a well-known device for finishing stones in the Greco-Roman world that may have arrived from the quarry slightly damaged. It was, however, a nod to Greco-Roman architectural and building forms that used what are still called "Herodian stones" to adorn the Western Wall, where they remain to this day. For me, this connects Jerusalem and Rhodes in a way that is much more than just about trade.

The drafted margins (so-called "Herodian stones") at the Temple of Apollo at the Acropolis of Rhodes. (Courtesy of the Avzaradel-Capuano Rhodes Excavations Project at the University of Hartford)

The Herodian drafted stones near the Western Wall in Jerusalem and Dr. Harry Jol of the University of Wisconsin-Eau Claire with GPR.

WHO FROM WHOM? HEROD'S STONEWORK
IN RHODES AND JERUSALEM

While there is no direct evidence to connect the Temple of Jerusalem and the Temple of Apollo, there is circumstantial evidence in the design of the drafted edges of the stones that appear in both locations. It is thought that part of the motivation for the restoration done by King Herod in Judea in the later part of the first century BCE of the Temple of Jerusalem was motivated by his viewing of other temples and structures in the Roman world. There was a competing Jewish temple in Leontopolis in Egypt in this period, and by this time synagogues had begun to develop in the Diaspora. In the eighteenth year of his reign (19 BCE), King Herod began a colossal expansion and refurbishing of the Second Temple, along with its artificial Mount, both of which were proving inadequate to the task of handling the tremendous number of pilgrims and visitors that came to Jerusalem.

What could have been his motivation? It was probably to honor himself as the master builder, but it is possible he knew that news of his renovations of non-Jewish temples in places like Rhodes would get back to his constituency, and he needed to show them where his loyalties lay. The renovation of the Temple of Jerusalem continued for thirty-four years, even after Herod's death in 4 BCE. He constructed a massive public entrance with stairs leading up into the main enlarged courtyards. In Herod's Temple, the Levites stood upon an area located between three vast courtyards—those of the priests, the Israelites, and the women—and the entire complex was situated on an elevation twenty-five feet higher than the Temple Mount, accessed by a terraced ramp. When it was finally completed, the Temple expansion created what must have been the largest religious institution in the Roman world. The sanctuary area, with a facade that had two separate areas for entering, became known to all of the pilgrims who visited Jerusalem. It was even remembered in the illustrations of one of the celebrated murals at the Dura-Europos Synagogue—walls painted two hundred years after the destruction of the Temple of Herod!

This is an important point: More than two hundred years after the destruction of the Temple, a synagogue wall preserved the memory of a pilgrim's last viewing of a now-destroyed entrance to the Temple. Not only is this view portrayed on the wall in Dura, but the same view is also captured in synagogues and cemeteries in ancient Israel. The view of the two entrances to the Temple courtyards is captured in the architecture of many of the synagogues, from the Capernaum Byzantine "white limestone" to the Beth Shearim entrance to the burial caves. They seem to be copying a well-known motif, of two smaller, shrine-like entrances and a larger central door. Where

The rabbinic-era Beth Shearim two aediculae and a door in the center entrance to the burial caves. (Courtesy of the Avzaradel-Capuano Rhodes Excavations Project at the University of Hartford)

did they get this view from? It does not really conform to anything in the Greco-Roman building form. Was this rabbinic-era tomb entrance intended to mimic a view that all ancient pilgrims had on their visits to the now-defunct Temple? Since the dead awaited their resurrection in these burial caves at Beth Shearim, were the tombs built to copy the last view of the Temple of Jerusalem that a pilgrim would have had? If so, it would give a special meaning to the synagogues and burial caves that had this configuration.

Most archaeologists have found it strange to have two aediculae (shrines) on two sides of the wall pointing east, with a central door. Some ancient synagogues have the two aediculae, and they are seen as simply placeholders. Dura-Europos preserves one of the earliest series of views of the Temple of Jerusalem, and they seem to project the singularity of the configuration. Five separate views of what is either the ancient Tabernacle (a stand-in for the Temple of Jerusalem) or the Temple of Herod are featured in the third-century-CE Dura-Europos Synagogue wall illustrations. It was a wonder when it was found. No other synagogue preserved so much representational art in one place. It shows the Temple as it was remembered in the third century CE, revealing that they still had a very clear sense of what it looked like. What can be seen in the picture are the three prominent door-like structures with the two winged victories at the top, at the front of the main structure; an unusual rosette in the center of the tympanum (a triangular decorated space on the pediment above the door); and what are *three door-like features*, but this time, with different Roman images on each. In the center is just a door, but the other two appear to be almost ark-like structures that are on either side of the central door, with a small triangular pediment. In the Tabernacle illustration on the Dura synagogue, however, it has three openings in a single wall, and in the background is the Holy of Holies. I want to be clear: These openings are not arks in the Temple, or even in the Tabernacle, but they do resemble the arks that I have seen in the Kahal Shalom Synagogue—two smaller, door-like structures with a central, larger door. They are clearly placed in such a way as to indicate that they were on the outside of the wall; this would have been the way a pilgrim would have seen the Temple of Jerusalem in the period before it was destroyed in 70 CE.

On one panel of the illustrated walls in the Dura-Europos Synagogue, there appears to be a Torah shrine and two smaller-shelled aediculae. This is clearly the Temple of Jerusalem, which has a rosette in the center of the pediment, two winged victories in the front of the building in the foreground, and four pillars on the side. Nowhere is this type of description found, with this level of detail; I believe this is not a literary invention, but rather the product of oral traditions of those who had been there some two centuries earlier. What is particularly powerful about this is that there are multiple images of the Temple of Jerusalem that worshippers in the Dura-Europos Synagogue would have been looking at as they prayed.

I think this is conclusive proof that the Jews' vision of the Temple of Jerusalem was one with two small, mirror-image, ark-like structures with a door in the center. They too wanted to sit in worship and see the Temple as it was before it was destroyed. The Kahal Shalom Synagogue is not only a "miniature temple" (*mikdash me'at*, as all synagogues are called in Hebrew by rabbis); it has gone one step beyond this, adopting the most famous image of the Temple of Jerusalem into the eastern wall of the synagogue that faced Jerusalem. I asked myself, Were they the only ones? As I started to investigate, I discovered there were many synagogues that adopted a whole series of architectural features that resembled this configuration. The worshippers at this KS synagogue not only symbolically faced Jerusalem as they prayed; they also "saw" Jerusalem as it was in the vision of the last pilgrims who visited the city.

The artist who drew this image of the Temple of Jerusalem on the wall of the Dura-Europos Synagogue reflected the memory of pilgrims who had come to Jerusalem for centuries. The artist wanted the illustration there on the wall of the synagogue so that the gathered could see what they were

The third-century-CE Dura Europos, Syria Synagogue wall illustration of the Temple of Jerusalem, with the two aediculae and the door in the center, from the 1933 excavations. (Maurice Le Palud, *L'Illustration*, July 29, 1933; public domain, via Wikimedia Commons)

praying about. As the worshippers offered prayers that remembered all of the Temple ritual, they could look around and see the stunning image of the Temple itself, a place of many entrances and access points. It is not a leap to understand how this image was translated into the architecture of the synagogue, where the central door remained in the wall that faced Jerusalem, and the two arks with the steps leading up to them were the original access points of the pilgrims as they mounted the stairs to the Temple Mount.

SOLVING AN ARCHAEOLOGICAL MYSTERY, AND A SHORT HISTORY OF SYNAGOGUES UP TO THE SIXTEENTH CENTURY

This is not a comprehensive study of the origins of synagogues in the Diaspora, but I thought it would be helpful for those who have not studied the question to have some background. Dr. Lee I. Levine has written what I consider to be the best study of this topic, entitled *The Ancient Synagogue: The First Thousand Years* (2nd ed., New Haven: Yale University Press, 2005), wherein he surveys the origins of the synagogue and the obvious innovations that emerged in each of the centuries. To many, it is clear that the origins lie in the Diaspora during a time when the Temple was either inaccessible—in the period of the Babylonian Exile, 586 BCE—or when it did not exist at all, after the destruction of the Temple and Jerusalem in the Roman period.

The "later" Roman period synagogues were institutions that were made to be Temple-esque, without being the actual Temple of Jerusalem, with its sundry animal sacrifices, priesthood, and separate and biblically defined artifacts. This later Roman period synagogue was a unique stylized building that had developed from "house synagogues" that were part of regular building structures, almost indistinguishable from the manor-like houses where many families resided in a common, gated community. The synagogue entered another stage of development when it turned into a prayer-oriented building led by rabbis. Some worshippers attempted to establish a closer connection to the architecture of the Temple of Jerusalem than others with their synagogues; I think this is what may have distinguished the two ark decorations in the Kahal Shalom Synagogue. The question is, was this a specific trend, or did it take place in just a limited number of places?

The synagogue was intended to model the Greek concept of gathering together, not to perform temple practices, but rather to "pray" about them. Those attempts by the Egyptian community to have their own temple—they also had some of the first synagogues, as well—with a priesthood and sacrifices, had ended by the Roman period, and seem to have been limited to two locations, at Elephantine and Leontopolis. The Egyptian temple reveals just how much the ancient Judeans and Israelites wanted to experience the Temple, even if it was not in Jerusalem.

I have spent thirty years researching the synagogues of ancient Israel and in the Diaspora. It seems to me that synagogue architecture was as much an expression of the imagined Temple as the local architecture. The descriptions of synagogues as *Batei-Knesset* (Hebrew for "gathering places") or the Greek word *synagogue* (also "gathering place") shows us that the Jews were not trying to have synagogues compete for the hope of Temple worship, but as a supplement to it. There were no synagogues in the Hebrew Bible, and none is mentioned through the Persian-period return of the Jews from the Babylonian Exile (in the period of Ezra and Nehemiah), so, if there had been synagogues in ancient Babylon during the Babylonian Exile, the "returning" flock may not have felt it was advantageous to mention it.

When did the synagogue originate? It is traditionally taught in rabbinic literature that the first synagogues were built in the time of the Babylonian

Exile; perhaps excavations may turn up something there in the future. I have to assume that synagogues emerged organically as expressions in multiple locations in the Greek period, and may have resembled other meeting places which other groups developed during this period. The earliest remains of synagogues have been found in Egypt and the island of Delos in the Mediterranean Sea. I assume that many more synagogues may have existed in the Greek islands, and await discovery. It means that the Rhodes synagogues, although destroyed in the Holocaust era, may yet yield many more pieces of the ancient legacy of the Jews of Rhodes and Greece. It means that the Jews of Rhodes—the city often called *La Chica Jerusalem* (the small Jerusalem)—really deserved the title, for reasons that many visitors may not realize.

• 7 •

The Origins of the "Final Solution" in a Forest and a Fort in Lithuania

How does one move from the destruction of the Jews of Greece to the destruction of the Jews of Lithuania? For me, it came in the form of an invitation from an esteemed colleague. We were working in Rhodes during our university term in January of 2015, and now we were planning to take our students to Lithuania during our summer term of 2015. I personally did not know if our students and staff were prepared for the gut-wrenching work of uncovering the Holocaust in Lithuania. It is one thing to tell students about how all of the Jews in Rhodes were rounded up on a single day; it is quite another to tell them about the details of the Final Solution that was implemented over three years in small and large cities all over Lithuania, with the collaboration of fellow citizens.

What does it mean to "discover" the origins of the "Final Solution" in Lithuania? Many readers have heard of the Nazi plan for the Final Solution of the Jewish Question that became a Nazi obsession from 1942 to 1945, referring to their plan to eliminate the entire Jewish people worldwide. It was the last step in a progression that started with ancient and medieval anti-Judaism, followed by the anti-Semitism of the modern period, and finally, by the Nazi movement that developed their formal Final Solution during—or perhaps, even before—the war. In fact, this Nazi plan may have been pursued at the expense of the war effort itself.

As I have mentioned, the term is usually linked to discussions held at the Wannsee Conference, held in Berlin in January 1942. The plan was to murder all Jews using death camps constructed in Poland specifically for this purpose. These camps only became operational in the second half of 1942.[1] Evidence I have discovered in Lithuania shows that six months *before* the Final Solution was formally discussed in Berlin, it was being carried out in the

141

Location of Study Sites

The map of investigation sites in Lithuania, 2015–2017. (Courtesy of Philip Reeder, Duquesne University, on behalf of the Vilna Excavations Project at the University of Hartford)

forests of Ponar, outside Vilnius, and in the forts surrounding Kaunas. I discovered the July 1941 evidence in the testimonies of survivors and locals, and while investigating the gruesome burial pits there, from 2015 to the present.

The archaeology of the Holocaust in Lithuania is different from the archaeology of the Holocaust elsewhere in Europe. In Rhodes, almost all of the people were rounded up on a single day, from a limited area. The stories of the Holocaust in Belarus, Poland, Lithuania, Ukraine, and Latvia vary because of the timing of Nazi atrocities in those areas, and because of the varying degree of active local participation in carrying out these atrocities. Although my work was not restricted to Vilnius, the depth of research my team and I completed in the Vilnius and Kaunas areas was greater than elsewhere, which made it possible to understand the lives of the Jews living there before the Holocaust, and thus, to appreciate just how significant their losses were.

I tell my students that in many ways, the massive implementation of the Final Solution began in earnest in a forest in Ponar, and in a fort in Kaunas, Lithuania. The stages of the Holocaust moved slowly, from the early anti-Semitic references found in Hitler's *Mein Kampf* (1925), to the rise of the Nazi Party in 1933, to the Nuremberg Laws of 1935[2] (which deprived Jews of their German citizenship, and forbade them from marrying non-Jewish Germans), to violence against them in the "Night of Glass" (Kristallnacht) in 1938, and to the 1942 Wannsee Conference that called for implementation of the Final Solution in Poland's death camps. Yet it is apparent that by the end of June and early July of 1941—a full six months before the "architect" of the Final Solution, Adolf Eichmann, met with other Nazi officials in Berlin—the Jews of Lithuania were being systematically exterminated in the Ponar forest outside Vilnius, and in Forts IX, VII, and IV in Kaunas, as well as in other locations. I place Lithuania in the center of the map in this figure because it was also at the center of a unique Jewish world—one which took five centuries to build, but only three years to obliterate.

WHY VILNA MATTERS

The Great Synagogue of Vilna—pictured at the center of the poster (overleaf) for University of Hartford's exhibit, "Vilna: The Jerusalem of Lithuania"—is the epitome of why Vilna was unique. Remarkably, the synagogue survived the Holocaust, albeit damaged, only to be entirely demolished by the Soviets, but that isn't the significance of the Great Synagogue. As you look at the 1929 photograph found on the poster, it tells an entire story. The Shulhoyf courtyard entrance had iron gates, originally donated by the "Tailors' Society"

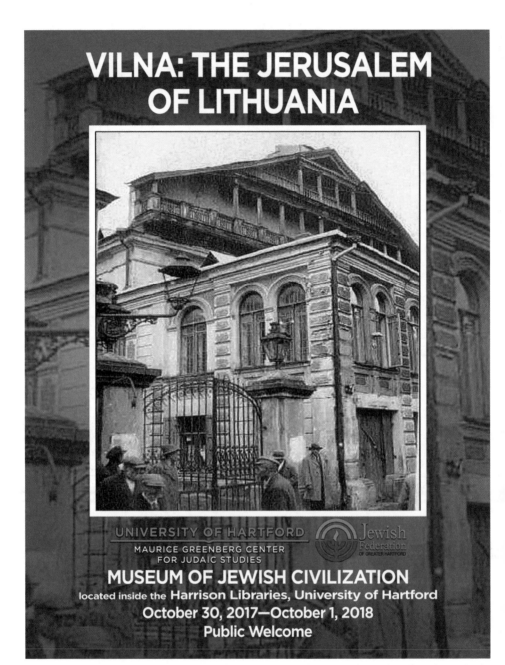

A poster of the "Vilna: The Jerusalem of Lithuania" exhibition at the University of Hartford's Museum of Jewish Civilization. (Courtesy of the Maurice Greenberg Center for Judaic Studies at the University of Hartford)

in the seventeenth century to protect the community of visitors inside. The gates were the entrance to the *durchhoyf*, a passage walkway that led to the different entrances to the many *kloyzn*, or prayer rooms, and tradesmen organizations and societies inside the Great Synagogue. The Great Synagogue and Shulhoyf of Vilna was a mini modern JCC, Vatican City, New York City Library, 92nd Street YMCA, and mini college campus, all rolled into one. It encompassed many parts of the Jewish community, from the secular to sacred. It had the famed Strashun Library on the second floor, with one of the greatest collections of rare Jewish books anywhere in the world; it had kosher food shops, multiple prayer and study rooms, and burial societies, as well as a massive bathhouse, with restrooms, a community well, and a water source, which flowed through pipes from the Dominican monastery nearby.

The university exhibitions attempt to capture the nexus between student and faculty work and the community. They display artifacts, photos, and short films made by students and faculty, and even include small digging boxes for teaching younger children about the importance of archaeology. Not every one of the excavation projects represented in this particular exhibition had an accompanying exhibition, as Rhodes and Vilna did. The exhibition poster above was for a yearlong photography exhibition of the work in greater Vilnius, and encompassed projects at Rasu Prison; the work in the Ponar burial pits and forest; a project at HKP (a vehicle repair facility and apartment complex that I will describe later); and the work in greater Lithuania, including the Silute prisoner-of-war camp, Forts IX, VII, and IV in Kovno (Kaunas), and the Jewish cemetery of Kovno. The exhibition allowed student docents to guide teachers, students, and members of the community through the University of Hartford's Museum of Jewish Civilization, located at the Harrison Libraries at the center of the University of Hartford campus.

For the past fifteen years, I have come back from excavations and presented the material we have collected to the public in a series of lectures and short films, and my colleagues and I participate in our professional societies' conferences, presenting the discoveries we have made each season. The material for the Vilna exhibition was especially plentiful. Not only did I have enough for a PBS television *NOVA* documentary, but, for the first time, I worked with virtual reality filming of the excavations, presenting that in the museum so people can see how it feels to be in the field without going to excavate the site themselves! Visitors can don the special viewing gear and reach out and "feel" like they are digging.

The computer-generated image in the figure was used in the *NOVA* documentary to re-create the interior of the Great Synagogue of Vilna for the viewing public, but it also shows the "real" secret of the Great Synagogue in a very clever way. There was an ecclesiastical rule in Vilnius that no synagogue

CGI re-creation of the interior of the Great Synagogue of Vilna. (Courtesy of *NOVA, Holocaust Escape Tunnel*)

could be built higher than the tallest church. Because of the great stature of the Vilna Jewish community, the Jews of Vilna wanted to build the tallest religious institution of Lithuania, but could not do it conventionally without violating the ecclesiastical rule. So instead of building up, they built down. They placed the Great Synagogue main seating area two floors below street level.

As you look at this darkened, misty photo featuring the area where the Torah was read, in the middle, you can see the windows at the top of the walls that peeked out from the first floor of the synagogue. When the massive basilica of the Great Synagogue above was destroyed during the Holocaust, it likely came crashing down into the two floors of open space below. When the Soviets came into Vilnius and finally pulled down the standing walls that remained, they bulldozed the area and built the elementary school on top of the location, sealing it like a time capsule and preserving the materials from the Great Synagogue.

Archaeology is not only about the small pieces of discovery; it is also about the small steps taken to reconstruct the history of a site. So much is known about the Great Synagogue because it was well documented by the Jews who went there, by the architects who worked there, and by the constant flow of Jews who preserved its legacy in photography and illustration. It is possible to learn a lot about the individual items in a single place like the Great Synagogue, but getting people to understand its power and grandeur and the culture it represents is not quite as easy. A reconstruction like the one here tells a story about the mystery and size of this magnificent building. This was not a re-creation from imagination. Reconstructions of archaeological finds often require educated guesswork based on comparisons with contemporary buildings in the region.

The Great Synagogue was different. It was one of the most photographed, illustrated, and sketched synagogues of the late nineteenth and early twentieth centuries. The architects who did the updates in the end of the nineteenth century left detailed architectural drawings with complete measurements. Of course, everything—even in the architectural drawings—may not have been realized, but the scale of documentation is unusual. The details of the complex are similar to some other religious institutions, but the main synagogue is enhanced by big and small discoveries.

In 2018, we began by far the largest and most extensive excavations under the elementary school. The discovery of the *bimah*—the altar where the Torah would have been read and the prayers offered—and the surrounding pillars, which held up the roof, made international news. In 2017, the discoveries of the *mikvaot*—the ritual baths located at the back of the elementary school playground—also made international news. The idea that an entire complex as big and significant as the Great Synagogue was hiding in plain sight for such a long time is as much a story of the archaeology of the Holocaust as it is a story about how much geoscience can contribute to establishing the foundations for archaeological work in congested cities like Vilnius.

The *bimah* (altar or raised platform for public reading of the Torah), from the Great Synagogue, discovered in 2018 under the principal's office in the elementary school in downtown Vilnius.

THE GREAT SYNAGOGUE AND SHULHOYF
OF VILNA: THE HOUSE THAT GAON BUILT

I must admit that one of the biggest draws of this entire project for me was the allure of getting to know arguably the greatest rabbinic figure of the premodern period: Rabbi Elijah ben Solomon, called the "Gaon of Vilna." One of the most famous illustrations of the Gaon, found in many Jewish homes, has him in his study, filled with books; he has a clock on the wall (symbolizing the modern world), a writing quill in his hand (symbolizing the ongoing work that he was doing), and his prayer shawl and his tefillin (phylacteries) of daily weekday prayer (symbolizing the personal piety he endorsed), draped over his shoulders. Born in 1720, at a time when the Enlightenment was just beginning, and dying in 1797, before the era of Napoleon, his role was to provide the "bridge" between the traditional rabbinic community and the new, more-organized Jewish community that would emerge in the nineteenth century.

He was known by the exalted title of "Gaon," meaning "outstanding sage," an honorific rabbinic term that dated back to the great academies of Babylonia a thousand years before his time. The Gaon was unlike any other great sage of the eighteenth century. His image appeared on printed posters (imagine a Mick Jagger poster in a dorm room!) that were nailed to the inside of Jewish homes all around the European Jewish world. These illustrations almost always included the clock, books, and writing quill, along with a substantial covering on his head. In other words, these illustrations were not merely portraits, but rather public relations material symbolizing the role he held in the world in which he lived. The Gaon was the quintessential premodern Jew.

The clocks that decorated the upper registers of the complex tunnels in the Great Synagogue and Shulhoyf also provided a touch of modernity. Prayer services for the morning, afternoon, and evening services were strictly regulated by time of day. Since most people did not have clocks in their homes or watches on their wrists, the introduction of a standardized dignified public system (rather than a town crier) to announce the services was an innovation. The Shulhoyf had clocks where everyone in the complex could see them to make sure that the Jews entering and leaving did not miss prayer times, or the start and end times for the Sabbath and holidays.

The entire life of Vilna's Jewish community was built around the Great Synagogue. Although there was a lack of running water in the Jewish quarter, the Shulhoyf complex had a well, a bathhouse, and latrines. It was more than just a synagogue; it was the entire world of the Jews who lived in the Jewish quarter. It was in many ways much more than the original Temple of Jerusalem was to the ancients, or the Second Temple was to that period. It was indeed a new Jerusalem, a "Jerusalem of Lithuania." (Jerusalem was added to a city's nickname when the city embodied the ancient Jerusalem in all of its ancient glory.) If you were a Jew in the Jewish quarter, you had to visit, regardless of whether you were religious. It was Starbucks, Facebook, a shopping mall, and a place of worship, all rolled into one.

I included a photo of the Gaon of Vilna statue here because it would be unfortunate to present Vilna without the enduring view that tourists see today. By the time the Gaon died in 1797, he was renowned in the European Jewish community. Because of his desire to go to Israel at the end of his life, and thanks to his devoted students, by the nineteenth century his influence

Richard Freund standing with the Gaon of Vilna statue near the elementary school. (Courtesy of the Vilna Excavations Project at the University of Hartford)

extended into the small religious enclaves of the ancient Galilean cities of Safed and Jerusalem. He wrote about many different aspects of Jewish life, not just Jewish law. His image was enhanced by the posters created for the one hundredth anniversary of his death in 1897. This bronze bust is not a particularly good resemblance of him, but it shows what happens when one goes to excavate a location like Vilna after the Holocaust. A product of the Soviet era, this statue stands next to where the Great Synagogue building stood, and is also near where the house of the Gaon stood. On the left of the statue you can see the elementary school built on top of the Great Synagogue. As you look at the statue, you see a man with a full beard (more like that of Karl Marx and Friedrich Engels than the illustrations that circulated in his time), obviously missing the signature head covering that was ever-present in the renderings of his own period. The Gaon would be mortified, I think, to learn that a bronze bust that does not even look like him sits near his now-destroyed home, without his trademark head covering.

Statues of Jewish scholars, especially rabbis, are questionable pieces of commemorative art. As another example, Maimonides, the great Torah scholar of the Middle Ages, was also given a statue, placed in what was once the Jewish quarter of Cordoba. It is now called the Plaza Maimonides (formerly Plaza Tiberiadus), located near the synagogue, a structure that was built after Maimonides's family had left the city, and ultimately made into a Catholic church in the sixteenth century. The attempt to connect Maimonides with this place is problematic. Maimonides's family was basically forced out of Cordoba while he was still a teenager, yet, in the statue, he is depicted in his later life, wearing a turban and sitting comfortably in his chair, as if to give the location some unfounded Jewish approval. He, too, would have been mortified with the creation of a statue in his honor.

I think marked areas of historic Jewish significance need to reflect what was appropriate to the Jews who lived there in that time, and to consider the sensibilities of the people who might come to view these locations. I tell students that the Gaon would have been disturbed to have a statue of himself anywhere (let alone that plaza in Cordoba)—not only because he was so humble, but because he would have considered it sacrilegious to represent himself in statue form. Many Jews do not consider statues of people to be an appropriate reflection of Jewish memory, in stark contrast to Christian art, for example. This statue in particular would have been objectionable because the Gaon is also depicted like a Communist founder, without his signature head covering!

Vilna was a crossroads of European Jewry during the eighteenth century. With the port of Riga to the northwest, the Russian empire to the east, the Polish Jews to the west, and Germany to the southwest, one might argue that Vilna, where the Gaon lived, sat at the geographic center of the largest concentration of Jews in the eighteenth-century world. If Vilna were the geographic center, the Gaon was the physical embodiment of the forces which would ultimately lead to the modern Jewish world. It was during his tenure as the rabbinic leader for Lithuanian Jewry that the Great Synagogue became *the* Great Synagogue. Many will argue that Vilna became the Jerusalem of Lithuania as a result of social forces that go beyond the Jewish community, but I think it started with the Gaon of Vilna in the eighteenth century. He was a rabbinic "bridge" between the world of the medieval study house—divorced from the changing world of Eastern Europe—and the engaged rabbis of the modern nineteenth century. He encouraged students to study mathematics and astronomy to ensure that the calendaring of the Jews was correct, but realized that the study of these elements also allowed these Jews to be a part of the greater Vilnius population. By the early twentieth century, the Jews of Vilnius represented 40 percent of the population.

The Great Synagogue, where the Gaon prayed (in his own *kloyz*, or prayer hall), is now buried under an elementary school built in the 1960s, and the cemetery where the Gaon was originally buried is now under what is still a decrepit concrete Soviet sports center, built in the 1970s. Many of these late-twentieth-century Soviet structures are ingrained in the landscape even today, and cannot be easily dismantled, which makes the use of geoscience even more important in order to retrieve the parts of history that may lie just below the surface.

THE EASTERN EUROPEAN SYNAGOGUE JUDAISM THAT LED UP TO THE GREAT SYNAGOGUE

As I mentioned previously when discussing the synagogues of Rhodes, synagogues, in general, were intended to be replacements for the Temple of Jerusalem. When Jerusalem was destroyed, in the year 70 CE, Judaism changed forever, but in order to maintain a level of continuity, synagogues became places for the practice of a new form of rabbinic Judaism that no longer included the burnt offerings of the Temple of Jerusalem. Although there were some synagogues in the Second Temple period, mostly in the Diaspora, the destruction of the central shrine of the biblical Jewish people led inextricably to a "Synagogue Judaism," which developed in the Diasporas of Babylonia, Egypt, and the Mediterranean.

This "Synagogue Judaism" struggled to create a new/old identity that tried to capture the grandeur of the Temple of Jerusalem, where a synagogue stood as a "mini version" of the Temple that was simultaneously similar to and different from the Temple. There were no more animal or incense sacrifices; the prominent role of the priests became a tiny peripheral status for priests and Levites, and a group of leaders called "rabbis" were suddenly the spiritual leaders of the Jews. The ancient rabbis were teachers, spiritual guides, judges, and scholars—professionals with income in the Jewish community. A few remarkable individuals had influence in- and outside of the community, and helped to move rabbinic Judaism from a potentially small and parochial faith to a major intellectual movement. Historians trace a direct line of unique rabbis from the first century CE, Hillel and Rabban Yochanan ben Zakkai; the second and third centuries, Rabbi Akiva and Rabbi Judah the Prince; the tenth-, eleventh-, and twelfth-century sages, Saadia Gaon, Rashi, and Maimonides; the sixteenth-century Joseph Karo; and the eighteenth-century Gaon of Vilna. To me, each made contributions of rabbinic creativity that were significant for the development of the modern world and modern Judaism. The Great Synagogue of Vilna is an example of how the rabbis continually went back to the Temple of Jerusalem, and even the Tabernacle from the biblical desert, for inspiration to reconstruct the life of the Jews in the different Diasporas of the Jews.

A NEW START: WHY THE JEWS CAME TO LITHUANIA

How and why the Jews originally came to Lithuania is not fully known. I think that I understand how and why the Jews came to Rhodes, but the question of how and why they came to Vilna is much more complex. All types of theories have accompanied the ascendance of the Jewish community in Vilna and the rest of Lithuania. Some place the movement of Jews from Babylonia and the Middle East to Europe back in the seventh through the tenth centuries.[3] Others claim the Lithuanian Jewish community foundations were a consequence of the movement of ex-Crusaders who brought along Jews who worked with them on their campaigns. Still others attribute it to the Grand Duke of Lithuania, Gediminas, who, in 1323, created the new capital of Vilna, which necessitated a new population that would follow the rivers to the new capital. It is thought that perhaps other Lithuanians did not want to move from their traditional villages to this new "capital," but that the Jews saw this as an opportunity in a very difficult time during the fourteenth century.

This view actually seems to fit the history of the period. Many historians think that the Jews came and stayed in Lithuania in the late fifteenth and early sixteenth centuries perhaps because Gediminas was still a worshipper of Perkunas, the local god of thunder and forests, and therefore the local population lacked the entire "baggage" of the rest of European Christianity. In this case, it meant that the Jews could enter Lithuania and set up all over as immigrants, without the shadow of the anti-Judaic laws that had hounded them in European Christendom. All over Eastern Europe the anti-Judaic views of Christianity followed the Jews into their migrations. Here, at Vilnius, perhaps for the last time, the charges hurled against them of being moneylenders, well-poisoners, the host desecrators, and the full-blown charge of *deicide* (the killing of Jesus) were not yet known. It is thought that this pagan worship so late in Lithuania's history may have indirectly contributed to the Jewish ability to immigrate to the area and be accepted as a motivated minority group with a different religion. The Jews were not seen by Gediminas as a threatening counter-religious identity; they were just another group of non-Perkunas followers who wanted to live and work out of his new capital.

It is also possible that the timing of the Jewish immigration to non-Christian Lithuania is linked to the post–Black Plague (1348–1350) expulsions of Jews from Western Europe. In Christian Europe, many Jewish communities were blamed for the plague and devastated by systematic violence. The plague, which killed millions of Europeans, was spread by contaminated water systems, and did not affect the Jews in the same measure. It appears that the Jews were less affected by the plague because they lived in areas separate from the Christian populations, had their own wells (because they were in separate areas), and followed very meticulous bathing and hand-washing rituals. The Jews who arrived in the greater Lithuanian area in the fourteenth century did not apparently face the same anti-Jewish Christian canards (blood libels, deicide charges, poisoning the wells, etc.) in the early years, although dark days would come. Gediminas, and, later, Grand Duke Witold, in 1388, may have accepted the Jews that were expelled from the plague-infested areas of Christian Western Europe into the growing capital of Vilnius. By 1400, Lithuania had offered the Jews a form of "tolerances," or privileges, that gave them religious, social, and economic (landowning) rights they did not enjoy elsewhere.

During the next period of growth, following the union of Lithuania and Poland in 1386, and the Christianization of the new area in the fifteenth century, the Lithuanians created a new model for the Jews of Lithuania to work with. Unfortunately, the anti-Jewish edicts of the rest of Christendom were suddenly transferred to this formerly pagan population by the middle of the fifteenth century. The ideas of deicide and blood libel, which had no basis in Perkunas worship, suddenly became a part of the new regime in the sixteenth and seventeenth centuries.

The Jews had to adjust to this new reality. The Polish Council of the Four Lands and the Lithuanian Council of the Jews organized local Jewish communities to create a sense of unity in this period of the fifteenth and sixteenth centuries, just as the new Christian order began. The individual self-governments, and an umbrella group like the councils, allowed the different Jewish groups in the small villages that spread to the north and east to unite into a more-cohesive group. Later, from the eighteenth century until World War I, the greater area became known as the "Pale of Settlement," created for Jewish life. It was an enormous area encompassing many countries that limited Jewish settlement in the region to what we could call a "super-ghetto," extending from Eastern Europe, including the Ukraine, to western Poland, and all the way to the Baltic Sea in the north and the Black Sea in the south.

The Pale of Settlement was a double-edged sword: While it created a unified Jewish identity and community, it also made concentrated non-Jewish violence against the Jews more likely. In many ways it is thought that the Pale of Settlement is what made the Holocaust not only possible but so horrific in Eastern Europe. The Jews were concentrated, even before 1939, in well-known areas that were defined over a century before. Either despite—or because of—this organization, the "Pale" made a unified Lithuanian Jewish community more identifiable. It encompassed more areas than just the modern state of Lithuania. The pressure to be organized was both an outside and inside issue in Eastern Jewish life. Commerce, shared resources, and a coherent and well-supervised Jewish religious structure made Jewish life in general vibrant, but also more susceptible to violence, as they were concentrated in specific locations.

A watershed event—or perhaps a foreshadowing of what was to come in the Holocaust, less than three hundred years later—happened in 1648–1649, when the Ukrainian Cossacks of Bogdan Chmielnicki led a revolt against the Polish nobility, in which the Jews of the region became the surrogate population for the pillaging and devastation. The Jewish chroniclers of the seventeenth and eighteenth centuries put the numbers of those killed by conventional weapons used by the Cossacks at 100,000, with 300 Jewish communities destroyed. Up until the period of the Holocaust, the Chmielnicki pogroms were seen as the greatest catastrophe of the European Jewish communities, second only to the Bar Kokhba revolt, 1,500 years before.

It appears that the Jews started to arrive in Lithuania in waves before the fifteenth century, and that an organized community may have only really emerged in the sixteenth century. The question is, when did Vilna become the Jerusalem of Lithuania? By the early nineteenth century, Vilna had already become legendary. On June 24, 1812, Napoleon Bonaparte crossed the Nemunas River with his huge army, heading for Vilnius. Napoleon stayed in Vilnius for eighteen days, until July 10, awaiting the Russian tsar's reply to his new peace offer. It is said that Napoleon himself was very surprised by what he found in Vilnius, a city so far away from the European mainstream, but with a lively Mediterranean mood and life. Napoleon was the one who started calling Vilnius "the Jerusalem of the North," and it would be the last "Jewish city" Napoleon would ever be able to compare it to. He had been on his famous tour of Egypt and Palestine thirteen years before, and had, at that time, declared that the Holy Land was not as beautiful as his picture-book biblical illustrations had taught him. He had gone all the way to Haifa only to be turned back at Acre, and made his way back to Egypt. He was no doubt aware of the Crusades, the Inquisition, and the pogroms and laws designed to discourage Judaic life in the Mediterranean and Middle East. The Jewish population that Napoleon must have encountered in Vilnius in 1812 was a group that would have constituted one-third of the city's population, and would have already heard about the proclamations that had been made in the cities of Italy, the Netherlands, and the German states. The idea that there was a "Jerusalem of the North" was interpreted to mean that the Jews would have in Lithuania what they had been afforded in other regions where Napoleon had been before: rights.

The idea of a Jerusalem of Lithuania became a reflection of the many different Jewish groups that were in Vilna in the period from the end of the eighteenth century and the death of the Gaon of Vilna until the Nazis took over in 1941. They included a large swath of religious groups, from Orthodox and Ultra-Orthodox Jews from the Musar and Yeshiva world to Hasidic and Enlightened Jews; from secular, Communist, and socialist Jews to Bundist and Yiddishist Jews. It was the place where the famed YIVO institute for Yiddish Language and Culture was built, the place where the famed Yiddish theater, poetry, and the writings of the Jewish authors were cultivated. In short, it was a very diverse Jewish community which encompassed the kinds of Jews that would have inhabited ancient biblical Jerusalem during the time of King Solomon, or even King Herod. By the twentieth century, Jews made up a large part of Lithuania (up to 40 percent of the Vilnius population), and had found their niche in the northern farming areas and villages as well as the large cities of Vilnius and Kaunas. By the post–World War I era, Jews had become an integral part of the newly declared Lithuania, and felt they could serve in the military, the government, many areas of education, the arts, banking, the law, and the literary community. It was a Jerusalem of sorts—until it was not.

PEOPLE OF THE PRESENT AND PEOPLE OF THE PAST

While working in Vilna in 2017, I participated in a screening of the *NOVA* documentary *Holocaust Escape Tunnel* at the Vilna Gaon Jewish State Museum. I finished work at the Great Synagogue that day and walked over to the museum, which administers the Ponar site, still in my work clothes. The evening was sponsored by the US Embassy in Lithuania, and the auditorium was filled with Lithuanians, tourists, staff from various embassies, some ambassadors, and my own excavators and students. The embassy staff and many of the Lithuanians who came after work to see the program were dressed in business suits, as was the director of the museum, Markas Zingeris, who chaired the evening.

After the documentary, I participated in a panel with the director and my colleague, Jon Seligman. I could see that it was not a total surprise to the attendees that the remains of the Holocaust were still present in the middle of the nearby forest, and under a school downtown. At that moment many realized that the evidence of the Holocaust could not easily be expunged from their midst, even with the passing of decades. Students later told me that many people in the audience commented that my appearance somehow seemed appropriate, given the subject matter. I hadn't showered or shaved, and the dirt of the field was still on my clothes. Perhaps I seemed like someone who had arrived from the past. In a way, I *had* come from the past, having walked to the event directly from the recently uncovered ruins of a synagogue which had been buried and preserved for more than seventy years. I think my derelict appearance was a visual reminder of the loss experienced at Ponar and at the Great Synagogue.

WHY I SEARCHED FOR MATILDA

At the end of the evening at the Vilna Gaon Jewish State Museum screening, I was approached by an American lawyer, Philip Shapiro, who said that he thought my work could be useful to the people who came from the small village of Rokiskis, in the north of Lithuania, close to the border with Latvia. He later sent me a parcel of information which I formed into a proposal for a project for 2018, a project I am working on as I complete the revisions for this book. This is the other archaeology of the Holocaust that few hear about. Instead of the big cities and institutions, or the extermination camps and mass burials in forts and in concentration camps and forests, this is a story of individuals.

The numbers of Jews in small villages varied, but there were literally hundreds of villages in Eastern Europe, and they formed the locations of the infamous "Holocaust by bullets." Philip recounted in e-mails the short history of Rokiskis: In the years before World War II, like the much larger Vilna, almost 40 percent of this village was Jewish (the businesses in these small towns were sometimes 75 percent Jewish-owned). In most of these villages, the synagogues (usually multiple, even in a small town), the *mikveh*, the study house, and the cemetery were almost totally destroyed during the Holocaust. Philip's idea was to mark the sites of graves and mass burials, and see what remained of the synagogues and *mikvaot*, all using noninvasive technology.

Philip introduced me to the story of one Jewish family in the small village of Panemunelis, near Rokiskis, which immediately caught my interest. While many accounts of the killings and destruction of the Holocaust are about anonymous victims, I realize it is the cases of individuals that help to personalize the Holocaust. I have investigated people such as Jacob Gens, Itzhak Nemenchik, and the survivors of the Holocaust Escape Tunnel, where there were compelling and multiple eyewitness testimonies.

Then there is a story like that of Matilda Olkin. I began to call her "the Anne Frank of Lithuania" because her diary and poems were recently discovered. The abundance of eyewitness testimonies and information about her life and death made the possibility of finding her more probable. Matilda Olkin and Anne Frank were both born in the 1920s. Both had relatively happy childhoods with wide-ranging educations (both Jewish and non-Jewish). Both had doting parents, local friendships, and went into hiding at the beginning of the Holocaust. Both were turned in and murdered. Both of these young Jewish women left a legacy of their lives and insights in diaries that were written, not in Yiddish or Hebrew, but in the language of the countries where they lived, the Netherlands and Lithuania. Anne died in an extermination camp, and nobody knows where she is buried. Matilda died on the side of a road near her hometown, and there were many eyewitnesses.

Philip asked whether I could find where Matilda was buried using the method I had developed elsewhere for Holocaust geoscience and archaeology, including critical analysis of testimonies, scientific comparisons of other local mass burials, historical and contemporary photographic comparisons, GPR and scientific mapping, and local museums that often have artifacts and archives of the region. All of this was possible in Rokiskis, so I accepted the project.

According to the records, Matilda was born on June 6, 1922, to Naumas Olkin (Noach was his Hebrew name), a respected pharmacist of the community of Panemunelis, and his wife, Asna. They lived near the railway station, and the family was part of a community of Jews that ran most of the businesses in this small village of perhaps two hundred people. By the time Matilda was killed, she had three siblings: her older brother Ilija, and two younger sisters, Mika (Mindel) and Grune. Her mother's sister, Sheina, married Elija Jofe, and they had one daughter, Judita, born in 1936. Naumas befriended the local priest at St. Joseph's Church, Father Joseph Matulionis. Apparently, the pharmacist helped the priest with medicine, and they are said to have had tea together on Sundays. Naumas even donated a confessional to the chapel. This friendship between a Catholic priest and a Jewish businessman is not a trivial footnote to the story, but a critical piece for my work in 2018, as I will explain.

This photograph of Matilda from the early 1930s shows her dressed in her Purim costume, with her friends and family. In these photographs, preserved in the Rokiskis museum (which sponsored the project), I came to know the young Jewish woman who was living the "Lithuanian dream." It all changed with the beginnings of World War II. Their village was almost immediately affected by the 1938–1940 Soviet nonaggression pact with the Nazis. In her poetry and her diary she writes about the beginning of the war in 1939, and the Sovietization of the towns, in 1940. She and her classmates felt the crackdown on Jewish status, and when the Nazis stormed back in June of 1941, the same Jews who had been terrorized by the Soviets now became the target of the Nazis, especially local Nazi sympathizers. Even though the Jews of Panemunelis had participated in local government, served in World War I, and fought for an independent Lithuania, they were nonetheless the victims of the first roundups and killings in the war, even after fifty years of relative integration into the daily life of the community.

It must have been a bewildering process, one that we cannot fully understand even today. These communities have been practically erased from the landscape of the country. Almost 95 percent of Lithuania's Jews were killed in the Holocaust. The nine members of the Olkin and Jofe families were part of this destruction. The biggest difference between Matilda and the many other "anonymous" victims is that she left behind a body of work and evidence of the life she lived before the Nazis came. An article in the online publication *Deep Baltic: Inside the Lands Between* chronicles the recent discovery and translation of her diary,[4] which reveals this young woman's experiences between 1938 and 1940. Like the diary of Anne Frank, this volume gives us a window into the inner world of a Holocaust victim, in both prose and poetry. How did the diary survive? The parish priest, Father Joseph Matulionis, friend to Matilda's father, preserved the diary (at the risk of his own life) by hiding it under the altar of his church.

The comparison with Anne Frank is an important one. Anne Frank is known primarily through her diary and its descriptions of hiding in the famous annex in Amsterdam. Anne's diary, made public through the efforts

Matilda Olkin, front left, dressed in her Jewish Purim holiday costume in the early 1930s. (Courtesy of Rokiskis Museum)

of her father, has inspired millions of people around the world because of the character it shows. Dr. Ronald Leopold, Director of the Anne Frank House, pointed out to us that Anne was one of the most influential figures of the 20th century and yet no one knows where she is buried so people make pilgrimage to the annex. It was for this reason that finding the burial place of Matilda, the Anne Frank of Lithuania, would be for me the moral equivalent of finding the unknown burial place of Anne Frank of Amsterdam. Finding Matilda was for me like finding Anne (and many others unnamed and un-marked Holocaust victims' burial places).

At the memorial stone placed by locals on the road near the mass burial site where Matilda is buried, in 2017. (Courtesy of the Vilna Excavations Project at the University of Hartford)

Recently a local Rokiskis area group created a play about Matilda, in which the actors read her poetry and told her story. It made an impact upon Lithuanian millennials, who saw in Matilda's words and story a great Lithuanian tragedy. On their own initiative, Lithuanian citizens have placed a wooden memorial dedicated to Matilda and her family in the Panemunelis (the village where they lived) village square, and on the road near where they were murdered, they have placed a memorial stone with Lithuanian and Hebrew inscriptions commemorating their lives. I came to Panemunelis to look for Matilda's actual burial site using testimonies, photographs and GPR. We were followed to Lithuania by writer Matthew Shaer, who wrote the story "Finding Her Voice" on Matilda for the November, 2018 Smithsonian magazine. He captured our own mixed emotions searching for and finding Matilda's burial some 70 meters from where the memorial stone sits by the isolated road.

It is rare to have all of the pieces available when you go to the field. My Lithuanian colleague, Romas Jarockis, provided us with photographs of 1944 Nazi flyovers of the area, where we were working to provide comparisons. Neringa Daniene, a local playwright, provided me with an article from the local press from 1998 that had a map of the location where they were killed during the summer of 1941, based upon local testimonies. I had the testimony (recorded by the local museum historian) of an eyewitness who watched the murder of the families from a farm overlooking the road. There were neighbors who came to the site after the murder of the Olkin-Jofes and reburied the remains in a more-dignified burial, and they also provided information.

Most important was that we also had one of the most experienced operators on-site to do the meticulous and large-scale GPR scans of the area. Professor Harry Jol of the University of Wisconsin–Eau Claire has now done GPR scanning of mass burials and graves in Israel, the United States, Spain, and Lithuania. He brought his students along to assist, not only with surveying the Olkin-Jofe mass burial site, but also another nearby mass burial site in the forest of Trakas. We listened as he explained how to trace a mass burial site using the various clues provided by topography, soil, compaction, and comparisons with the nearby mass burial site.

I took the testimonies seriously (but not literally), and followed the clues to find the burial site in the woods—a difficult task to accomplish—just as it was described by the eyewitnesses. I went to the church and scanned the great altar where the priest had hidden the diary, sought out the house by the railroad station, and interviewed neighbors and friends of Matilda. I think this is the way to find an individual from the Holocaust.

IMAGINING SIX MILLION VICTIMS— AND SIX MILLION INDIVIDUALS

An estimated six million people died during the Holocaust, but the true number will never be known. Whatever the number, it is so mind-boggling that it often trivializes the deaths. Each death represents an individual with a story. I believe my work as an archaeologist of the Holocaust is to uncover the details of the stories I research, to personalize history, so that it is impossible to forget. I cannot research every individual who perished at the hands of the Nazis; that would take a thousand lifetimes. Perhaps those I do elucidate, like Matilda Olkin and Jacob Gens, will serve as standard-bearers for the millions more who remain anonymous.

My students often feel that my work is only about the mass burials of Jews killed in the Holocaust. It is not so limited, but it is mostly about that. While I was in Lithuania, I consulted with museums and institutions about other killing fields and mass burials; for example, where the KGB distributed their victims during the Soviet era, or where the French buried the war dead of the disastrous Napoleonic invasion of Russia, and even the burial sites of medieval plague victims, all of which potentially could be sites for geoscience and archaeology. It is good, scientifically, to examine sites of mass killing and burials not specific to the Holocaust, to serve as points of comparison. I often cannot calculate exactly how many people are in a single mass burial, but the geophysicists have created a formula for the compaction and size of an excavated area. It is a technique that allows scientists in many fields to estimate what they may not be able to count.

In 2017, I was contacted by the US Embassy to help locate three US airmen buried in a prisoner-of-war camp in Silute, Lithuania, during World War II. The Nazi POW Stalag Luft VI, or airmen camp, was located deep in Nazi-conquered Eastern Europe, to intimidate POWs from considering escape. The airmen were sent to Lithuania from Western Europe. Many people may remember the famous 1963 film with Steve McQueen, entitled *The Great Escape*, based on the real 1943 escape from Stalag Luft III in Zagan, Poland. These escape attempts by POWs were rarely successful, but in the meantime siphoned valuable resources from the Nazi war effort. The Nazi creation of Stalag Luft VI in Lithuania was a diabolical plan, which put thousands of US, Canadian, British, and Australian airmen at terrible risk of being used as hostages, especially as the war dragged on. The unexpected Soviet thrust into Lithuania in July of 1944 made the Nazi plan unworkable. The Nazis evacuated thousands of POWs from the camp. Yet, three Americans died there prior to the Soviet liberation.

The search for these Americans had nothing to do with the Holocaust, but everything to do with the methodology and equipment I use in my archaeology of the Holocaust projects. I was not looking for mass burials, nor was I looking for three Jewish POWs. I was looking for American servicemen who died while in captivity at the Macikai POW camp in 1944. The policy of the US Department of Defense is to bring every soldier home. I remember that when I was approached, I asked my team whether they were all in agreement about spending a day searching for the servicemen. They were. We were in-country, and we believed we could provide services that no one else could. I was not being asked to excavate the remains—only to find them. It was a perfect use of our noninvasive methods. The disinterment and DNA verification would all be up to the US government, working with the Lithuanians.

Once I was satisfied that I had as much information as possible and determined that I could spend a day on the site to do the work, I accepted the proposal. This search would attempt to give closure to the families of the American airmen who had been waiting seventy-three years to learn more about what happened to their loved ones. I took out one more permit for work with a Lithuanian archaeologist from the area and proceeded to take everyone from the Kaunas site to the cemetery in Silute, three hours away. We left very early on July 27, 2017, driving mostly in silence, the students catching up on their sleep in the back of the van. I expected to be met by the regional archaeologist. Instead, we were greeted by local leaders, and, later, by the mayor, with great fanfare, before setting out to look for three graves in a ten-acre area of the cemetery grounds.

This is not a secret site; it is quite well-known by the locals. There is Lithuanian literature on the site from its time as a POW camp, and its time under Soviet control. This search would have been much easier immediately following the war, but the situation between the United States and the Soviet Union at the time precluded this collaboration. Only after the new independent Lithuanian state emerged in the 1990s did this become possible. The three airmen have a symbolic stone located at the front of the cemetery which simply states ". . . who died here and never returned home: Sgts. George Walker, Walter Nies and William Teal," but the stone does not mark their actual burial site. We were accompanied by US Embassy staff at the site.

At first, I felt that doing this seemed somehow inadequate, but as I looked around during the day, watching students and staff set out the grids, decide where the most likely sites might be, and then do the work in the field, I realized the importance of this kind of search. GPR, ERT, digital mapping, drone photogrammetry, and comparisons with photos from the 1940s provided a lot of help. At the end of the day, the team packed up and drove back to Kaunas and went to dinner. The results were sent out overnight to GPR-SLICE director, Dr. Dean Goodman, in Los Angeles. By the morning, I knew that we had probably located the graves. As in much of our work, we leave our results for the local government to follow up on, telling them where we think they should excavate, or not excavate. These results would be given to the US Embassy in Vilnius, and they would handle the follow-up. For the families of the airmen, missing for so long, perhaps the discovery of their loved ones' graves would finally provide closure after a very long wait.

· 8 ·

The Road to Vilna

$\mathcal{I}$ have been asked many times in the past few years what brought me to Vilna. The answer can be found in my own DNA. The discovery that the Great Synagogue of Vilna was still possibly lurking below the surface of modern Vilna was what brought my research team to Lithuania. The opportunity to work with great archaeologists (Jon Seligman of Israel and Zenonas Baubonis of Lithuania) on a project of great cultural significance to Jews and Lithuanians was another reason. To test the limits of the technologies at a multilevel and very significant site was yet another reason. What I also discovered was that this was an opportunity for self-discovery, since my own ancestors came from Vilna in the early part of the twentieth century.

I always start with a clear "large perspective" on every site, even in the cramped area of a modern bustling city like Vilnius. Here, in this photo (overleaf), is the innocuous drone view of the site where the synagogue sat for nearly four hundred years, from the sixteenth century until the 1940s. This photo reveals the top of the central flat roof of the elementary school, in the middle; the trees are all post–World War II growth around the school, with the apartment buildings surrounding what was the heart of the Jewish Quarter. The marked basketball area to the left faces the now-destroyed Ramayles Yeshiva, and the open area behind the school is where the playground is located, and the excavation site. The Great Synagogue was hiding in plain sight, underneath the school.

This project began as many of my projects do: with a discussion and a suggestion. The research group was working at the time in Israel and Rhodes, and had no specific projects in Lithuania. I had done work in Poland almost a decade before, but wasn't even considering anything in Lithuania until I was approached by Dr. Jon Seligman of the Israel Antiquities

A drone photograph of the elementary school (center), under which is buried the Great Synagogue. (Courtesy of Paul Bauman, Advisian, on behalf of the Vilna Excavations Project at the University of Hartford)

Authority (IAA). Jon and I were together at an archaeology conference at the University of Nebraska in 2014. I have known Dr. Seligman from his work as the head of the research and permits department at the IAA, and had followed his work on Byzantine monasteries along the Dead Sea, and especially in Jerusalem. His work there made me think that perhaps he was interested in bringing my team of geoscientists to work on a project at one of the monasteries, or in Jerusalem.

That was not the case. He explained that he had been investigating the Great Synagogue and Shulhoyf in Vilna, and thought this would be an important excavation site—if the ruins of the building were indeed still there. I was surprised, since this was so far out of his comfort zone as a researcher. During our discussions, I realized that Jon was motivated as much by a personal connection to Vilna as a professional curiosity in the synagogue. His extended family had also come from Lithuania, in particular, Vilna.

As I listened to Jon explain his own personal connections to Vilna, I realized that I too had a similar story. My great-grandfather, Nathan Ginsburg, had left Vilna in the beginning of the twentieth century, and I had listened to his Vilna story many times as a child. My grandmother (my father's mother), Celia, and her sisters, the daughters of Nathan Ginsburg, were the center of my family's visits for celebrations, burial commemorations, holidays, and weekends. I knew very little about Vilna other than what I had studied. I knew about its central role in religious Jewry and in Yiddish language and literature. I had heard my teachers speaking in hushed terms about the YIVO Institute for Jewish Research, which had started in Vilna in 1925. Of course I was familiar with the pivotal role of the Vilna Gaon, and even knew about the famous yeshivot of Kovno, but all of this was secondhand. My grandmother, her sisters, and my great-grandfathers were the real "Litvaks," an endearing Yiddish term for Jews of Lithuanian background, as my mother's family stemmed from the Ukraine. The idea of exploring a destroyed synagogue from my great-grandfather's hometown, using geoscience, was too compelling to pass up. Thankfully, my colleagues—who knew nothing about Vilnius other than the fact it was a major city in a former Soviet-bloc country—agreed.

The University of Hartford research group is actually a partnership of many universities, institutions, and private industries, which involves geoscientists, geophysicists, geographers, historians, archaeologists, and the biological sciences, both in-country and out, and brings students, both undergraduate and graduate, to work in the field. It is really a "we" project, since without them there would be no geoscience. The group is unique because we have all agreed to share all of our information with our colleagues in-country, and with each other, and to include our students and colleagues in all of our publications and presentations. We raise our own funds for the work we do, and we do not take salaries. One of the most important aspects of these projects is to teach students and colleagues about the process of using noninvasive archaeology. All students participate in the conducting, and writing about, the research. Most of the research is published in a vast array of geography, geology, and geoscience regional and area studies and journals, and not necessarily in archaeological volumes, and we are all committed to teaching about what we do, both to our professional societies and to the general public.

My colleagues realized early on that I was very passionate about this Vilna project, and readily agreed to join me. Universities often commit funding to projects through competitive grants, and the group applies to funding agencies outside the universities to pay for personnel expenses. We have done more than forty projects together in the past twenty years, taking on those we feel we can do in a short period of time (two to three weeks), often multiple sites in the same country or region, but only if we think that traditional archaeology or the local population will benefit from our efforts.

I knew there was good reason to suspect that a major part of the Great Synagogue in Vilna was actually still there, buried under the elementary school. The Lithuanians had opened sections in front of the elementary school in 2011 to discover that there were artifacts, walls, parts of the columns, and even the demolished frescoes from the roof. They closed up the site they had excavated after sampling the areas, but it was from their work that Dr. Seligman developed the Great Synagogue and Shulhoyf project, with partnerships in Lithuania, Israel, South Africa, Canada, and the United States. The goal of my work was to prove that there was indeed enough still buried to excavate.

The Israeli team organized by Dr. Seligman included some of the best art historians and architects, and all of the expertise of Israeli archaeology. Together, their team and mine began to map the subsurface of the areas around the elementary school, which revealed that the entire complex had a "secret" that may have saved the Great Synagogue from total destruction during the Holocaust. I'll return to this later. We created a partnership that also includes the Jewish Community of Lithuania, the Vilna Gaon Jewish State Museum, and even Vilnius University. During the presentation that the Jewish community of Lithuania made to me in June 2015, I realized the enormous complexity of the task. The organization's president, Faina Kukliansky, stressed the sheer number of sites they have to oversee with their small staff. Most of these sites in Lithuania—cemeteries, synagogues, schools, bathhouses, and mass burial sites—need their constant oversight. I explained my expertise in noninvasive subsurface mapping, and the costs involved, and they asked for my help in defining the project, using the noninvasive technologies.

According to the Jewish community's accounting, there were as many as 250,000 Jews in Lithuania by 1941, many drawn to Lithuania because it was so well known as a vibrant cultural and religious center, with many Jews living in more than two hundred small villages and big cities. More than 90 percent of Lithuanian Jews were killed by 1945.

The center of Jewish life in Lithuania was Vilnius, known in Yiddish as Vilna. At the heart of the city was a single institution, the Great Synagogue of Vilna. There were great synagogues (*shtot shuls* in Yiddish) in almost every major city, and with each great synagogue, there were also "great" study houses (*batei midrash*), bathhouses (*mikveh*), and Jewish elementary schools (*heder*). One could say that the Great Synagogue of Vilna was just one of many of the same types of institutions throughout Lithuania, but it was the circumstances of the Jewish Quarter, the central role of the Vilna Great Synagogue, and the singular rabbinic leader, the Vilna Gaon, that made the Vilna Great Synagogue stand out.

There were over one hundred prayer halls in Vilna before World War II. Not all of them are exactly what we would call "synagogues" today. There are actually big distinctions between synagogues and *kloyzn* (prayer halls), *shtibls* (small prayer settings), and *batei midrash* (study houses), which often doubled as prayer locations. The Yiddish term *kloyz* (pl., *kloyzn*) is presumed to have come from the Latin *clausum*, which literally means "closed," and refers to a building or closed complex of structures connected to a monastery (and also the origin of the word "cloister"). The term first appeared in Ashkenazic culture in the sixteenth century, and referred to a house where scholars assembled—a place of study intended for mature, adult male scholars. By the second half of the seventeenth century, there were *kloyzn* in many centers of both Western and Eastern Europe. The term by then had gradually come to refer to a private house of study, existing separately from the institutions of the community, and financed by a patron or a wealthy family. It was usually headed by a prominent leader, like the Gaon of Vilna (his *kloyz* contained only twenty members), but sometimes the *kloyz* was known not for its prominent rabbinic figure, but instead for the work or cultural background of the group.

A place like the Shulhoyf, with its large open courtyard and gates, had many private *kloyzn* which represented individual groups from various professions, including scholars, merchants, and landowners. They were individual classroom-like areas each stylized according to the students they attracted. A functioning twenty-four/seven institution like the *kloyz* provided a variety of functions which would border today on a type of social club for some and a form of higher education for others.

The first "Great" Synagogue of Vilna was probably built between 1633 and 1635, in Renaissance-Baroque style, after permission was given to build a stone structure to replace the old (wooden) synagogue purportedly built in 1573. This is based solely on literary evidence, making it important to look for physical evidence. One of the goals of my study of the Great Synagogue was to track the stratigraphy of the synagogue as it changed and grew—first from wood to stone, then from one building to many, probably oriented in the same place. This is the ultimate in cultural micro-superimposition, because the ancient foundations (and destructions) of the many iterations of the synagogues of the Jewish Quarter of Vilna were built on that site. Iron gates were added to the Shulhoyf by the tailors' guild in the seventeenth century to protect the Jews inside the complex from crowds that rampaged through the Jewish Quarter. The placement of the gates after 1661 is one way of distinguishing the earlier and later versions of the synagogue. The Jews were expelled for a time after a number of events in the 1650s, and so protection and a stable building structure for the synagogue was seen as important.

Later additions carefully follow architectural plans, which are accessible even today. The early original work, done in the seventeenth century, is hard to track. But by the beginning of the eighteenth century, the Shulhoyf took shape. The many different *kloyzn* and *batei midrash* developed around the court. Most of the small *kloyzn* were small rectangular or square rooms with wooden pews, bookshelves, and a small ark for the Torah. Over the course of time the Great Synagogue was surrounded by other buildings within the labyrinth-like Shulhoyf, a complex of twelve prayer settings and other communal institutions. (They used the holy number twelve, even though it appears that more would have been possible.) I do not think it was an accident that the number of prayer settings reached twelve. This was a well-known "holy" number, honoring the ancient twelve tribes of biblical Israel that surrounded the ancient Tabernacle in the center, in the desert stay following the Exodus from Egypt. It was a symbolic number that is probably significant in demonstrating unity.

The main floor of the Great Synagogue was approximately seventy feet by sixty feet, and probably only had seating for about 450 on the main level (although illustrations make it seem like there were thousands of seats). This was augmented by the seating in each of the different *kloyzn*, *batei midrash*, *shtibls*, and women's galleries. The large number of Jewish institutions around the greater Vilnius area meant that by the early twentieth century, the Great Synagogue stood at the center of multiple, ever-expanding circles of dynamic Jewish life, from secularists to the most religious Jews. It also had a unique architectural secret that preserved it even after the Nazis and the Soviets thought it had been destroyed.

THE "SECRET" OF THE GREAT SYNAGOGUE

The significance of ERT, the scan used in this image, is that it can trace layers of earlier structures at the same time that it gives a contemporary history of a site. The photo reveals where future excavations might be conducted and what might be found. Not only am I investigating the synagogue that was destroyed by the Nazis and built over by the Soviets, but also the original location and size of the structure before it became "the Great Synagogue." I assume that the area where the Great Synagogue is located was the same location for the original synagogue, from before the era of the Gaon, perhaps going back to the sixteenth century. The color-coded layers indicate occupation at four meters, which I interpret as the layer of the Great Synagogue before the Holocaust. When I "see" defined layers/strata that fit together at

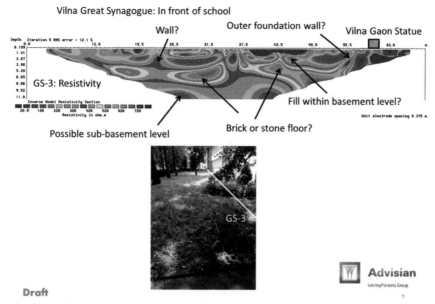

The front of the Great Synagogue of Vilna, scanned by ERT down to five meters, in front of the elementary school. (Courtesy of the Vilna Excavations Project at the University of Hartford)

seven to eight meters below the surface, and then see layers that start again at eleven meters below the surface, it raises the possibility of uncovering the origins of Lithuanian Jewry in Vilnius. As I plan a work season, I think about how to do more subsurface mapping at the excavation site to see clearer and more-defined layers below.

The "secret" of the Great Synagogue does not involve buried gold or silver, but rather an architectural feature that was built into the synagogue in the nineteenth century. The history of the Great Synagogue probably begins in the sixteenth century and pauses in the late 1950s, before it picks up again with my work in 2015. According to local Jewish literary tradition, the Great Synagogue of Vilna was established in 1573, on a plot exempted from municipal jurisdiction. One of the many goals of my work would be to know whether there are any remains of the early synagogue. Since the subsurface mapping can indeed establish a "stratigraphy," it may be possible to determine where there is likelihood of finding early remains.

In 1592, this early incarnation of the synagogue was plundered by a Christian mob, according to literary traditions. Apparently, in 1593 this event caused Jews to make efforts to obtain "privilege" (a legal permission) from Sigismund III Vasa (1587–1632), which would allow them to settle in the city, build a synagogue, establish a cemetery, and engage in trade. In 1606, the synagogue was again attacked by a Christian mob. On February 25, 1633, Władysław IV Vasa (1632–1648), responding to the Jews' request, granted a privilege, which reads: "[F]or the purpose of security and better protection from fire, permission is given to build a synagogue in our city of Vilnius, on Jewish Street, which is densely lined up with buildings [. . .], on the same plot where it stands now." In this way the construction of the stone Great Synagogue was sanctioned on the same site as the earlier wooden synagogue.

The Shulhoyf grew around the Great Synagogue, and by the early twentieth century it included the twelve prayer halls that represented a whole variety of different groups in the community. In 1633, by a separate permission, Vilnius Jews were assigned a quarter limited by the streets designated today as Zydu (Jewish) Street, Vokiečių (German) Street, and Šv. Mikalojaus (St. Nicholas) Street.

The literary histories of the synagogue tell us much about its rise of significance in the eighteenth century, and the reasons for necessary remodels in the middle of that century. The Great Synagogue was damaged by fires in the years 1737, 1747, and 1748, and it was rebuilt several times into the iconic large, squarish, brick building that most know from photos and illustrations. The Torah ark at the center of the southeastern wall was renovated by the *Bedek Bayit* (Hebrew for "Synagogue Maintenance Fund") Association after either the fire of 1737 or 1748, but by mid-century the famous shield with the Tablets of the Ten Commandments above the ark was donated by a well-known Vilna philanthropist. The shield, the doors of the Torah ark, and the metal shell of the place reserved for the leader of the prayers were apparently rescued after the Holocaust and are preserved in the Vilna Gaon Jewish State Museum.

Reaching the roof height of twelve meters was an enormous architectural feat in the nineteenth and early twentieth centuries. The original synagogue had been ransacked and rebuilt in the seventeenth century, but it was never done with heavy equipment; apparently they just built upon the ancient floor, making possible the type of geoscience and archaeology project we had planned. The fires in the mid-eighteenth century meant that the synagogue was truly developed architecturally into the Great Synagogue as we know it only in the time (or right after) of the Gaon of Vilna, at the end of the eighteenth century.

One of the reasons why we know so much about this synagogue in Vilnius is because of the pioneering and tireless work of Dr. Vladimir Levin, of the Center for Jewish Art at the Hebrew University of Jerusalem, Israel. He is co-editor of *Synagogues of Lithuania: A Catalogue* (Aliza Coen-Mushlin, Sergey Kravtsov, Vladimir Levin, Giedrė Mickūnaitė, Jurgita Šiaučiūnaitė-

Verbickienė). When Vladimir came to meet my students and staff in 2015, he helped the whole team focus on what to look for below the surface. His book is a comprehensive, two-volume work containing much of the comparison literature on the Great Synagogues of Lithuania. It puts into perspective why the Vilnius synagogue was arguably "the Greatest of the Great Synagogue structures" in Lithuania. (While many cities had *shtot shuls*—literally, "city synagogues," we are differentiating here by calling them "Great Synagogues" to distinguish them from the many other synagogues in a particular city.)

Vladimir Levin's knowledge of the synagogues of Lithuania was encyclopedic. In 2015, we sat eating and drinking in an underground portion of a downtown Vilnius restaurant as Dr. Levin presented to the students and staff a lecture on why the Vilna Great Synagogue was so special. I have recounted this to students since as an example of interdisciplinary cooperation—the rare sharing of insights, in chronological and detailed form, which can only be gleaned from field research. Of the more than one hundred prayer houses in Vilnius, there were only a few true, architecturally unique structures that were called "synagogues," and the Great Synagogue was the largest and most complex in Vilnius.

Dr. Levin spoke specifically about the four Corinthian and eight Tuscan columns that held up areas of the roof; these types of columns had become a staple. While this Tuscan Baroque style may be found in many European churches and synagogues, what makes the Great Synagogue of Vilna so significant was more than just the main synagogue; it was also the many *kloyzn* and the full complex and bathhouse behind it, and the Shulhoyf.

The column style used to hold up the enormous roof is important, since it was developed in the fifteenth and sixteenth centuries for large buildings in Europe (e.g., St. Paul's Covent Garden, in 1633), but was not a regular part of synagogues in Europe. The four-pillar style that held up the roof may have originated in Eastern Europe, with the principal problems being the *bimah* (raised platform) and the need to have a central focus for the worshipper. If you look back at the CGI illustration done by *NOVA* for their film, it is clear that this multitiered work in the center of the large space was a well-known feature. This kind of space relationship was partly anticipated hundreds of years earlier by the double-naved, two-pillared synagogue with the *bimah* between the columns. It was possible, of course, to emphasize a centralized layout by other architectural means, as indeed is shown in the domed synagogues throughout the centuries, but never was the centrally designed *bimah* so strongly and meaningfully stressed as when it was integrated in the structural system of pillars, vaulting, and buttressing, creating a four-pillared subspace within the shell of the building, as in this case. Synagogues where the four pillars create a close group include the buildings at Vilna, Nowogrodek, and Lutzk.

The *bimah* was not only a central feature of the synagogue, it was also the heart of the worship service. It is a symbol of a symbol. We knew that leading luminaries as well as common students had graced the central *bimah* during the last three hundred years. Its discovery in 2018, therefore, was hailed by Jews all over the world. While we cannot bring back the Jews of Vilna, we can uncover the physical elements that gave their lives meaning in the period before the Holocaust.

In many ways locating the *bimah* was the equivalent of the unexpected discovery of the Dead Sea Scrolls in 1947. It took more than sixty years to translate and reconstruct the history behind that discovery. Locating the *bimah* of the Great Synagogue was also unexpected, and truly the convergence of a number of factors in Lithuania that go beyond just geoscience. My colleagues and I thought we would not see the *bimah* for a number of excavation seasons, primarily because it sits under one of the classrooms of the school. Suddenly, almost inexplicably, the mayor of Vilnius, Remigijus Simasius, decided right before we began our 2018 season to close the school and allow us to excavate under the classrooms. Several press reports include what he told us personally: "The school will be demolished within two years, and by 2023, when the city celebrates its seven-hundredth birthday, we will create a respectful site, displaying Vilnius's rich Jewish heritage."[1]

He asked if we wanted him to take down the school entirely, but realized that we were going to need the school building to protect whatever we found until such time it is decided what they will do with the artifacts and discoveries. That process has begun, but in the meantime, I am still shocked by how quickly the decision was made to allow us to excavate under the school, and how we knew almost immediately exactly where we needed to excavate. We know that some of the most important finds from the upper floors fell onto the main floor when the original roof fell down. These artifacts were pushed into the open spaces when the Soviets pulled down the building in the 1950s. The many add-ons throughout the building—including a multilevel wooden gallery that expanded into an existing women's gallery—might provide new discoveries right up until we are asked to stop excavating in two or three more years, when a final plan for what will be done at the property is decided, and a new structure is built on top.

Some of the more-exaggerated illustrations of the size and interior of the main synagogue floor, by Franciszek Smuglewicz (1745–1807), show more of what people thought of when they were in the synagogue, rather than the actual dimensions. Smuglewicz shows a dramatic and massive central *bimah* that hinted at the Temple of Jerusalem rather than the Great Synagogue of Vilna. It was painter Marc Chagall who painted a true portrait of the main synagogue interior in 1935, including the central *bimah*, in a colorful but realistic way. The photographs taken in the early twentieth century preserve details that provide, for the excavator, the most important information to coordinate GPR and ERT subsurface mapping.

The double-naved synagogue was like the medieval synagogues of Worms and Prague, but it was a unique structure in Vilna. The lower tier of the *bimah* was composed of twelve columns, while the upper supported an ornate dome. Columns are usually associated with architecture of churches in the medieval period, but for the Jews there was also a parallel to the columns associated with the Temple of Jerusalem. Using massive columns to hold up the roof is both an architectural and ritual issue. The idea that the Great Synagogue of Vilna was a tribute to the Great Temple of Jerusalem would have been aided by the locals' own reading of biblical texts associated with the building of the Temple of Jerusalem, found in the books of Kings and Chronicles.

Looking at the descriptions, illustrations, and photographs of the Great Synagogue, you can see that it had a two-tiered area (Holy Ark) on the eastern wall decorated with stucco carvings of vines (conforming to my view that nonrepresentational art was the most acceptable form of Jewish art) and vegetation, along with animal and Jewish symbols. The ark was approached by two sides of steps with iron handles. Numerous bronze and silver chandeliers hung from the walls and ceilings, and the synagogue also contained a valuable collection of ritual objects (many of which were removed for safekeeping to Russia during the World War I period, and never returned).

When I was asked by the press what I was looking for, I responded by saying that GPR would provide clues to the architectural features of the synagogue and shulhoyf in every different stage of the work. I would give reports that prioritized what was worth excavating for the archaeologists by figuring out the likelihood that objects had been sealed in an archaeological context that might still be excavatable—in other words, large pieces of the architecture that would have been difficult for the Soviet builders to move, especially among the detritus of the largely destroyed Jewish Quarter that surrounded it.

When I was in the midst of working on the Great Synagogue in 2016—this was after the information on the Holocaust Escape Tunnel had been released worldwide—we would be visited daily at the excavation site by curious onlookers. Everyone was asking the same question: How could the most important Jewish institution in the country be found "hiding" in plain sight, under a school in the middle of the city?

A few stories reveal much more about the relationship between people and artifacts, and are worth telling. One day, a man got on a plane and flew to Vilnius to return something that belonged to the Great Synagogue. After reading about the excavation in his local newspaper, he decided that it was time for him to bring back a Torah scroll, in his possession for more than

Some of the "rescued" artifacts from the Great Synagogue that were brought to the Vilna Gaon Jewish State Museum after the war. (Courtesy of the Vilna Excavations Project at the University of Hartford)

sixty years. During the Soviet era, his father had rescued the scroll (five books of the Bible, read every week in the synagogue) from the Great Synagogue and smuggled it out of Lithuania, to safety. Now the son wanted to return the Torah to its rightful place.

This was an extremely emotional encounter for him and everyone present at the work site. It took some time to authenticate that this was indeed one of the Torah scrolls that would have been in the Great Synagogue in any number of the settings. It turned out that this was indeed an eighteenth-century Torah scroll of the type used in one of the many *kloyzn* prayer services at the Great Synagogue. It is the type of artifact an excavator always hopes to find in situ. In this case, it came with its caretaker and a real provenance backstory that certainly provided as much, if not more, meaning to the artifact than if it had been uncovered on the site. I was glad to see that it figures in the Holocaust Escape Tunnel documentary, because it shows just how close a connection there is between the institutions I excavate and the people behind the artifacts.

The location of the Great Synagogue artifacts from the end of the nineteenth century to the time of the Nazis in 1941 is not fully known. Some of the artifacts were smuggled out of Lithuania to Russia before or during World War I. Some items from the Strashun Library collection, which occupied the second floor of the Great Synagogue, were probably among those rescued and recently found in the basement of a Vilnius church. In 1991 and in 2017, books belonging to the Jews of Vilnius were recovered.

As I planned the work in Vilnius for 2016, I sought out experts to give me a sense of what might still be found in a building like the Great Synagogue. When Professor David Fishman, author of *Embers Plucked from the Fire: The Rescue of Jewish Cultural Treasure in Vilna* (YIVO, 2009), came to the University of Hartford in 2015, he spoke about the possibility that some books and documents might remain hidden in Vilnius, in the Great Synagogue. It was only two years later, in 2017, when information came out about 170,000 new documents recovered in the basement of the St. George Church.[2] I know that my students are inspired by the idea that there are so many new discoveries to be made about the Holocaust, seventy-five years or more after the killing ended. At the Vilna Gaon Jewish State Museum (VGJSM) in Vilnius, there are pieces of the ark and prayer houses from the Great Synagogue. Every year when I bring students to Vilnius to excavate, I bring them to the VGJSM and have them stand in front of these artifacts, and explain to them that this is what we are looking for. The question was, where might I encounter something like this in its original (or hidden) location in the nooks and crannies of the buried synagogue?

The Holocaust history of the Great Synagogue of Vilnius began soon after the Nazis arrived. The city was captured by the Nazis on June 24, 1941. I was working to excavate the synagogue exactly seventy-five years after the creation of the two ghettos began. On September 6, 1941, the murder of tens of thousands of Jews began in the nearby Paneriai (Ponar) forest. The synagogue sat empty and divested of its silver and wood, and the Jews were driven into two ghettos situated in the territory of the historical Jewish Quarter and the surrounding streets. The small ghetto in the old Jewish Quarter, including the Great Synagogue and Shulhoyf, was liquidated on October 21, 1941, and all of its inmates were shot in Paneriai. The second, larger ghetto was liquidated on September 23, 1943, and approximately seventy thousand Jews were killed.

The Great Synagogue and Shulhoyf were not totally destroyed during the period of 1941–1945, which is why I thought there still might be promising places to excavate. The buildings were seriously damaged and mostly destroyed, but much of the main walls were still standing in 1945. They were stripped of their wood and silver ornaments (that were not hidden). It's possible that the Torahs were moved to what would have been perceived as "safer" areas, but it's doubtful that they were saved. The search for artifacts does not include only books and larger objects, but also the original stone foundation and the different layers of synagogues that were located at the same site during the past four hundred years.

The entire Strashun Library and its thousands of rare books is one example which encourages efforts. It contained some of the most significant works of medieval Judaism, which were smuggled into the ghetto and hidden during the period of 1942–1943. People in the ghetto with work permits would clandestinely bring back books and important papers one by one (at the risk of their own lives), which is documented in Professor David Fishman's most recent book, *The Book Smugglers: Partisans, Poets, and the Race to Save Jewish Treasures from the Nazis* (ForeEdge, 2017). His 2015 presentation at the University of Hartford had left my students shocked; they asked me whether it was true that people had actually risked their lives for books. It was at this moment that some millennials took away a lesson that is impossible to teach in a classroom. The lesson was that the designation of the Jews as the "People of the Book," was more than just an empty title. It meant during most of Judaism's history but especially to many Jews in the Vilna Ghetto during the Holocaust that they loved their books as much as life itself.

WHY WE STARTED WITH THE BATHHOUSE

Our mandate in 2015, 2016, and 2017 was clear: We did not want to disturb the elementary school, so I began in the playground, which was dirt, and

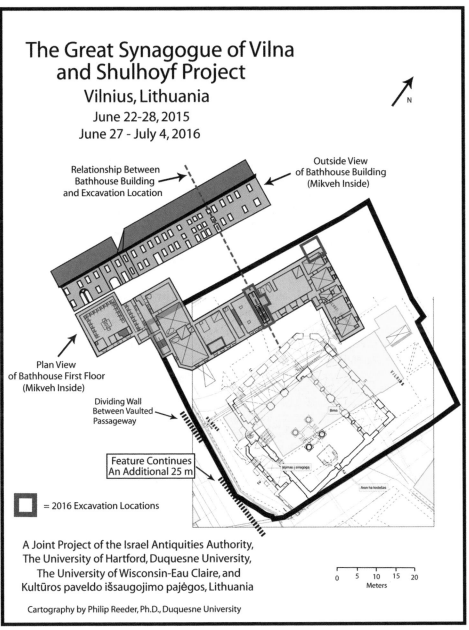

The Great Synagogue of Vilna
and Shulhoyf Project
Vilnius, Lithuania
June 22-28, 2015
June 27 - July 4, 2016

N

Relationship Between
Bathhouse Building
and Excavation Location

Outside View
of Bathhouse Building
(Mikveh Inside)

Plan View
of Bathhouse First Floor
(Mikveh Inside)

Dividing Wall
Between Vaulted
Passageway

Feature Continues
An Additional 25 m

= 2016 Excavation Locations

A Joint Project of the Israel Antiquities Authority,
The University of Hartford, Duquesne University,
The University of Wisconsin-Eau Claire, and
Kultūros paveldo išsaugojimo pajėgos, Lithuania

0   5   10   15   20
Meters

Cartography by Philip Reeder, Ph.D., Duquesne University

A draft of the map of the bathhouse excavations behind the Great Synagogue in the playground of the elementary school. (Courtesy of Philip Reeder, Vilna Excavations Project at the University of Hartford) which I knew held an important discovery: a massive bathhouse. I was asked by my staff and students why I was beginning the work in the back of the school and not in the front. The elementary school is outlined in the map, but the largest area that presented itself was the playground in the back of the school, which did not contain any fixed structures. This meant that instead of beginning with the synagogue, I would begin in the back of the Shulhoyf, in the large bathhouse that itself was a multitiered building. This is the structure about which the least is known in the synagogue complex. Although most people do not think of the bathhouse as a Jewish location, in many ways it is the quintessential cross between a social, religious, and cultural Jewish site.

Part of the work involved orienting the excavations so that they would blend seamlessly from year to year into one another. The open area of the bathhouse presented a target that could be closed and covered up after each season and returned to without creating a problem for the school and its students. Furthermore, culturally, the bathhouse was one of the best places to start the work. Many of my colleagues have been working on bathhouses with me in Nazareth, Israel; Rhodes, Greece; Burgos, Spain; and elsewhere. I have found that bathhouses are excellent places to excavate because people go there, remove all of their clothes and personal items, and inevitably lose things that are found by archaeologists hundreds (or thousands) of years later in the drains, pipes, and changing rooms. I can attest to the fact that beyond any other part of daily life, this would have been a place where all Jews would have gathered in Vilnius.

There is another "secret" to the Great Synagogue rarely mentioned by historians, but which became an obsession in my study of the history of its location: the story of water. The Jews of the Jewish Quarter in Vilnius did not have in-house water (even in a period when other places around the city did), which meant that they had to come to the Great Synagogue to get water for cooking, to use the bathrooms, and to perform their ritual bathing. Whether they were pious and prayed in the synagogues, or they just came to relieve themselves, Jews of all backgrounds in the Jewish Quarter came to the Great Synagogue multiple times each day.

WHY A BATHHOUSE MATTERS: THE GREAT EQUALIZER FOR ALL JEWS

Some readers may be scratching their heads and asking: A bathhouse? The bathhouse was for the Jews what a pub was for the English: It was a gathering place that provided more than just a place to clean up; it was a place where Jews would go in the middle of winter to enjoy the company of one's colleagues. With no running water at home, the bathhouse, located inside the shalhoyf's secure boundaries, where people could get warm, prepare for prayer, and share intimate conversations of life.

Preserved in the beautiful language of Mendele Mocher Sforim (pen name of Sholem Yankev Abramovich, one of the greatest Yiddish writers of the nineteenth and early twentieth centuries) is an indication of the importance of the bathhouse for the lives of Jews in a place like Vilna. It is likely that Mendele describes the bathhouse I was excavating in this excerpt below:

> The comfort was none other than the bathhouse, by which they meant quite literally an actual bathhouse and all its accessories, with its broad benches, long beams on which to hang trousers and stockings and miscellaneous items of men's clothing, with an expert healer sitting in the corner, a lighted candle before him, shaving and bleeding* our fellow Jews in the approved fashion . . . The only place for Jews to fish out what is going on, to complain about their own troubles and listen to those of others, is the bathhouse. There, one hears many secrets repeated. Many business deals are closed there. The place has more activity than the marketplace . . . Up above the notables, the fine Jews, the men of good birth sit in a little group. Their conversation revolves around business and politics; the kosher meat tax, the troublemakers of this generation, the recruiting of soldiers, the choosing of town councilors, the appointment of a rabbi, about one thing and another, and also about the new police chief. ("Fishke der Krumer," translated by Gerald Stullman, New York: T. Yosseloff, 1960, p. 50) [*bleeding is a common term for a treatment used by Jewish and non-Jewish practitioners for many different ailments]

Mendele studied in Slutsk, and was in Vilna until he was seventeen, so his experience would have been from the 1850s, before the bathhouse had been updated. It was a place where the Jews created a whole world of experience. It was not the prayer house or the study house. It was a place where Jews mixed and lived. The bathhouse (*bod* in Yiddish) should not be confused with the ritual bath (*mikveh*, discussed later in the chapter). The *bod* was probably the larger three-story structure.

My research team has spent the better part of thirty years looking at shorelines, rivers, marshes, wells, bathhouses, *mikvaot*, and buildings that housed the intimate moments of ritual and personal bathing all over the world. I have researched the bathing practices of Jews at Qumran on the Dead Sea, Nazareth and Bethsaida in ancient Israel, and the Jews of Spain and Greece. I am sometimes hard-pressed to explain to students what is distinctive about the Jews. I have always argued that the ancient Israelites, and then later, the Jews, survived and prospered in so many different cultural contexts all over the world because of elements that are often subtle and understated. One of the most distinctive elements of Jewish life is not one of the most well-known. The dietary laws, the Sabbath and the holidays, the prayer services, the use of the Hebrew language (and especially the use of the Hebrew lettering system, with the creation of a specific dialect in each country of the Diaspora), and the Hebrew Bible and Talmudic texts used in weekly study and prayer are all distinctive elements of the Jewish faith, but these are derived from ancient prohibitions and celebrations that the Jews adapted as their own. Some of the most important—yet frequently overlooked—elements of Jewish life are the daily and weekly ritual washing and bathing practices that have characterized Jewish life, from biblical times through to the modern era in Vilna.

In the past thirty years archaeologists have become extremely sensitive to the stepped pools that they have been discovering in sites all around Israel. In my excavations at the ancient city of Bethsaida, Israel, for example, early on in the excavations, I thought I had found a *mikveh*. Now, this may not sound like an amazing discovery, since Bethsaida was a Jewish village, but a *mikveh* that was part of the life of the first apostles of Jesus would be an interesting find. It had steps going down into it, and just enough internal volume to support 191 gallons of water; it had the appropriate stretcher stones to give the top some coverage, and it had what I thought could serve as a reservoir. I dug it for one whole summer only to discover it was probably a wine cellar! It had stored wine jars at the back of the enclosure.

This left me confused. Was it a *mikveh* that had been turned into a wine cellar, or was it just a wine cellar? For a time I developed what some students called "*mikveh* envy." I had students write about the *mikvaot* at other sites, and we all came to the conclusion that at ancient Bethsaida, on the shores of the Sea of Galilee, and adjacent to the Jordan River, a *mikveh* would have been redundant. This is relevant to the bathhouses and *mikvaot* I would study later in Eastern Europe. There, where the rivers and lakes were abundant, the bathhouse and *mikveh* were generally located in direct proximity to the river or lake. Even when they were built back from the water, the groundwater was sufficiently close to allow the natural flow of the water to these *mikvaot*. The Great Synagogue bathhouse and *mikveh* were far from the spring and the river, and the piping system and the cost for the water to be channeled into the bathhouse, the latrines, and the well, made up a very big part of the Great Synagogue's budget, according to archival information.

A SHORT HISTORY OF THE *MIKVEH*

I mentioned the *mikveh* of the Kahal Shalom Synagogue in my work on Rhodes. A *mikveh* is essentially always the same type of structure, but often tailored to the local materials (stone, ceramic, tiled/untiled). It is a bath with a series of innovations and steps that can make the complex larger or smaller. In Rhodes, I discovered that the large local *hamam* (or "Turkish bath") had served some of the Jewish community, as well as the small *mikvaot* that I assume were part of the synagogues of Rhodes. The building of *mikvaot* is so specific that it does allow for comparisons. A *mikveh* is an architecturally unique structure used for Jewish ritual immersion which is approximately six feet by two feet by two feet, and which minimally contains 40 *se'ahs* (191 gallons) of collected rainwater. How that rainwater is collected or directed into the *mikveh* is important. The rainwater off of the roof would not have been sufficient for the large population of Vilna's Jewish Quarter. The *mikveh's* size and exacting standardization are defined by the rabbis in the earliest rabbinic collections, but they often added elements that are not mentioned.

Archaeology has shown that the *mikveh* was a central pillar of Jewish life, not only in the ancient Land of Israel, but in the Diaspora, from almost the beginning. It is really one of those types of ethnic markers for determining the Jewishness of a group. It was part of fulfilling public needs as much as a road or other public building. Here is a rabbinic pronouncement: "They [Public Commissioners] go forth to clear the roads of thorns, to mend the broadways and [main] highways and to measure the [ritual] pools; and if any [ritual] pools be found short of forty [cubic measures] *se'ahs* of water, they train a continuous flow into it [to ensure] forty *se'ahs*" (Babylonian Talmud, tractate Moed Katan 5a). I was lucky to have a colleague who is an expert in the study of *mikvaot*. I consulted with Professor Stuart Miller at the University of Connecticut, whose work on ancient and modern *mikvaot* has set the standard for research.[3] He is not only interested in ancient *mikvaot*, but has also been involved in the discovery and research of a *mikveh* from the twentieth century in Chesterfield, Connecticut. He has served as the "*mikveh* expert" on a variety of sites.

The definitive history of *mikvaot* in the Diaspora has yet to be written, presumably because the institution developed in different ways in different parts of the Diaspora and the Land of Israel. The physical structure is interesting and varied, with a lot of commonalities. Although medieval installations have been found in Syracuse, Sicily; in Besalu, Spain; in Amsterdam, Holland; and in a number of sites in Germany and Poland, they are not all the same. Most of these *mikvaot* use groundwater and placement on the edge of bodies of water (rivers, lakes, and underground springs), but many of them are dug deep into the ground and accessed via deep shafts surrounded by staircases. This is often because these locations were too exposed for Jewish communities, which were sited in less-desirable areas.

While a detailed regional study of the *mikvaot* in the Hessen region of Germany discusses a series of these installations, no study of those located in the Pale of Settlement or Lithuania exists, and it would be a good comparison. It should be noted that *mikvaot* associated with the bathhouse are very important, not only because of the *mikveh*. They are often the only places for bathing, and are associated with public latrines, as well. They have been found at Plungė and Alytus (Lithuania); Sokolka (Poland); Indura and *Lyubcha* (Belarus); Labun, Kretinga, and Iziaslav (Zasław); and Merkine, Švėkšna and Aizpute (Latvia), and are documented mostly by Yad Vashem and the Center for Jewish Art in Jerusalem. Interestingly, the bathhouse and the *mikvaot* of the Great Synagogue were not only different; they were also from different periods! When I began my project in Rokiskis, Lithuania, in the summer of 2018, one of the first areas I asked about was the placement of the *mikveh* and the synagogue.

In 2016, a stone arched area below the center of the bathhouse at the Vilna Great Synagogue excavations caught my attention. It became known as "the *mikveh*" because it resembled many of the other *mikvaot* entrances found throughout Europe. The excavations in 2016 did not extend all the way down to the actual water source, but the structure and its siting did resemble the types of stone chambered *mikvaot* of what I would call the late medieval type. Most of the medieval *mikvaot* were located at the lowest area of the buildings (and bathhouses). They were mainly brick and stone installations, often constructed adjacent to a water source or, as in the case of the Vilna Great Synagogue, the water was channeled into the *mikveh* from springs nearby. Dr. Jon Seligman visited both the nearby springs that were described in the literature and found the architectural renderings of the bathhouse in the Vilnius archives. The two together give us a sense of how the water got to the bathhouse and what the installations might have looked like.

WATER IS THE KEY TO EVERYTHING

The search for the ancient mikveh was aided by both ERT and GPR that placed a large structure under six feet of dirt and debris. This photo shows Shuli Levinboim, an Israeli restorer, who worked with me and my students on the excavations of the Great Synagogue bathhouse in 2016-2018. As I write this we still have not reached the ancient mikveh, and given the descriptions in the literature from the 1920s-1930s written about it, the old mikveh was a nasty place.

The search for the old *mikveh*. (Courtesy of the Vilna Excavations Project at the University of Hartford)

Shuli Levinboim, together with her husband and sister, were among the most motivated of all of the excavators and were excited at the prospect of uncovering the ancient mikveh. These arches were not only distinctive; they also served a serious architectural purpose. I have photographs of other medieval and premodern *mikvaot* that resemble this kind of stone construction, and actually correspond pretty well to the descriptions of the Vilna *mikveh* before the new *mikvaot* were built in the twentieth century. It was clear that the bathhouse, probably in use from the beginnings of the synagogue in Vilna, would have evolved and changed. The *mikveh* was built in the lowest part of the bathhouse to ensure that the water flowed "uninterrupted" to the *mikveh*, as prescribed by Jewish law. This meant that it would need to be in an area where the running water could be directed down and collected in what would have been a stone receptacle, which had stone steps to a stone enclosure.

Bathhouses should have been built on or near large bodies of water, but this was not always possible given the allocation of land to the Jews in various countries. In reviewing the bathhouses of Europe, it is clear that the

Jews built their bathhouses wherever they were allocated land, which was not always on a body of water that would make water readily accessible. The Jews in antiquity even developed a rule that said snow could be brought in naturally to fill a *mikveh*, because not all Jews had access to water in cities where they lived.

The excavations of the bathhouse and *mikvaot* in Vilna began in the playground of the school, and did the least amount of damage to the area. Slowly, information emerged that allowed the piecing together of where this bathhouse, landlocked and far from the main rivers of Vilna, got its water. Starting from 1759, the *mikveh* and bathhouse were connected with a wooden (and later, a metal) pipeline to the Vingrių springs that belonged to, and were controlled by, the Dominican friars. The communal bathhouse and public lavatories were placed nearby, and from 1772, sewage and garbage pickup were connected to that of the Jesuit monastery.

I have collected an enormous amount of documentation regarding how much the Jewish community was paying for their water and sewage, to the Dominicans and Jesuits, respectively, despite the fact that by the beginning of the twentieth century, there was running water in many other areas of the city. The new building of the bathhouse was reconstructed in 1823, and is a regular part of the writings of Yiddish and Maskil (Enlightenment Period) Hebrew authors. In short, the bathhouse played a central role in the lives of the Jews of Eastern Europe during the entire nineteenth and twentieth centuries, yet little detail is known about the inner workings of the bathhouse, its design, changing rooms, or its location inside of the structure. There are very few photographs, perhaps for obvious reasons of propriety, of the inside of the bathhouse, despite the fact that there are many photographs of the accompanying synagogues.

The architectural floor plan of the bathhouse at the Great Synagogue is known exactly, since it was renovated in Vilna in the late nineteenth century, and a plan drawn. The plan, which was found in the city archives in Vilnius, shows that the bathhouse consisted of two main floors, with a single room on the third level. At the southern end are what seem to be the latrines, divided into two rooms on both floors of the building. These are likely designated for men and women. The latrines were divided into cubicles that line the walls of the rooms. At the center of the latrine, and in many of the rooms, is a square feature cut through with a diagonal line. The finding of two separate modern *mikvaot* on two sides of the bathhouse building in 2017 seems to confirm this construction. (Often an architectural plan is not fully followed in the construction phases of a project.) In the center of the bathhouse map is the 2016 excavation of a metal stove which was probably used to heat each of the rooms.

GEOSCIENCE TECHNOLOGY AND METHODOLOGY: BATHHOUSE AND SYNAGOGUE RESEARCH

By my accounting, this is the tenth synagogue and bathhouse that my team has been asked to examine worldwide. Between Spain, Greece, Israel, Poland, and Lithuania, my group has provided significant data on synagogues, some of which were excavated afterward. Most of them were buried under other structures and were not excavatable—and even when they were, it wasn't always convenient to do so. The size of the field necessary to excavate safely down to three or four meters (up to twelve feet) is enormous.

It was decided to open three separate areas of the site in the playground behind the school, starting from behind what was the outer area of the destroyed synagogue. Since I knew there were elements that had been discovered in 2011 in the front of the school, I decided to use that as a guide for the back of the building. I completed the first piece of research of the site in the summer of 2015, and in the summer of 2016, I revealed more of the larger grid that extended beyond the school's present gates.

THE DISCOVERY OF TWO "NEWER" *MIKVAOT* OF THE BATHHOUSE IN 2017 AND 2018

A discovery only a few feet below the surface yielded one of the most exciting moments of 2017's work in the Great Synagogue. In order to know what the bathhouse looked like, it was very helpful to have the architectural designs from the later nineteenth century, when the bathhouse was redesigned. It was also helpful to have a comparison site in Lithuania, described by a Holocaust historian who included a full chapter on a bathhouse in her own city. The author is Yaffa Eliach, and her book is titled *There Once Was a World: A 900-Year Chronicle of the Shtetl Eishyshok*. Published in 1998, it is a landmark study numbering more than eight hundred pages, including photos and sections on most aspects of life in one small Lithuanian city. Her descriptions are based on firsthand testimonies of people from the city.

I wish I had more such stories on every aspect of daily life for the people I study. Although I have explored bathhouses in Israel, Spain, and Greece, and am aware of many of the technical elements of a bathhouse—water grade, heating elements, wall materials, types of artifacts found inside—it was Eliach's book that gave me the most useful information. She collected important descriptions of basic daily rituals, and her descriptions offer a detailed picture of the culture of a place like Vilna:

The modern *mikveh*, discovered in 2017, in the bathhouse complex in the playground. (Courtesy of the Vilna Excavations Project at the University of Hartford)

The first stop was the "cold room," where one undressed and left one's clothes . . . and to which one returned after bathing. Because the dressing room was unheated, there was less of a shock to the system when passing between it and the outdoors after bathing in wintertime, and therefore less chance of getting sick. Next was the lukewarm room, where some people like to immerse themselves (at least in warmer weather) in the cold *mikvah*,[4] and where all of the shtetl boys and men got their hair cut and their *peot* [sidelocks] and beards trimmed. . . . The third of the three bathhouse chambers, the steam room, was where most people did their actual bathing and where they immersed themselves in the *mikvah* after bathing. In both it and the lukewarm room there were buckets of water to be poured over the body and a shallow gutter that drained the water away. The bathhouse attendant was kept busy bringing bucket after bucket of hot water, both for bathing and for pouring over the burning coals that were under a grate in one corner of the room. Ringing the room were five step-like wooden bleachers, which one ascended according to one's tolerance of the heat level. Young boys stayed at the first level, most adults at the second, third, or occasionally fourth, and the bravest of all, the elite of the classless bathhouse society climbed to the fifth. Stretched out on the top bleacher, wreathed in steam, glistening with sweat, the men abandoned their bodies to the intensity of the heat, and revived each other with the thrashings of the twigs. Not only did those little birch bundles improve the circulation, but when the moist steam penetrated the wood, it released wonderful fresh smells, recalling the meadows and forests from which it had been gathered by local shepherds. (Meir Wilkanski, published in Tel Aviv in 1933, as quoted by Yaffa Eliach in *There Once Was a World*, p. 202)

The communal well was at the center of life in any Jewish community, from the ancient to the modern period. This is significant because it is often the development of a water and drainage system that often preserves remains from ancient settlements. In my work on "Mary's Well" in ancient Nazareth, for example, I found there was pottery in the pipes still stuck together with the mud and silt. The pipes that brought the water to a communal area often became clogged with ancient artifacts (including coins and glass fragments), which help to date the well, even after people in other periods were living in the area. Wells preserve history.

You may not think about how simple changes in the environment of a place can affect the possibilities for growth. Archaeologists constantly think about these changes when they are excavating a site. Since Jews were generally restricted to a very specific location in most towns in the medieval period, the possibilities of growth were linked to the possibilities of bringing the resources to that specific location. One of the major changes in a European location like the Jewish Vilna area of the city was the inclusion of a "modern" water system. How does a Jewish community go from a few thousand people in the eighteenth century to a hundred thousand in the twentieth century? Water and a water system are key to that development.

A bathhouse is not a *mikveh*, and a *mikveh* is often not found in a bathhouse. In Vilna, because the Jews did not have the water rights, all of these were part of the Great Synagogue complex. The bathhouse was the multistory building unique to the area. In Vilna, the bathhouse fulfilled both secular and holy purposes. There were renovations to the bathhouse and especially the mikvaot which happened in the twentieth century. According to documentation two new mikvaot were built probably around World War I and which we discovered in 2017 and 2018. These two were probably used in addition to the old *mikveh*, which continued to exist, albeit as a sort of relic. The bathhouse complex inevitably had all three *mikvaot*. Future research will probably provide a much better view of the whole bathhouse.

The central area of the excavations in the back of the school revealed some major parts of the old infrastructure of the bathhouse, with massive stone arches and rooms that extended nine feet below the level of the surface, along with the upper area of the twentieth-century refurbishments, located less than three feet below the surface. The decision was made to follow the contours of other more-modern areas of the bathhouse, and areas A and B (see the map) were opened in 2017, based on what appeared to be the more-recent improvements in the designs of the bathhouse *mikvaot* and water systems.

The true meaning of a discovery in the archaeology of the Holocaust depends upon its context. It is not just about mass burials and destroyed buildings; it is also about what you can find that is still unbroken, and can contribute to our understanding of life before the Holocaust. It is really amazing to discover an almost-intact *mikveh* in a place like the Great Synagogue of Vilna, in what is now the playground of an elementary school. There must have been hundreds of *mikvaot* in Lithuania in the nineteenth and twentieth centuries, but inside the Great Synagogue and Shulhoyf complex is not just some random location; it is a holy place that was visited by many scholars over the years. It was not the *mikveh* that made them holy, but rather, they that made the *mikveh* holy. This partially destroyed *mikveh* is a physical reminder of the people who used it. The interesting part of the discovery is that in 2018, we discovered the "sister" *mikveh* on the opposite side of the playground. It was decorated in a similar tile pattern, ostensibly built in the same fashion, and located near the entrance of the bathhouse, just like the 2017 "new" *mikveh* (on page 191).

There is even documentation about why a new *mikveh* was built. An early-twentieth-century mikveh was described in correspondence between the Great Synagogue authorities and the Joint Distribution Committee's offices, which invested in the facility. On the other side of the same playground was another *mikveh* structure—again, with what looks like a lavatory and changing room at the back of the bathhouse structure. Just as the Great Synagogue's excavations are significant reminders of the history of a lost world, perhaps the bathhouse also serves as a reminder of the lifestyle that was lost, as well.

People often ask me, "What is the greatest discovery of the Great Synagogue?" I do not tell them it is the thousands of pieces of ceramic, bricks, coins, keys, bowls, cutlery, or small and delicate fragments of glass or metal. It is not even the discovery of the hundreds of beautifully designed tiles that decorated the bathhouse heaters. The most important discovery for me was indeed the discovery of the two different tiled floor mikvaot on two sides of the playground. I could imagine boys and girls; men and women waiting on a Friday afternoon for their turns there to prepare for the Sabbath. The tiles of the mikvaot were quite modern looking and lacked any Jewish decoration or markings. It could have been found on any floor or wall in Eastern Europe.

The explanations of the way the mikvaot worked were discussed amongst the staff and students and it remains a teaching moment of great significance for me personally. It is one thing to talk about the concept of a mikveh in a classroom or read about it in a book. It is another thing to discover it in a playground of a school in downtown Vilnius. It is the epitome of archaeology of the Holocaust. There was one other discovery I made concerning the mikveh and this has to do with my young Lithuanian colleague. As the National news

The second modern *mikveh*, discovered in 2018, in the bathhouse complex in the playground. (Courtesy of Lena Stein, on behalf of the Vilna Excavations Project at the University of Hartford)

media came to hear and film interviews about the mikveh discovery I made sure that he explained the significance to the Lithuanian viewing audience. A Lithuanian archaeologist describing a Lithuanian discovery from a significant Lithuanian institution destroyed during the Holocaust but still there. The most important part of the discovery for me was indeed the moment he began telling the Lithuanian public about its significance.

The local Lithuanian news crews, which began to cover the excavation after the big discoveries in 2016, had come to interview me in 2017 about the discovery of the new *mikveh*. My colleague, Mantas Daubaras—a young Lithuanian PhD candidate in archaeology—asked me to explain the meaning of the *mikveh* for the nightly news. I told him it was important that it be explained by a Lithuanian, for the Lithuanian public.

So there I stood, watching a young, non-Jewish Lithuanian archaeologist explain the meaning and significance of the discovery of a pre-Holocaust *mikveh* in the midst of the excavation of a playground in downtown Vilnius. This discovery for me was not only the recovery of the artifact itself, but how it would be understood by the public, thanks to Mantas having worked with Jon Seligman and me on this project. It meant far more for him to explain the discovery of a Lithuanian *mikveh* in a Jewish bathhouse and a Lithuanian synagogue to a Lithuanian (albeit, non-Jewish audience) than to have an American or Israeli Jew explaining it. The real innovation here was that a Lithuanian was explaining part of their cultural (albeit, Jewish) history to Lithuanians. Again, it proved my rule: Archaeology is really about people—in this case, today's Lithuanians.

In 2018, similar events occurred when we discovered other *mikveh* locations. First, we located a second "new" *mikveh* in the school playground in Vilnius, and another young Lithuanian archaeologist, Justinas Racas, was inevitably pressed into service to explain to the Lithuanian public the customs of the *mikveh* and Jewish ritual bathing, which differed from the bathhouse bathing that the Lithuanian public might have been familiar with. That same summer, 150 miles to the north, I found myself in the village of Ponedel examining a *mikveh* and bathhouse complex located in a resident's backyard. The woman allowed us to examine it as part of our work in the region. In this case we had a seasoned Lithuanian archaeologist, Romas Jarockis, who explained to the press and the local population what the site was all about, even as we worked to learn what state of disrepair it was in.

The process of engaging the Lithuanian public and getting them to understand the customs of their Jewish neighbors, who are no longer there—as well as the institutions located in their homes and backyards—is one of the most important parts of the archaeology of the Holocaust. The more we educate people in these areas about what was there, the more they will be attentive to telltale signs of what might still remain.

· 9 ·

An Altruistic Nazi and
the Descendants of Hope

$\mathscr{T}$he photogrammetry image on the next page was taken by a drone, and is in reality not one, but thousands of photographs, stitched together to provide an image that has contrast. It includes topographies that would be lost if captured by just one photograph, no matter how well positioned the camera. Today this technique of macro-photogrammetry (of an entire site) and micro-photogrammetry (of individual artifacts) is another tool in the arsenal of noninvasive archaeology. The ability to see tiny changes in the landscape that will give us an idea of where to do a survey is important. It not only saves time, but can also narrow down a field to make the work more efficient. This photo shows a perspective of an area where the central two apartment buildings are aligned in parallel fashion, with the parking area in the center and the green areas around the outside. This rather idyllic photo hides what lies below the surface, and in the walls and basements of the buildings, even today. We were looking for two mass burial sites, and the photogrammetry together with survivor testimonies gave us a clear idea of where to start.

These apartment buildings are a unique site for an archaeological survey of the Holocaust. Most places that I am called upon to research are destroyed buildings, mass burial sites located in the middle of a forest, or reconstructed sites that hint at the devastation below. This one is unique in that it is a Holocaust-era Jewish labor camp where people still live today, going about their daily lives, unaware that mass burials took place under the playground where their children play. One of the most inspiring stories of the Holocaust took place in their very apartments—one of rescue—and all of the evidence is still there. These apartment buildings housed 1,257 Jewish men, women, and children from September 1943 to July 1944, and held a closely guarded

Photogrammetry of HKP 562, with markings for ERT and GPR. (Courtesy of Paul Bauman, Advisian, on behalf of the Vilna Excavations Project at the University of Hartford)

"secret" of the near-miraculous efforts of one Nazi officer to save the last remnants of the Vilna Ghetto.

There are few Holocaust sites of any kind that have been virtually untouched by the past seventy-five years. When I was brought to the site of the World War II HKP 562 ("HKP" is the German designation for "Heeres Kraft Park," an army vehicle repair shop) by Irina Guzenberg, then a senior researcher at the Vilna Gaon Jewish State Museum, and author of the definitive book on the HKP 562 Jewish labor camp, she emphasized the immediate need for an intervention. The apartments were built at the turn of the twentieth century by the famed Jewish philanthropist Baron de Hirsch as inexpensive and efficient housing for the poor of Vilna. More than one hundred years after construction, they are still impressive, but in need of significant renovations. The nearby shops have suffered in the past decade, and the possibility of total urban renewal was real when I visited in 2015. In 2017,

I arrived to do my project here; it was clear that my work would be crucial to determining what was left of the Holocaust in this location, using noninvasive techniques. The story behind my work is not simply a list of the people who were brought to HKP 562 by Major Karl Plagge, the commanding officer, in August 1943. It is the ultimate test of how the archaeology of the Holocaust can reveal the complexities of a rescue event that is little known, without disturbing the residents who now occupy the location where it all happened.

HKP 562: FROM INEXPENSIVE JEWISH HOUSING TO A LIFESAVING JEWISH REFUGE

From 1997 to 2002, I worked on the Cave of Letters on the Dead Sea in Israel. It was a series of interconnected limestone caves used as a refuge by Jews who were hunted during the First and Second Wars against the Romans. My work—chronicled in my book *Digging through the Bible* (Rowman & Littlefield, 2008) and captured in the PBS *NOVA* television documentary, *Ancient Refuge in the Holy Land*—shows how I came to the cave looking for the archaeological detritus of the refugees that had been buried for 1,800 years. In the cave were found burial niches for the dead, their letters and documents, their kitchens and implements, and their religious objects.

Going to HKP 562 in 2017 reminded me of the Cave of Letters.[1] The camp was made up of two brick buildings containing 216 apartments where Jews had hidden from the Nazi killings that were going on all around Vilnius. I had the testimonies of those who survived to guide me. In the Cave of Letters, I had some of the documents of the people whose lives probably ended in that cave to guide me. While the two groups of Jews are separated by 1,500 years, their experiences were eerily similar. The big difference was that the Jews at HKP 562 had a rescuer: Major Karl Plagge. The site of the camp is located only a few minutes from the downtown area, on Subačiaus Street 47 and 49, in Vilnius. There are playgrounds and parking lots in the areas of the apartments where I did some of my work.

In 1898, the Jewish Colonization Association allocated funds for the construction of *biliker* (cheap) housing for the Jewish poor of Vilna. A Healthy Homes Association was established in Vilnius, and the two buildings, with a total of 216 apartments, were built in the year 1900. The architect was Eduard Goldberg. Poor Jews, students, and young Zionists who were preparing to take up agricultural activities in Palestine could all tend the gardens of the new buildings. In the fall of 1941, the residents of the buildings were murdered at Ponar, along with many other Vilnius Jews, during initial extermination operations. By 1943, the buildings had been emptied of people for a second time.

At this point a Nazi officer, Major Karl Plagge—an engineer who had been assigned to Vilnius to run HKP operations—came up with a new use for the building: It would now serve as a place to house a skilled labor force, thereby saving the remnants of the Vilna Ghetto. It is rare for archaeology and geoscience to provide evidence of an act of altruism, but in the case of Major Plagge at HKP 562, it exists in the form of personal testimony, and the physical remains of the place where he worked, which provides insight into his character.

I wanted to see what the physical evidence available today at the site would tell me about this unconditional act of altruism by Major Plagge. Did the physical evidence match the story, or was it simply a rationalization by the survivors, created after the fact, in an effort to understand the meaning of their survival? Altruism—helping others, often at the risk of one's own health, comfort, or very life—is often hard to identify. Usually historians and philosophers find less-obvious and unstated ulterior motives—power and control over others, financial gain, sexual favors, and so forth—that diminish a seemingly selfless act to a cost–loss ratio. I have studied the case of Karl Plagge, and, given the conditions and timing of his act, find it to be one of the least known "points of light" during the Holocaust in Lithuania. Those who escaped HKP 562 make up the largest single group of survivors from Vilna.

It is not clear when and why Plagge changed from Nazi to savior, but the documentation presented at his denazification trial after the war provides some clues. Although Plagge joined the Nazi Party early on (in 1931—two years before Hitler came to power) out of what would seem to be idealistic reasons, the storm of ideological Nazi anti-Semitic legislation (the 1935 Nuremberg Laws) made him uneasy. Plagge seems to have thought he could have more of an impact on changing the Party if he had greater involvement. He was "denounced" in this period for not accepting the working theories of racial inequality that the party had made policy, and his personal contact with one particular German-Jewish family during this period may have tipped the scales of his moral decision-making.

By the time war had broken out in 1940, Plagge was no longer an active Nazi supporter, although he was still a functionary in the service of his country (he had served in World War I, as well). When he was brought into active service in the Wehrmacht (German Army) at the beginning of the war, he was a changed man. His assignment in the fall of 1943—to take command of the HKP 562 site—allowed him to both serve the Wehrmacht, and to save Jews.

Why was Plagge different? I think he was different because he had had personal contact with Jews before the war. Perhaps it was his contact with the Jewish workers he supervised in Vilnius when he got there which allowed him to know them as people. Perhaps it was the brutalization of the Jews in the ghetto that he must have witnessed daily. Perhaps it was the ever-present movement of Jews from the center of Vilnius to the Ponar forest, which would have been evident to someone who supervised some of the vehicles used to transport them there. Or perhaps he had heard from his workers and fellow Nazi officers about the fate of those Jews who were being taken from the Vilna Ghetto—or he was aware of the planned liquidation of the Vilna Ghetto.

Whatever the case, by September 1943, Plagge had become "an altruistic Nazi" who put himself and his career in possible mortal danger in order to save those Jews he could. His HKP unit had existed from 1941 to 1943, staffed with Jewish workers who were treated humanely. Just weeks before the Vilna Ghetto was liquidated, he brought its last residents to staff this new camp. In the end, Plagge's lists would include 1,257 Jewish men, women, and children who were brought into the apartments at HKP 562, just days before their compatriots were sent to the Ponar forest for extermination.

HKP 562 was not the only HKP in the German Army (there were hundreds), and like all of the others, it was devoted to the maintenance and repair of Nazi vehicles for the war effort. HKP 562 is distinctive not only because it is still intact today, but because it still has the original buildings that housed the workers at the site. The workshops on the other side of town are still standing, as well. Many areas of Vilnius which were part of the war effort were destroyed in the Battle of Vilnius in July 1944, or during the reconstruction efforts by the Soviets. It is unusual for a forced labor camp from the Holocaust to still be standing. It's an excellent target for geoscience, precisely because most of the original site is intact. I had known about this site for more than a decade, and then forgotten about it until 2016, when I decided it would be one of the seven sites in Lithuania of which I would do a complete geophysical scan in 2017. After the Great Synagogue; Forts IX, VII, and IV; the Jewish cemetery of Kaunas; and the Silute POW camp, in the summer of 2017, I came back to Vilna to see what was left of the events that took place at HKP 562, and to see whether archaeology could answer the question of "Why here?"

The reason I feel so confident about the information from this site is because of the survivors who gave their testimonies, and because of the groundbreaking work of two individuals who gathered much of the evidence about HKP 562 in the 1970s and 1990s, and wrote about it. Irina Guzenberg, a senior researcher at the Vilna Gaon Jewish State Museum, wrote my first resource on the subject.[2] Her book, a tersely written, three- and often four-language text of 190 pages, is a gem for archival specialists. *The H.K.P. Jewish Labor Camp: 1943–1944* contains the history of the apartment buildings, including the lists of those brought there in 1943. It shows what happened in those final days of July 2–4, 1944, and mentions the work of Major Karl Plagge. What she does not answer is why Plagge did what he did.

For the answers to that question, I went to Dr. Michael Good's book, *The Search for Major Plagge*.[3] Why someone like Plagge or frankly any historical figure became transformed mid-life into someone different is at the core of historical studies, but is difficult to assess, even for the best historians. How do we change (or can we change) ingrained behavior when it is reinforced by the society around us? It is a problem that has vexed the best philosophers, sociologists and anthropologists. Plagge not only changed himself but to succeed he had to surround himself with like-minded Nazis who shared in his altruism. I have always wondered if archeology could help us to understand behavior? I think it can. Why a site is configured the way it is sometimes figures in archaeological studies. I had two goals in my work at HKP 562: the search for multiple mass burial sites, and the search for the *malines* (Yiddish for "hiding places"; you may recall the ancient significance of hiding places in Jewish culture) that saved those who were not captured and killed outright.

First, while studying the survivor accounts, I saw that the Jews who were killed on July 2 and 3 were not all sent off to Ponar; rather, many were killed at the site. The survivors actually could hear the shootings from their hiding places. From this, I assumed that the killing and initial burial sites would most likely be within earshot of their hiding places. I was looking for physical evidence of the killings, and the initial sites where they may have been buried. There is a "memorial" burial monument located at the modern camp site, the spot where the survivors indicated most (but not all) of the bodies were later moved. The other goal was to see whether the *malines* were ubiquitous, as to allow so many people to survive. Perhaps more important, I wanted to see whether their construction would have been known to Major Plagge and his soldiers (certainly, they were unknown to the SS who occasionally entered camp).

When I am surveying a site for geoscience and archaeological work, I always want to know whether the historical information is confirmed by physical evidence. In this case, I wanted to know what the Nazi guards knew, and when they knew it. The documents of who was there and what happened are at the core of Guzenberg's book. The SS left HKP 562 on July 4, 1944, after killing those who could not find hiding places, or those who showed up for roll call on Sunday, July 2. Irina's assessment of the information (including many of the document exchanges between Plagge and his superiors) reveals the numbers of people who were interned there, who they were, and who survived. She personally directed me when I visited the site in 2015, but in 2016 she began to worry that since it was located very close to the downtown, it might be part of the urban renewal going on all over Vilnius. She wanted me to find what evidence still existed at the site before it was torn down.

After my visit in 2016, I shared Irina's concern and sense of urgency. Our shared interest in the site was not the reason I wanted to do a full-scale survey, however; it was because I was hoping that Michael Good's book, *The Search for Major Plagge*, would lead to physical evidence about how Plagge, a Nazi officer, risked his life to save the Jews in Vilna in 1943–1944 at HKP 562. Dr. Good, a Connecticut physician, had written his book based upon unique materials from his parents and grandparents and their circle of fellow survivors. He presented his findings at a Holocaust Educators' Workshop in 2005. At the time, I remember thinking how unusual it was to hear about a "good" Nazi, and I wanted to know why Plagge was so different from his contemporaries. I thought this would be a good topic for teachers to hear about. Michael Good gave his talk and sold his books, and I did not think of him again until more than a decade later, when I stood at the HKP site with Irina and realized this was the site that Michael had written his book about! It is rare to have such exacting information, and to have people like Irina and Michael to consult with as you do the work.

When I finally arrived at HKP 562, I wanted to see whether the physical evidence of the site might confirm the work of the two books, and help me understand what the evidence reveals about the character of Major Karl Plagge. I tried to call Michael back in the United States from the HKP site in 2016, but he is a busy physician, and he was seven hours away. The two of us did not connect until I came back to the United States. When we finally met, I asked him what physical evidence I might be able to discover through a geoscience and archaeological survey of the camp. He pulled out a single sheet of paper that would become my guide: a hand-drawn map of some of the *malines* that had saved people, a chart Plagge seemingly allowed to be constructed under his watch. This map was featured in the poster used to promote the documentary, *The Good Nazi* (produced by Associated Producers, a company in Israel and Canada). Plagge was a "good" Nazi not only because he brought Jewish men, women, and children from the Vilna Ghetto to HKP 562 before the ghetto was liquidated, but also because he allowed them to prepare themselves for the day when Plagge knew he could no longer protect them from the SS.

This is a clear example of how geoscience and archaeology can actually document more than just walls and artifacts; it can also document altruism. The book that I had read back in 2005, *The Search for Major Plagge*, was now a very real event that needed to be carefully documented with science. We needed to see if there was evidence of the *malines* that could be identified by GPR and ERT, and then filmed. We wanted to identify the mass burial sites of those who were not brought to Ponar, but rather shot at HKP 562. In order to know what those *malines* looked like, we had to investigate to see

The Good Nazi poster for the documentary by Associated Producers, featuring the HKP 562 site with the map of the *malines* embedded at the bottom. (Courtesy of Associated Producers)

whether they were still there. Geoscience is particularly good at doing this—especially when you have testimonies and maps to direct you.

Michael Good was convinced that HKP 562 would show more about the character of Plagge and his soldiers than all of the documents combined. Investigating the site was one of my highest priorities in 2017 in Lithuania, and I had the good fortune of being accompanied by Michael, his son, Jonathan Good, and Sidney Handler, who, as a child at the camp in 1944, was saved by his mother in the hiding places the Jews had been able to develop under the watchful eye of Major Karl Plagge.

On September 16, 1943, Plagge transported more than one thousand of his Jewish workers and their families from the Vilna Ghetto to the newly built HKP camp. The cheap housing that had been built by the Baron de Hirsch Foundation in 1898 was already in disrepair, but its basements, attics, and brick construction all allowed for the creation of *malines* for the Jews there. HKP 562 and the Jews placed there emerged from the ashes of the Vilna Ghetto—but only because Karl Plagge made it so.

The final liquidation of the Vilna Ghetto came on September 23, 1943. Karl Plagge tried to save hundreds of his Jewish workers, arguing to his superiors that they were vital to the German war effort, even as thousands of Jews from the ghetto were herded off to Ponar for extermination. His own superiors in Vilna did not agree. Plagge traveled to Berlin to try to convince people in high places of the need to have a repair unit ready, despite the impending Nazi retreat from Vilnius. Plagge's unit—located outside the ghetto in HKP 562's two buildings—contained workers that could be utilized right up to the last minute, Plagge argued; he could house the workers even as the ghetto itself was being liquidated.

It was as if Plagge had created a self-contained "third ghetto" which did not require a Judenrat or the structure of the Vilna Ghetto. The 350 original Jewish male workers he chose for HKP were saved from certain death in the Vilna Ghetto. This would have been enough to justify his act as altruistic. Instead he went further and was able to create an even larger unit at HKP, one which included women and children, because he also proposed a plan where wives would see uniforms for the German Army at the same location. This was a grand altruistic plan that brought with it a risk to Plagge and his men who were essentially protecting the Jews of HKP as much as they were guarding them. His plan is known from his correspondence, and from the survivors of the camp's last days, who, thanks to his ingenuity, were warned, and, on the evening of July 1, either escaped, or hid at the site.

On Saturday, July 1, 1944, at about seven p.m., Major Plagge entered the HKP camp and made an informal speech to the Jewish prisoners who gathered around him. In the presence of an SS officer, he told the Jews present that he and his men were being relocated to the west, and that in spite of his requests, he did not have permission to take his skilled Jewish workers with his unit. This was all to take place on Monday, July 3. According to survivors who were present, his motives were clearly to give the Jews a "coded" message: They were no longer safe, and should take every measure possible to save themselves.

Survivor William Begell says that the coded words were understood by many, but not all, of the Jews on July 1. He remembers Plagge's words as: "You will be escorted in this evacuation by the SS, *which, as you know, is an organization devoted to the protection of refugees.* Thus there is nothing to worry about"[4] (testimony of William Begell, HKP 562 survivor). Of course, every Jew in Vilna knew about the murderous tactics of the SS. The five hundred prisoners who did appear at roll call the next day were taken to the forest of Paneriai (Ponar) and shot.

Over the next couple of days, the SS searched the camp and its surroundings. They found half of the missing prisoners, and immediately took them to the camp courtyard and shot them. However, when the Red Army captured Vilnius a few days later, approximately 250 of the camp's Jews emerged from their hiding places. The survivors apparently took many of those who were still lying in shallow graves by the building where they were killed and transferred them to a mass burial site that is today commemorated by a memorial.

I was looking for two separate elements using geoscience: mass burial sites, and the large attic, cellar, and apartment *malines*. Based on the accounts of Sidney Handler, and others, I assumed there might still be human remains at the site of the killings, near the side of the building, and at the "official" burial site established near the memorial. The *malines* were more complicated, as they were located inside the buildings.

After the war, Plagge's efforts were not generally recognized, even by him. In fact, as a member of the Nazi Party, and a commander of a forced labor camp, he was required to appear in front of a committee that dealt with war crimes, where he barely defended his actions. The testimony of a couple of the Vilna camp survivors helped to clear his name and offer his legacy as a "Righteous Among the Nations" at Yad Vashem in Jerusalem. This is a designation created by the State of Israel at this combined Holocaust resource, archives, commemoration, and museum, established in the 1950s, when no other institution of its kind existed. This special designation is for individuals who put their own lives in extreme danger to save Jews. To date, almost 27,000 individuals have been named as Righteous Among the Nations. While this may seem like a large number, I imagine there were almost half a billion people living in the areas where the Holocaust took place, and to find only 27,000 who qualify for this title is actually heartbreaking. One must go through a rigorous vetting process to achieve this lofty status. Eyewitnesses and documentation are required, and as the years have passed, it has become more difficult to substantiate claims to get into what I think of as the "Ethical Living Hall of Fame."

Plagge died in 1957, childless, never having totally appreciated what he had done. In his postwar defense, he did not even fully exonerate himself, but the survivors of HKP 562 did. It made it all the more difficult for the Plagge research group to argue that Yad Vashem should accept him as a "Righteous Among the Nations" when he did not put forward a strong defense of his own work at the original trial. I believe this was the case because, like Oskar Schindler, Plagge never quite felt he had done enough. The experience of how and when a person like Plagge becomes a "Righteous Among the Nations" is not altogether clear. Was it from the moment he entered Vilnius and learned about the plight of the Jews? Was it when he became aware of the Ponar mass killings? Was it when he learned that the ghetto was to be liquidated, and his small attempt now demanded much more of him than he had hitherto been giving to the enterprise? Was it when he allowed the Jews to create their hiding places? Was it during that July 1 roll call when he sent his "coded" message? Or was it what I call the daily kindnesses that must have presented themselves as the Jews watched and waited to see what would happen next?

On March 27, 1944, the SS implemented a *Kinderaktion*, rounding up all of the children below a certain age and shipping them out of the camp to their deaths. Some of the children survived by hiding in the *malines* (I will mention this again, later). After the *Kinderaktion*, the daily sounds of the hidden children who had survived the roundup required Plagge and his staff to look the other way and put themselves at risk, as the SS could have shown up at any time. It is clear that he is one of those unique soldiers who saw the evil aspect of Nazi orders that differed from the normal requests his superior officers were making of him. Plagge made the decision to thwart Nazi efforts to exterminate the Jews almost every day during the years he was in Vilna. Slowly at first, and then with one bold gesture, he committed himself in 1943 to the housing and care of 1,257 men, women, and children in the apartment buildings.

The HKP 562 survivors who knew him were particularly generous in their praise of the man. Samuel Esterowicz, Michael Good's grandfather, who wrote an unpublished post-war memoir of his time in the Vilna Ghetto and HKP has a unique perspective on assessing good and evil in this period. Esterowicz found the actions of the Jewish head of the Vilna Ghetto, Jacob Gens, wanting, but had many good things to say about Plagge. (Gens, Jewish director of Vilna Ghetto's Judenrat, was murdered by the Nazis on September 14, in advance of the liquidation of the ghetto some nine days later.) Writing in his memoirs about the days following the execution of Gens, Esterowicz writes: "During the ensuing dismal days while we feared for our lives, there came a sudden ray of hope; tidings came to the ghetto that Major Plagge, the chief of HKP 562, had succeeded, after many requests, to contrive a work camp for the Jews working in his establishment."

It all seems so incongruous: a Nazi officer risking life and limb to save the remnants of the Vilna Ghetto. Indeed, Plagge's nomination to achieve Righteous Among the Nations status was rejected multiple times by Yad Vashem. His case was very unusual; the committee at Yad Vashem could not easily accept that Plagge hadn't had some ulterior motive. When none could be found, they decided to offer the designation, and Plagge was finally inducted in 2004. Since he did not have a living relative, the certificate was accepted by the president of the Technical University of Darmstadt, where he studied, and where there is a building named after him in Darmstadt. The German Army named a military base after him; in fact, Plagge's method of resistance to what he considered to be immoral orders is studied there in the officers' classes.

I am working to add material culture finds among the buildings and the burials at the site to the literature and testimonies that exist about Plagge's work. While we work long and hard in the archaeology of the Holocaust to demonstrate how "evil" was done, I think we need to work equally hard investigating how "good" was done. We need to learn who performed these altruistic acts, and where, and seek to provide physical evidence of the places so they will stand as a testament to future generations about the choices that were made.

Our work at the HKP 562 site concentrated on what the SS did, and where they did it. Those Jews who showed up for roll call following Plagge's final message to them (done in the presence of the SS) were killed on the spot. When the surviving Jews emerged from their hiding places after July 4, they found the dead in a trench on the side of a building. In 2017, the bullet holes were still present in the side of the building. This helped to guide our GPR and ERT lines, where we found the now-buried trenches adjacent to the building and under the bullet holes. But it was Sidney Handler who truly helped guide our search. As a ten-year-old in July of 1944, he had heard the shooting, and remembers seeing the dead bodies, bloated from the heat, when he came with other Jews to dig them out of the shallow trench and deposit them in a more dignified burial spot, in the center of the two buildings near where the memorial stands today.

CAN ARCHAEOLOGY HELP TO IDENTIFY ALTRUISM?

I have been asked many times if archaeology can tell us anything about the character of the people at a site. I see a certain symmetry between my work in Rhodes and Vilna. In Rhodes, there was a diplomat like Selahattin Ulkumen who stood up and—at the risk of his own job, and his very life—issued visas for Jews. In Vilna, it was Major Karl Plagge, a Nazi officer, who risked his job to create HKP 562. In Kaunas, we have the example of Chiune Sugihara, the consul general of Japan, who issued visas to Jews who escaped to the east.

The archaeology of the Holocaust should attempt to identify and if possible collect data at sites where acts of compassion took place, in addition to exploring places where unspeakable crimes were perpetrated. The thousands of places where children and adults were hidden, and the offices of those brave consuls who saved thousands of Jews, from France to Lithuania; this kind of research represents a unique opportunity to teach about the moral decision-making of victims and perpetrators alike.

Finding the places where these people worked is one part of the research that archaeology can do. Finding the testimonies that give meaning to the actions of people on the ground at the time gives us an archaeology of the Holocaust which is beyond the artifacts themselves. Reading the records of what happened, listening to the survivors tell where their hiding places were, and then going to those places in the apartment buildings, does give a sense of how Plagge colluded with the Jews to save them. He not only "looked the other way," as many directors of camps probably did on some occasions; he also created the conditions that allowed them to build these spaces in the apartment buildings. According to the survivors, many of Plagge's soldiers—his inner circle, for example—were in on the deception. Just finding these hiding places speaks volumes for the cooperation that Plagge must have had with his Nazi troops, whose job it was to guard the camp. As I stood at the places where machine gunners were positioned, it occurred to me that in addition to what we think of as the guards' primary mission—keeping the inmates in—they were also protecting the Jews from the realities of Vilnius.

One of the most difficult elements to trace in history is the "motivation" for a person's actions. The ethical evaluation of someone who lived at a precise moment in history cannot be easily assessed by present-day standards. This is the reason why many Holocaust scholars are divided on the issue of "intentionalism" versus "functionalism" in the way the Holocaust unfolded. To listen to the accounts of survivors and then see the physical evidence of the *malines* at HKP 562 brings home how difficult it would have been to create these spaces without the cooperation of the Nazi overseers, and explains much about the success of those who survived the July 2 and 3 roundups at the camp. If they had not had Plagge's commitment to them, none of them would have survived the SS roundups.

It is bad scholarship to take available literary accounts at face value. Often, I am aided by comparative, contemporary eyewitness accounts. I have experienced many moments of finding elements in archaeological context that provide me with insights into an ancient person's personality. For example, finding second-century letters from Bar Kokhba in the Dead Sea Cave of Letters in Israel—written to his compatriots during the middle of the war they were waging with the Romans—gave me a fuller sense of the ethical dimensions of the real, historical Bar Kokhba, distinct from the literary Bar Kokhba, derived from later Jewish, Christian, and Roman sources. What I wanted to know was who Bar Kokhba really was, and the letters told me that he certainly was not a perfect person.

Altruism is an ethical and philosophical idea which states that individuals will, at times, go beyond their own natural instinct for self-preservation, and attempt to save others, at the risk of their own lives and comfort. It does not always imply total self-sacrifice and death. Often it just implies a major or minor expense, damage, or disruption to the lives of the individual who has extended him- or herself for another individual. Philosophers debate whether there is such a thing as altruism, since motivation is an important part of the assessment. Even if there is no remuneration for the altruistic behavior, the altruistic person does receive personal satisfaction, and therefore is in some form compensated. Biologist Richard Dawkins has written about this extensively in his book, *The Selfish Gene*. He says that humans are basically hard-wired from our DNA to think primarily about our own survival, and not the survival of others outside our clan, family, or group. In the past thirty-five years, I have taught Jewish, Christian, and Islamic ethics as part of my course offerings at the university, and I find that students are bewildered to learn that if Charles Darwin taught us anything, it is that being human means we have overcome our DNA.

During the days of work at HKP 562, the most-often-asked question among staff and students was: Why was Plagge different? We discussed his life, his losses, his family, his assignments, and what he asked the Jews to do each day. In my work at the site, I felt that I was teaching archaeology and ethics at the same time.

During much of the 2017 HKP 562 project in Lithuania, Michael Good had his own book with him. He also had the diary of his grandfather, Samuel Esterowicz. He and Sidney Handler directed the students and staff and the TV film crew that was documenting the research, capturing the spirit of the work in video form. I knew from the documents that on September 16, 1943, Plagge transported more than one thousand of his Jewish workers and their families from the Vilna Ghetto to the newly available HKP 562 living quarters. It had been used to house other groups, and, in 1943, was available for Plagge's Jewish workers. The site offered much better housing than what they had experienced in the Vilna Ghetto. It is unlike any other Holocaust site that I have ever seen in Lithuania, because the people who reside there now actually live and play in areas where there are mass burial sites, and the walls of the buildings still bear the marks of shootings that were carried out in the last days of the Nazi occupation, in July 1944. It is for this reason an excellent target for Holocaust archaeology and geoscience.

I knocked on the doors of the current tenants in the apartments, explained what I was doing, and asked for permission to scan the walls and floors of their homes to find out whether any of the *malines* still existed. For the most part, the tenants were accommodating, although there were those who were concerned that I might turn up elements from 1944 that would need to be fully excavated. I assured them that my work was totally noninvasive. I only wanted to see whether the spaces existed, and, if they did, to map them for future knowledge. It was the noninvasive nature of the work that put the residents at ease.

WHY WAS MAJOR PLAGGE DIFFERENT?

The final liquidation of the Vilna Ghetto came on September 23, 1943, about a week after everyone on Major Plagge's lists had come to HKP 562 from the ghetto. Plagge probably knew in advance what was coming, and made a supreme effort to provide a detailed list to the SS to save 1,257 men, women, and children—his workers and their families—by arguing that they were vital to the German war effort. His own superiors in Vilna did not agree, and Plagge had to travel to Berlin to convince Nazis in high places of the need to have an active repair unit available. Plagge was able to maintain his unit from September of 1943 until the end of June 1944. By then, it was clear that the end was rapidly approaching. On July 1, 1944, many of the Jewish workers in the unit went into hiding, and several made an escape; the rest were murdered by the SS the following day. When the Red Army captured Vilnius on July 13, 250 of the camp's Jews emerged from hiding. They were the largest group of Jews to survive Vilnius's destruction.

Karl Plagge, like Oskar Schindler in *Schindler's List*, never believed he had done enough. There are moments—emphasized by survivor testimonies in the documentary filmed about this work, in 2017—which most likely contributed to Plagge's own sense of remorse. On March 27, 1944, during Plagge's absence from HKP 562, the SS implemented a *Kinderaktion* (literally, a children's roundup, or "child (capture) order"). In a matter of a few hours, children were rounded up by SS troops and taken away in transports to be killed in Ponar. The only thing that saved many of them was the planned escape to the *malines* that the adults had been creating for their own final concealment. The *Kinderaktion* was much bigger than HKP 562, but if Plagge had been on-site at the time, he may have been able to control what became one of the most tragic moments of the Jewish camp.

From the end of March to July 1944, when the camp was being prepared for liquidation, to be a child at HKP 562 was a sort of death sentence. Children had to be constantly hidden from the possible squads sent in to monitor the camps. We found multiple *malines*: one in the roof, where the children hid under the wooden floorboards; one in the apartment of a woman who allowed us in, which we were able to image using a concrete scanner; and one, the largest, in the basement of the building where Dr. Good's parents hid during the final fateful days at the end of the Nazi occupation, The *malines* were safe havens that took on even greater significance after the *Kinderaktion* in March 1944.

It was this part of the geoscience and archaeology work at HKP 562 that became one of the more inspiring parts of my time there. Even though I located mass burials which I assumed were from the final days of the camp, finding the *malines*—thanks to the presence of Dr. Good and Sidney Handler, we had a firm handle on where to look—was truly powerful. The students sensed that the search for the *malines* was both scary and reassuring; scary, because it reminded Sidney of where he had experienced his most traumatic moments, but reassuring, because he also saw the *maline* as the place that saved his life.

DO ARTIFACTS SPEAK?
THE DISCOVERY OF A TOY IN A *MALINE*

One debate amongst archaeologists is whether we can extract meaningful information just from artifacts. They ask whether indeed stones, coins, architecture, ceramics and glass objects found in a specific context. One might say that of course you can but it is far richer when we have oral and written

A child's toy found in a *maline*. (Courtesy of the Vilna Excavations Project at the University of Hartford)

testimonies to add to the assessment. It is rare to find children's toys from any period but the Holocaust presents a rather different context. How did Anne Frank play in the Annex? How did a child pass the day in the Ghetto or extermination camps? Toys and playthings are rarely preserved unless there is a rare discovery and the researchers have the presence of mind to examine them. As Sidney Handler put it, "We had no time to play!" After the *Kinderaktion* at HKP 562, the surviving children had to be hidden for most of the day—from possible further SS sweeps, but also from the grief-stricken parents who had lost their own children during the events of March 27. It was a near miracle when we discovered a child's toy wagon hidden in a *maline* in the basement of one of the buildings. It served as a poignant reminder of what exactly I was doing there.

This toy does speak to us in a way that other Holocaust era artifacts cannot. It was probably constructed during the time of the Holocaust. This toy may have been repaired or in use in the Soviet era judging from the state of preservation. It was not used for scarce firewood during the post-Holocaust Soviet era when deprivations were the rule. It was constructed from materials that would have been readily available to those interred at the camp (or in the repair shops where they worked), but it is impossible to know whose toy it was, and if indeed it belonged to any of the children who had hidden in the maline where it was discovered. It appears to be a crudely handcrafted toy circus wagon, with an animal cage and oversized wooden wheels. The irony of this particular toy in this particular place was not missed on my staff and students. A caged animal circus wagon would have been a toy for a child who might have seen him-or herself as a "caged animal" first at the Vilna Ghetto and later at HKP 562. I can imagine a HKP child who had to pass endless days in hiding playing with this and seeing in it a way of controlling his/her lack of freedom. When I searched I found the popular original toy manufactured and available in Vilnius in the 1930s where several circulating circuses came in this period. It is how artifacts speak that makes them powerful.

I have seen toys from the Holocaust in museums before. They are quite rare, since so little remains of the world of children from the Holocaust era, including their shoes, clothes, and any parts of their childhood. On display at the University of Hartford Museum of Jewish Civilization is a toy doll that belonged to Ruth (Tutti) Lichtenstern. Ruth carried the toy throughout the Holocaust, the family's fortune hidden inside the doll's head. The doll is featured in a special exhibit at the museum called "Tutti's Promise," a favorite with school-age children. The children who come can imagine themselves with a favorite doll or toy, and it distracts them from the reality of the situation.[5] The doll also shows how toys were often more than just playthings. During the war, Tutti's father told her that he'd hidden some money inside her doll, and that she must keep that fact a secret. "I promise," she told him solemnly. "I'll take care of her . . . and I won't tell anyone." Eventually, the Lichtensterns were sent to Theresienstadt. They ultimately survived, and ended up in Connecticut, largely because of that toy.

From the beginning, I wanted to discover what, if anything, made HKP 562 different from standard labor camps. It was most unusual for Jewish families to be allowed to live together in apartments, which were not what they had been used to in downtown Vilna. Beyond that, the ability to create hiding places with the knowledge and cooperation of Major Plagge was the main difference. I have researched Plagge's life, looking for hints as to the reason for his actions. He experienced health scares—he had had polio—which may have taught him about suffering at an early age, and left him unable to have his own children. He was educated as a scientist and engineer, which may have made him skeptical of the racial theories and less susceptible to the Nazis' hateful racial ideology (although there were many scientists and engineers among the Nazis). He had personal connections to Jews throughout his life, doing business with several, and serving as godfather to a Jewish child, even after the Nuremburg Laws in 1935. One might imagine that his posting in Vilna during the period that included the liquidation of the ghetto, as well as the Ponar shootings and burnings, must have exposed him to the worst forms of violence an officer could see. It is impossible to know for sure which of these experiences helped to make him what he was, but he was not like most Nazi officers of the period.

Representatives from Plagge's family flew from Germany to attend the ceremony held at the memorial stone, located between the two HKP buildings where the SS had murdered the Jewish workers. They also attended a dinner at the US Embassy in Vilnius, one of the supporters of our work at the site. At both occasions, they described the archaeology of the Holocaust as science in service to humanity.

What type of resistance would we call Plagge's work? It is not exactly active resistance, nor is it passive. It is not really subversive in nature, but it is certainly what I would call *humanistic resistance*. To do your job and live your life as an altruistic human being is one of the great lessons that Plagge taught us by his actions. Our work at the HKP site—preserving a Holocaust labor camp where a single individual practiced his moral convictions in the face of murderous evil—is yet another example of how archaeology and geoscience can help to preserve the elements of light in the midst of the darkness of the Holocaust.

WHY ARCHAEOLOGY OF THE HOLOCAUST IS DIFFERENT

I treasure this photo of the memorial service, because it captures a moment unlike any other I have ever experienced in an excavation. My team has worked on many archaeological sites over the past thirty years, all over the world. They all involved some measure of death and destruction. The presence of human remains instills in students and staff a sense of humility. Finding the jewelry or personal items of a man, woman, or child from antiquity makes you pause to think about what you will leave behind. The devastation of an ancient home or religious institution (or even a bathhouse) never ceases to impart a sense of loss.

I have found that the archaeology of the Holocaust is different—not only because there are still living survivors, some who participate in the work, but because it is so close to the present that I can't help but wonder whether anything learned from the excavation might help stop a future disaster from occurring. It is unusual to work at a Holocaust site and not feel that it's an opportunity to reflect upon the events that took place there.

In the case of Rhodes, I have taken staff and students to Sabbath services in the Kahal Shalom Synagogue so they can experience the way of life that

The memorial service at the HKP 562 burial site, following the excavations near the monument commemorating the mass burial. (Courtesy of the Vilna Excavations Project at the University of Hartford)

was lost. One of my students, Jacob Greenberg, a pre-cantorial student, led a service on a Friday night that showed everyone present how a building preserves in its acoustics and setting the memories of the former occupants. At the end of the service, as I intoned for them the Kaddish (the prayer for the dead), it brought many of them to tears, understanding the depth of the loss.

Each season at Ponar, my colleague, Jon Seligman, and I have brought the staff and students to the memorial in the center of the burial pits to listen to Yiddish readings from the Yiddish writers of Vilna, and to read aloud in English from the literature that made Vilna great. I read the Kaddish, and again, after a season of working on these projects, it sinks into the consciousness of everyone that we are doing a "special" type of archaeology and geoscience.

At HKP 562, I had a similar experience. Lithuanians, Israelis, Canadians, and Americans all gathered on the last day to reflect upon the work. There were scientists, a famed Jewish member of the Holocaust era Partisans, our students, a rabbi, a survivor of HKP 562, children of survivors, the leader of the present Lithuanian Jewish community, group of local Lithuanians, and even a relative of Plagge's who had flown in for the ceremony. It is not similar to any other professional or religious experience that I have had at any other excavation site. The rabbi intoned the words of the prayers for the dead; Sidney Handler, HKP 562 survivor, spoke of his feelings about being back at the site of his greatest trauma and triumph. The grandnephew of Karl Plagge spoke about his own need to be there. The idea of speaking to and about people who died in the Holocaust, and what happened to them, is preserved in the lives of the survivors, but also in their descendants.

• *10* •

Why the Discovery of the "Holocaust Escape Tunnel" Gives the World Hope

*W*orldwide interest in the discovery of the Holocaust Escape Tunnel during the month of July 2016 reached a fever pitch, and continued throughout 2017. It was trending as one of the most well-known news stories in 2016, and even included as one of the top science stories of 2016 in the *New York Times*. I was mystified by the interest, as were my colleagues. An escape tunnel in a far-flung forest of Lithuania did not seem to be one of the great discoveries of the year, yet it was obvious from the many interviews that I gave that it fascinated people in Africa, Asia, the Middle East, Australia, and North and South America. I received many notes and letters, and I started to wonder whether I had missed something that others saw in the project. It was not necessarily the story of the Jews, or Jewish history, or even the Holocaust that drew people's interest; I think it was the possibility of being able to escape from the most horrific conditions imaginable to freedom that most captured the imagination. It was the idea that there can—and should be—hope against all odds.

It was the idea of hope itself.

I was not present when *NOVA* filmed and photographed the actor in the "created" escape tunnel in Lithuania, on a film set far from the real Holocaust Escape Tunnel. All of the reenactments, which were some of the most powerful moments in the documentary, were filmed with local actors, in period costumes, and held to exacting standards of the period. They were based on the scientific data I had collected, and the testimonies of the escapees. The thought of being on set just made me uncomfortable. I could not bring myself to watch the reenactments, but I knew the rest of the staff and students were there, watching and marveling at how a discovery like the escape tunnel can be translated into a meaningful experience for the viewer.

213

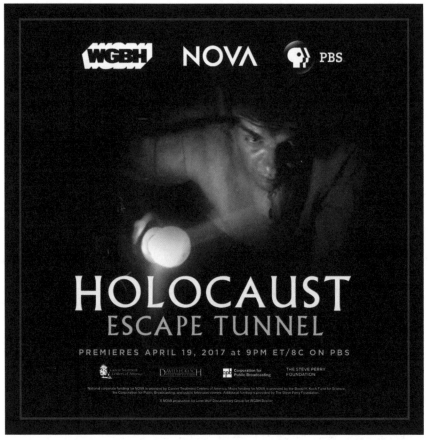

Holocaust Escape Tunnel **poster from** *NOVA.* **(Courtesy of** *NOVA*)

This poster is at the center of the University of Hartford exhibition of my work in Vilna. Students and community members who come to the museum always ask, "Who took that picture?" and I have to remind them that it was a reenactment. Most museum visitors and attendees at my lectures want to know how I knew the tunnel was there. That is the mystery of science in general, and geoscience and archaeology in particular. I did not know it was there when I started! Science is about discovery. You set a hypothesis, and then you follow it. In the case of the tunnel, many survivors mentioned a tunnel in their testimonies. I started with the assumption that the collective memory of these survivors involved at its core a dynamic but real historical event and not a fantasy or a joint conspiracy to somehow lionize their past or mythologize the situation. If remains of a tunnel existed, perhaps I would be able to find one part of it. In fact, our work exceeded all expectations. The tunnel was discovered almost completely intact, often ten or twelve feet underground.

I assumed that the escapee testimonies were accurate, since I knew they had been recorded in different times and places, without consulting one another; but when I began, I didn't know whether the tunnel had been found earlier and destroyed or filled in, whether it had collapsed or become integrated with the surrounding soil, or whether it was an exaggerated version of a shortened escape route. In the end, the tunnel turned out to be even longer than the estimates found in the survivors' accounts, and the conditions present at the site even more horrific than their descriptions.

I did not go to Lithuania to look for a Holocaust escape tunnel. It would have been problematic if I had based the entire project on a possible discovery of a mythical escape tunnel (or, perhaps less dramatic, a tunnel that had been completely destroyed after the war). I went to use the noninvasive geoscience and geophysics equipment on behalf of the work of the Great Synagogue project in Vilnius; I went to search for Jacob Gens in Rasu Prison; and I went to Ponar forest to look for additional burial pits that might still be hidden there. The escape tunnel was an extra piece.

As I have mentioned, I work with local archaeologists, donating my time, expertise, and equipment to help them uncover their own history. Thus, they can benefit from the cutting-edge techniques, and both they and my students can benefit from international connections and collaboration. In Poland, I worked on projects in Luta, Otwock, and Sobibor. In Rhodes, I worked on two medieval synagogues and searched for a third, another ancient synagogue, and we worked on two other projects with the local authorities using noninvasive technologies. In Lithuania, we have now worked in three areas of the country: In Vilna, we worked on the Great Synagogue and Shulhoyf, multiple sites in the Ponar forest, HKP 562, and Rasu Prison. In Kaunas, we worked on projects at three forts, and a Jewish cemetery. In Rokiskis, we did five separate projects, and in Silute, a POW camp for many Allied airmen. These projects are about scientific and historical discoveries, but they are also about international collaboration among students and professionals in different countries, in an effort to introduce them to a different way of doing archaeological work, especially when it comes to the Holocaust.

TWO PROJECTS IN ONE PARK

Although I came to Lithuania to do projects which benefited local and Holocaust history, I was totally unprepared for the discoveries at Ponar. Ponar is a site on par with Auschwitz in terms of its brutality and significance. Throughout this volume I have introduced you to the reasons why I hold

The Ponar (Paneriai) sign, administered by the Vilna Gaon Jewish State Museum, in Lithuanian, Yiddish, and English. (Courtesy of the Vilna Excavations Project at the University of Hartford)

the site in such reverence. In my view, it was one of the first killing sites of the infamous "Final Solution to the Jewish Question." The Vilna Gaon Jewish State Museum (VGJSM) administers the park at Ponar, as well as a small museum on-site that tells the story of what happened there. In 2015, I met with staff of the VGJSM at Ponar, who asked me to look for possible burial pits that still existed in the forest, but were not marked. The search for the escape tunnel was almost an afterthought. The VGJSM had commissioned a lidar study by a local geo-tech company, which showed some elevation changes under the tree canopy that suggested man-made features. This form of mapping is invaluable in the search for lost buildings, caves, and hidden features under tree canopies and other heavy vegetation, and it is important at many Holocaust sites. With the local lidar study and a vintage 1944 air photo of the site, I could detect that some of the original burial pits extended beyond the parameters of the present-day "prepared" park. I decided that this was a project that GPR and ERT could best handle together, given the depth of the pits and the contents (held to be the burned remains of the victims, based upon the testimonies). Thanks to the LIDAR data and comparisons with the 1944 air photos, I had a better idea of where to look. This project's main goal was to assess the size of the burial pits that would have extended in a circular fashion, like the well-marked pits that are part of the park's established memorial areas.

It is interesting how a discovery begins. During my discussions about a potential project in Ponar, I was asked whether I would be interested in looking for the escape tunnel which the survivors of Ponar wrote about in their testimonies. These chilling testimonies appear in many of the panels at the Ponar museum, accompanied by grainy photos. They all chronicle the existence of an escape tunnel, roughly one hundred feet in length, that led from a burial pit, under the barbed-wire fences and guards' positions, and out to the forest. The idea of the tunnel was fascinating, of course, but with such a small amount of information, and such a large park—with possibly several unknown pits—it seemed like a daunting task. Nevertheless, I agreed that, if there were any chance of finding such a tunnel, geoscience would be the methodology best suited to the task. The geoscientists agreed to run long ERT lines across these areas, and then construct a GPR grid over the ERT survey to confirm any discoveries. It seemed like a workable plan, and allowed me to do the rest of the work I had to do in Lithuania with the equipment involved.

We work in-country usually for no more than two weeks. We then collect all of the data, and at the end of the season, we pass all of it to the chief cartographer, Dr. Philip Reeder. He adds this information to his own "Total Station" data. A Total Station is a device that fits into a box for the upper technical brain, the theodolite, and is an electronic/optical instrument used for surveying and building construction. You may have seen them in use along highways or construction sites. The theodolite fits on top of a tripod that Dr. Reeder brings with him from his university. He moves strategically around the grid for ERT and GPR, and then the entire site beyond our grid, to give it context. He continues to monitor with a student to measure the topography of the area, and also to establish GPS coordinates for all of our maps.

Many archaeologists use only Total Stations as their guide to the depth of the excavations and the pits and natural dips in the landscape, which are often critical to our initial setting of a grid. It is even more important after the fact. We use Total Stations as a check and balance to the geoscience. The theodolite communicates with an electronic distance measurement (EDM) device to measure both vertical and horizontal angles and the slope distance from the instrument to a particular point. An on-board computer collects data and performs triangulation calculations. Professor Reeder's method involves using a base station location and then connecting the areas that we decide to work on to the GPS coordinates of the site. He does take notes throughout

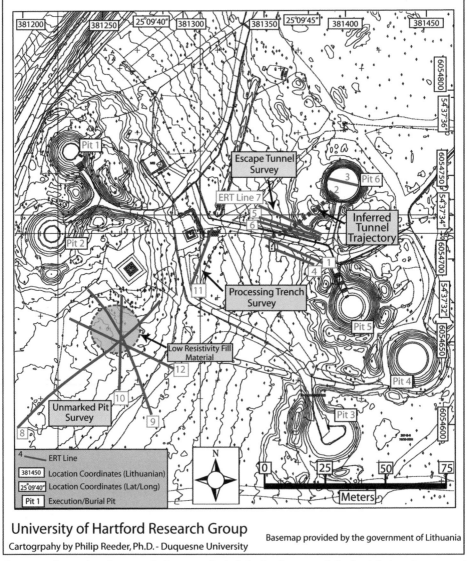

Ponar Forest Site
Vilnius, Lithuania

Pit 1

Escape Tunnel Survey

ERT Line 7

3 Pit 6
2

Inferred Tunnel Trajectory

5
6

Pit 2

7

1

4

11

Processing Trench Survey

Pit 5

Low Resistivity Fill Material

12

10

9

Unmarked Pit Survey

8

Pit 3

Pit 4

4 — ERT Line
381450 Location Coordinates (Lithuanian)
25°09'40" Location Coordinates (Lat/Long)
Pit 1 Execution/Burial Pit

N

0   25   50   75

Meters

University of Hartford Research Group
Cartogrpahy by Philip Reeder, Ph.D. - Duquesne University

Basemap provided by the government of Lithuania

The Ponar forest site, the tunnel, the unmarked pit in the forest, and the burial pits. (Courtesy of Philip Reeder, Duquesne University, on behalf of the Vilna Excavations Project at the University of Hartford) about each reading, and involves the students by having them move the EDM around the field, collecting the data. He also explains to the students what he is doing and why it is important. Students often marvel at his ability to slowly build a map that he can then use to explain all of the findings. I cannot emphasize enough the importance of these maps. They are unlike a standard map, because in their digital forms they contain layers of complex data that can be summoned up or turned off, and yet, they are also readable by almost anyone, even those without a scientific background in archaeology.

The map in this figure is truly a remarkable piece of work. It represents the sum total of our work in the field, a "snapshot" of the discoveries made there. In one map you can see the whole perspective on the killing fields: The seven lines of data confirm the existence of the tunnel; the work I did evaluating the trench where the Jews were processed before entering the pits, where they were killed; the other pits, already known, and now numbered; and the unmarked pit in the forest, which I investigated. It is the epitome of archaeological science. It looks like a simple map, but as Dr. Reeder will tell you, embedded in each digital layer of the map are multiple levels of information that document what is found in each layer, so that a scientist at a later point in time could go back and examine a specific one. It is not dependent upon the memory of the survivors, nor on whether or not any future changes to the location will be prevented. The GPS locations are embedded in the map despite any efforts to erase the past, or lose data as the Ponar park is developed in the future. I look at these scientific maps as the best monuments to the past available to us in the twenty-first century.

THE OPEN SECRET: THE BURNING BRIGADES

More than 100,000 people were murdered in the Ponar forest, of which 70,000 were Jews. From July 1941 to July 1944, the killings continued right up until the Soviets came from the east and displaced the Nazis in Lithuania. By December 1943, the Nazis decided that the evidence of their war crimes needed to be destroyed by burning the bodies of the victims. That decision resulted in the infamous *Aktion* 1005, a horrific "secret" order issued when the Nazis started losing the war, which included numerous areas where there were many bodies and no crematoria.

In Vilna the Nazis brought in eighty Jews as slave labor from nearby camps; some came from the now-destroyed Vilna Ghetto, but others came from different villages. The Jews in the squads detailed to destroy evidence realized early on that when they were finished burning the bodies, they would probably be the final victims. By the end of January 1944, the Jews assigned to one burial pit, now designated as Pit #6, hatched a plan: to dig a tunnel out of the burial pit to freedom. From the testimonies of the survivors of the tunnel escape, I learned about details of their everyday lives in the pit. There is agreement that there were seventy-six men and four women assigned to this detail, and that their main task was to disinter thousands of the dead and burn their bodies on makeshift pyres. These were the so-called "Burning Brigades."

The pits had been built by the Soviets during their short period of occupation from 1940 to 1941 (stemming from the compact between Hitler and Stalin), to serve as future fuel depots in preparation for the building of a new airport. The circular pits were dug near the train lines that ran through Vilnius, to a depth of twelve feet, with vertical stone walls. When the Nazis displaced the Soviets, the Ponar pits became a place for Nazi killing, starting in 1941. The 1943 Burning Brigade for Ponar was a group brought in from many different areas, but some were originally Vilnaites who had been interned in work camps after the liquidation of the Vilna Ghetto, in September 1943. Those who were originally brought in to construct the pit housing also started to chop wood in the forest, not knowing the exact purpose of this task. They would eventually use this collected wood to construct massive pyres to burn the bodies of the Jews. The makeshift living quarters for workers at Pit #6 were built in what is assumed to be one of the early killing and burial pits at Ponar, but its central location made it the obvious choice for the prisoners. The tasks of the new Burning Brigade at Ponar were slowly revealed to the prisoners. The level of detail in the testimonies is amazing, and since they were recorded in different places and times after the war, they appear to be reliable.

One question I have been asked is how the Jews came up with the tunnel plan in the first place. It appears to have emerged from multiple sources. A Soviet Jew (Yuri Farber) with engineering and military training arrived as a prisoner at the end of January 1944. He may have been the catalyst for an idea that was brewing among the other prisoners. There is a possibility that the prisoners may have been inspired by the audacious escape of the Jewish Burning Brigade from Fort IX in Kaunas, on Christmas Day, 1943. The manhunt for these Jews continued through the beginning of January, and it appears that news reports may have filtered down to both the guards and the Jews in the Ponar pit by January 1944.

Although the Ponar escape tunnel is quite different from the escape at Fort IX—at Fort IX, they did not actually have to build an escape tunnel; they just figured out a way of escaping through an already-existing tunnel— the idea that they should even attempt to escape by a tunnel was bolstered by reports coming out of Kaunas. The fact that the Jewish prisoner, Itzhak

Dugin, an electrician, was pressed into service by the Nazis to help with the lighting for the Ponar site gave the group in burial pit #6 a clear perspective on where they had to get to in an escape. They knew they wanted to find the partisans in the forest nearby. This not only drove them; it was what happened when they did escape.

One Jew in the pit at Ponar had more experience than anyone else, and may have been instrumental in formulating the idea of tunneling. Joseph (Blaser) Kagan escaped twice from Ponar, and also had experience before the war in tunneling. When asked "Who came up with the idea of digging an escape tunnel?" my answer is simple: "It was a group effort." I see elements in each of the diggers' biographies that contributed not only to the plan, but also the execution of the tunnel, as well as the strategy of linking up with the partisans. I see, for example, Mordechai "Motke" Zaidel as a youthful, strong-minded prisoner who would push the project through despite the risks that would have stopped others. I see Shlomo Gol in his post-escape partisan uniform, with his machine gun, together with the other partisans, and I know that this is what he saw every day as he dug the tunnel.

I have made notes on each of those who got out and were able to re-cord their testimonies; I understand how each one contributed to the Ponar escape tunnel. To me, the idea of an escape tunnel, conceived and built by Jews for their ultimate survival against all odds, seems vaguely like that of the second-century-CE group of refugees in the Cave of Letters on the Dead Sea, which I had excavated eighteen years earlier. Which one of those earlier Jews formulated the plan to bring them to this almost-inaccessible cave, to try to wait out the Romans? Clearly, it involved a series of skill sets that each one possessed. If there is one thing I have learned from studying multiple destroyed Jewish sites, it is that the will to survive is embedded in the Jews, and was more than just an ethnic marker.

THE BURNING BRIGADE: WORK AND ESCAPE

The testimonies reveal horrific details of the preparations for the digging and escape. Every day the Jewish men, who were shackled, were brought up from the depths of the pit where they lived. (The women stayed back to do their work in the living quarters at the pit.) The Jews in Pit #6 went about their assigned tasks, which included Nazi-ordered scavenging for valuable objects among the dead (in addition, they were also collecting items they would need for the escape); digging up the bodies; placing them on pyres of wood that they had prepared; and then burning the bodies. The descriptions in the testimonies are difficult to read. They were not only disinterring Jews (who, in some cases, they knew, or were related to), they were also performing one of the most objectionable acts in Jewish life: cremation. Cremation is forbidden in the Bible (Jews must bury their dead in the ground), and later proscribed in Jewish law by the rabbis (because it was being done by local populations). Thousands of years of anti-cremation prohibitions, and now the Jews were being forced to cremate their coreligionists. It was an act that must have stirred enormous passion, even for these Jews who had become hardened by their experiences. The Jews of the Burning Brigade were being forced to perform an act that was undignified and objectionable, knowing that if they refused, they could face death at the hands of the Nazis.

I am still haunted by the case of Itzhak Dugin, one of the tunnel escape survivors whom I came to know intimately through his testimony. One day, in February or March of 1943, while digging up the buried Jews, Itzak encountered members of his own family. He recognized them by their clothes, and it traumatized him to the point where he was almost unable to continue. When I spoke to Dugin's daughter, Sabina, in Israel, she mentioned that it was difficult for him to recover, but in the end, he returned to his work for the Nazis, and also continued digging the tunnel, for an escape route. His comrades rewarded his efforts by allowing him to be the first person out of the tunnel on April 15, 1944. Sabina's work on her father's testimony was a labor of love. I had long interviews with her, and she sent me the published book of her father's story in 2017 that was only in manuscript form when I met her in August of 2016.

The Nazis ordered the Jews to keep track of the number of unearthed bodies, perhaps so the Nazis could know whether they were nearing the end of the *aktion* at Ponar. Hana Amir, whom I met in Israel in August 2016, told me that her father, Mordechai "Motke" Zaidel, was keeping count, both for the Nazis, and for himself. As far as I can tell, the total number of the buried—100,000—is based upon their systematic accounting, and an extrapolation that was done as part of the early Soviet trials after the war, with evidence collected there by forensic teams. The work the Jewish Burning Brigade did each day from late 1943 into early 1944 convinced them that they needed to keep track of the evidence even as they were destroying it.

It is with this in mind that the prisoners planned their escape, carrying out their tasks during the day while digging the tunnel at night. In the course of seventy-six days, a small group of shackled Burning Brigade members in Pit #6 dug a tunnel of more than one hundred feet using only spoons and metal objects they discovered among the dead. Their work had a storybook finish. On the last night of the Jewish holiday of Passover, April 15, 1944—known by the Jews as "the holiday of liberation from Egypt," and the darkest night for the lunar month of April—the escape began. Just as the Fort IX prisoners had planned, those in Pit #6 decided to act when the guards would likely be distracted by their own holiday (Easter was two days before the last day of Passover, in 1944). According to their testimonies, two days after Easter, April 15, 1944, between nine and ten p.m., the first group escaped. The leaders of the tunnel escape had divided the entire eighty prisoners into groups of ten. Many in Pit #6 knew little or nothing about the tunnel until the evening of the escape, in order to protect its existence. Most of those who got out in the second group were shot while coming out into the forest, but twelve to fifteen actually escaped, and eleven survived the war to tell the story.

A COMPASS, A LIGHTBULB, THE WOOD, AND THE SAND: DETAILS OF THE TESTIMONIES

In reading the testimonies I kept asking myself, "Was this tunnel ever finished?" I needed to see whether I could find multiple "slices" of the tunnel using ERT and GPR. I assumed that the entrance and the exit would have been badly damaged by the Nazis during their investigation following the escape. I looked for details in the testimonies that would give me clues as to the direction of the tunnel, and an indication of anything inside the tunnel that would make it easier to find. There were hundreds of small details in the testimonies that corroborated one another, and a visit to Fort IX's museum collections of artifacts from the Burning Brigade prisoners certainly confirmed many of the details from the Ponar testimonies. A scientific approach to studying the testimonies allowed me to evaluate the testimonies for internal accuracy and agreement, but also question the details as presented by the testimonies themselves. Some of these testimonies were taken right after the war, while others were recorded in the 1950s.

Since the discovery of the tunnel, the five most prominent questions I have been asked are:

1. How did the prisoners make sure they were digging in a straight line?
2. How did the prisoners see what they were doing in the dark tunnel they were digging?
3. What did they do with the sand they were digging, and how did they shore up the tunnel itself?
4. Why didn't all (or more) of the prisoners get out?
5. Why couldn't they find the tunnel after the war?

Fortunately for history, all of these issues were addressed in some of the testimonies, which demonstrate that the people taking the testimonies, and the survivors themselves, realized just how incredible the escape had been. Certainly, with respect to the first three questions, the presence of Yuri Farber, the Jewish prisoner who was a trained engineer, made a difference. It was not until his arrival in the pit, in January 1944, that the tunnel began in earnest. Somehow, they had "commandeered" a compass that provided them with the directional decisiveness that made the tunnel digging possible. Another critical person in the escape was the previously mentioned Itzhak Dugin, a skilled electrician. A tunnel of the configuration they were digging (two feet by two feet) would not have allowed enough oxygen for a candle to light their way after they reached twenty lateral feet. Dugin found a way to string electrical cable through the tunnel and provide light at the end with a single lightbulb. In 2004, when the Lithuanians excavated the entrance to the tunnel, they found the remains of the electrical cable. This and other details were probably not missed by the original Lithuanian excavator, Vytautas Urbanavicius, whose report documents how he opened the entrance to the tunnel in 2004 and then recorded what he found and closed off the opening. We came back in 2016 and found his original excavation site and then traced it back through the forest.

The sand they excavated from the tunnel was an issue, but it did not present as big a challenge as did the famed *Great Escape* tunnel, from Stalag Luft III, the subject of the Steve McQueen movie (1963). The prisoners in Pit #6 at Ponar were living in the sand and squalor of the burial pit. The wood they received to burn the bodies ironically provided a means to shore up the tunnel. The diggers dug in teams and emerged from the tunnel each night dragging the sand around the camp; it was indistinguishable from the floor of the pit. More important was the fact that unlike the officers in Stalag Luft III, nobody dreamed that the Jews, who were shackled and working all day, would be digging a tunnel all night. According to the testimonies, there were usually two diggers in the tunnel at the same time—one to dig the tunnel, and the other to ferry the sand out. Fortunately, the tunnel never collapsed, which would have been tremendously demoralizing, and possibly would have revealed its existence.

The issue of secrecy was one of the most problematic aspects. I mentioned above that only a small group of diggers was involved in working on the tunnel. The Nazis could be brutal, and could find ways to get tired and half-starved people to reveal whatever secrets they might have had to tell. If the tunnel had been known to everyone, it would have soon been discovered by the Nazis, and the consequences would have been fatal. Therefore, the tunnel was kept secret from all but the few digging it.

Nevertheless, although it was located in an obscure part of the pit, and the entrance covered up each night, it still could have been stumbled upon by others in the pit and revealed to the guards. The tunnel was literally a matter of life and death to the Jews in Pit #6. If they succeeded in building it, it would be a path to freedom, and life; if they failed, their eventual murder was guaranteed. Once they began to dig, an extra level of anxiety and stress was now manifest. Whereas before, they were living under the constant fear of death, they may have been resigned to their fate. With the tunnel came hope, and a race against the clock to finish and escape before they were discovered. The story unfolding in the testimonies is a collage of hope and fear, rather than a purely linear event. The gruesome nature of the task and the fears for the dynamic of the group make the testimonies even more compelling, and give them an added measure of authenticity.

I am well aware of the skepticism surrounding these testimonies. It was something I had heard many times from historians when I was beginning my research into the tunnel. Testimonies are not newspaper accounts of events, but rather personal recollections subject to all the failings of memory, recounted years later under conditions that often made these survivors question why they had survived while others had not. The issue for most scholars of the Holocaust is how the memory of survivors works to protect the survivor from deep trauma, while retaining those details of their experiences that they want others to understand.

The consensus is that survivors try to create intelligible accounts of the events they have experienced, remembering those elements that for them were significant because of who they are. Not all survivors involved in the same sets of events remember what happened in the same way. This creates a lot of confusion for historians, and is a point of contention exploited by many Holocaust deniers. "How," they ask, "can people who say they experienced the same event have such different recollections of it?" I remember how difficult it was for us to understand the different maps made by various people who survived Sobibor. It is a product of where these people spent their days in the camp, but also what registered in their memory because of who they were as people.

There are multiple survivor testimonies about the Holocaust Escape Tunnel. The survivors did not always have the luxury of consulting each other to confirm details while they provided their testimonies. When I wrote about the escape of the Jews from Sobibor and Treblinka in Poland, I interviewed some of the people who had survived the escape. I learned details about how it was planned and executed from their perspectives. I later read their accounts, many of which have been given to the Spielberg and Fortunoff archives of official taped testimonies.

Reading and listening to their personal reflections, I realized just how difficult it must have been to plan an escape when day-to-day necessities—such as food and water, sleep and health concerns—were hanging in the balance. It meant that individuals in the group often had to put aside their own daily needs in favor of a goal that might aid the entire group. This not only provided insight into the planners of the escape tunnel at Ponar, but also helped me to understand something about how my own research group works. We start with the general parameters of what we wish to accomplish, each of us coming to the field with different methodologies, training, and personal backgrounds. We all contribute in a group effort, our goal not only to uncover some particular site, but also to teach colleagues and students about how we do this work. If there is something I learned from our work on the many sites covered in this book, it is that a group is much more than the sum of its parts.

Regarding the Holocaust Escape Tunnel, in particular, it was extremely challenging to attempt to locate its remains in the short space of the week that had been allocated for this project. I know that I was amazed the prisoners were able to dig the tunnel. I think my colleagues and I were also amazed that we were able to find it.

One of the most important and least understood issues that all archaeological teams face when working on a Holocaust site is the difficulty of doing this work more than seventy years after the events unfolded, and how the places have changed. In the case of Ponar, the creation of the park, the need to put in parking lots, to create a museum, to landscape, to create walking paths and orient the visitor so they have a meaningful and safe experience in a camp—all of this has meant that the site has been completely reoriented.

Other Holocaust sites are similar. Hannah Amir and other children of the tunnel escape survivors, who came with their families to Ponar in the 1980s, could not locate the tunnel. The camp had been reorganized as a result of park planning and upgrades. Part of what I did was to locate the original path into the camp from the original 1940s entrance. Jon Seligman, who walked this route while we were working at the burial pits, showed the filmmakers just how different the entire camp looks in these undeveloped forest areas. The work of future Ponar expeditions should fully document, and perhaps excavate, the original entrances to provide a clearer context before they are developed. The major changes in the configuration of the nearby train railways at Ponar totally changed the entire orientation of the park-ironically preserving them for future investigators. The next generation of Holocaust archaeology must always keep in mind that a site may have been totally reconfigured for visitors and the original site might still be available for research.

PHOTOGRAPHING A HOLOCAUST SITE

One of my students pointed out to me in one of my lectures that I rarely appear in the photos of a site. This is perhaps a result of my own desire to make sure these photos are scientific evidence—not selfies—but also because many

A drone photograph with infrared overlay of the burial pit at Ponar, where the escape tunnel began. (Left to right) Richard Freund, Paul Bauman, and Mantas Siksnianas. (Courtesy of Paul Bauman, WorleyParsons, Inc., on behalf of the Vilna Excavations Project at the University of Hartford)

of the photos are directed by me to ensure that I have a particular view of the site. I want to have people in a photograph to give a sense of perspective, but not too many people, which would obstruct the view of the site. When I get to the point of photographing one area, I am usually already looking at the next area of research, since my time at a site is limited.

The moment captured in this photograph, when the drone hovered over Pit #6, was different. I had already discovered the tunnel. I am sitting closest to the entrance of the escape tunnel, as my colleague, Paul Bauman, operates the drone that is photographing us. The photo serves as a reminder of where the work began, but also as a pointer to where the work will continue, directed by multispectral imaging from drones.

In 2016 and 2017, I had Paul Bauman and Alastair McClymont of WorleyParsons Inc. (Advisian is their consulting group) working together with the local people and my students. Over the years Paul has brought some of the most indefatigable, curious, and tireless workers to the field. He tells me that this is the fortieth project we have worked on together, experiences including caves, deserts, shops, religious institutions, cemeteries, buried ancient synagogues, churches, mosques, burial pits, individual graves, and whole cities. He has a whole host of software applications that I have been testing over the past twenty years.

It all began when I saw how the gas and oil industry used technologies to map the subsurface of sites looking for gas, oil, and, later, precious metals, and I realized that our goals (the oil companies' and mine) were similar. We were both in pursuit of treasures below the surface; we both needed to know what materials (bone, stone, metal, glass, wood, ceramic, sand) composed the substrate; and we both wanted to do the work in the most efficient way possible. The oil companies, with their deep pockets, possessed technology that could map up to twenty or thirty meters below the surface with extreme accuracy.

All of my work depends on receiving the support of local staff and archaeologists. At Ponar, Rokas Vengalis, the assigned Lithuanian archaeologist of record at the site; Markas Zingeris, the museum director; Zigmas Vitkus, the administrator of Paneriai; and Mantas Siksnianas, the head docent, all worked together to get the information I needed to plan the initial survey of the site, and continued to update the site, thanks, in part, to the ERT, GPR, and digital GPS mapping from 2016. I try to make maps that will be useful to scientists and laypeople alike, in hopes they can be helpful for additional projects in the future.

WHY TWO GEOSCIENCE TECHNIQUES?

I will repeat a short mantra regarding scientific confirmation that I have made throughout this book: I use two different geoscientific, noninvasive technologies on the same site. I call this the "find and verify, in one operation" method. I will usually not get a second chance at working on a site. It may seem redundant, but on the extreme ends of their ranges, each technology can spot things the other misses; when the different data sets support each other, it provides strong confirmation of a hypothesis. Any archaeological site is fragile and irreplaceable. I need to collect as much data as possible on the off chance that something may happen after I leave.

With the tunnel project, I had seven slices of ERT that showed me single pieces of the tunnel. On top of the ERT, I constructed a GPR grid that confirmed the details. Remember from earlier chapters that GPR cannot locate a tunnel (or anything) that is more than fifteen feet below the surface. If I had been using only GPR, I would have missed the tunnel. The ERT lines scanned deep into the ground. The GPR grids are much larger and more extensive than ERT, because the GPR unit can easily move back and forth over the area. The grid contains everything between the ERT slices. Although GPR can do a massive grid, it cannot look down as deep as the ERT, nor can it capture the details that ERT can, such as the color-coded materials below the surface. Only ERT can provide the details, but without GPR to confirm some major sections of the subsurface, the ERT would not have been as valuable.

THE SECRET OF ERT AND THE
INDUCED POLARIZATION SCAN

There was one other "secret" I had brought with me, along with ERT, which allowed me to see a detail of the tunnel that otherwise would have been lost. I started with ERT on June 8, 2016, at Ponar, because it can scan very deep (the escapees had to dig very deep to get under the obstacles in front of them), and ERT software interpretation identifies very specific elements in the subsurface, such as metal, wood, stone, bone, etc. On June 9, I knew that I had located sections of the tunnel. The University of Hartford research group, together with WorleyParsons, Inc., of Calgary, Alberta, Canada, made the discovery of the escape tunnel only a couple of days after we began the search.

In recent years, ERT has yielded a new tool, called induced polarization (IP), which identifies metal in the ground once the electricity *is turned off!* Normally, ERT draws a picture based on different substances' resistances to electrical current. Wood can be detected because it has a different resistance from sand or stone (or other substances). In the case of IP, the capacitance (ability to store electrical charge) of substances can be measured after the source current is turned off. I learned about this function of IP scans from Paul three years ago, when we used it in a cave in Nazareth. We now use it at many different sites to "see" the metal present in a site. I can understand why a gas and oil company might want to know about other natural resources, like metal deposits. For archaeologists, the IP function can provide an important insight into a delicate metal object still located below the surface.

Because of the nature of the tunnel-building process described in the testimonies, IP seemed likely to yield results. The testimonies indicated that the tunnel still had metal artifacts inside. They may be the metal used to shore up the wood or they may be the metal shackles that the escapees removed before they left the tunnel. Earth materials generally have no capacitance. Clay surfaces have a little. Metal has a lot, and IP can detect it, even in small amounts. Often, I could not tell exactly how large the metal fragment was, but I know that it was there. In each one of the IP scans where I found a metal signature, it was between seven to fifteen feet below the surface in a "rounded," tunnel-like area that measured approximately two feet by two feet, and the slices of the tunnel I found were oriented in the same direction. I had seen the metal objects that were found at Fort IX in the museum where the other Burning Brigade had worked, and escaped. It gave me a sense of what my Burning Brigade must have had. The metal IP discoveries were perhaps the biggest "little" discovery. These scans also stand out because the area of the tunnel is surrounded by uniform sand (the blue in the scans in the figure is the sand). I do not know exactly what metals were captured on the scans, but I remember looking at the ERT IP scans with the geophysicists, and, they, too, were excited by the simple "smudges" that appear inside of the rounded edges of the tunnel.

Geophysicists now regularly use the IP technique to distinguish conductive landfill leachate from conductive landfill domestic waste with only small bits of metal. IP was originally developed as a technique for companies to locate copper. Although it was not designed for the purposes I use it for, it has become an important tool for archaeologists. The escapees gathered many different artifacts in the tunnel in preparation for their journey (metal pieces, money, personal artifacts) to take with them for bartering after their escape.

There were multiple sections of the tunnel that were captured in the IP ERT scans. I discovered one just over thirty meters from IP ERT #6 (see figure below) that led to the bunker in the pit. This indicated to us that the

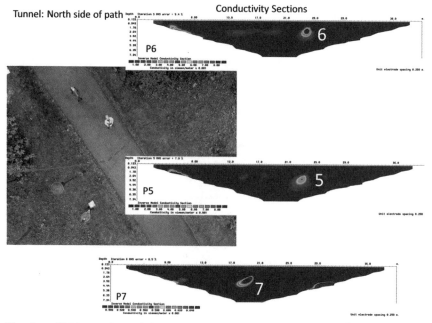

The three IP ERT sections of the Holocaust Escape Tunnel at Ponar; numbers 6 and 7 clearly have metal inside. (Courtesy of Paul Bauman, WorleyParsons, Inc. on behalf of the Vilna Excavations Project at the University of Hartford)

tunnel may have been more than thirty feet long. The exit continued into the forest across the path that had been paved, unknowingly disturbed by an aboveground shallow asphalt laid during the past twenty years. The walkway changed the entire area where the exit would have been. The thought that graves might be located below, and the need to manicure the lawns and create paths through the forest, indirectly protected this entire tunnel section. The exit must have been open to the elements, and was probably one of the first places destroyed by the Nazis, who immediately launched a search for the escapees, killing the remaining members of the Burning Brigade, either in the tunnel or in the pit. The tunnel exit was close enough to the surface that it was inevitably affected by all manner of very wet, cold, and snowy winters, and the year-round rain. Tracing the tunnel in the same direction for such a length, from the edge of Pit #6 to a trench which led to the open forest, was science at its best.

IT STARTED WITH KILLING SQUADS

Instead of taking Lithuanian Jews to the death camps in the west (even after the camps became operational in 1942), the Nazis created killing fields in areas such as Moldova, Estonia, Ukraine, Belorussia (now Belarus), and Latvia (among other locations). There were never enough German Army regular soldiers to do this work, so the killing squads in Eastern Europe were made up of locals employed to kill Jews in these open, mass burial pits. The Ponar exterminations took place in the forest near Vilnius over a three-year period, beginning in July of 1941 and continuing through July of 1944 (even after the tunnel escape). The killing site duties became well known to the locals who lived nearby, and many would wait every day to collect some of the clothes and artifacts left by the troops.

Finding these additional burial pits is extremely important—not only for the families of the victims, but also for posterity, as part of the entire documentation method for mass burials worldwide. By educating people about mass murders and burials of the past (and showing people that one can never destroy all of the evidence!), it is possible to deter or even prevent future genocides. If you know that you cannot get away with a crime it will inevitably make people think twice about committing a crime.

In 1944, as the Soviet armies were approaching from the east, and during the actual battles leading up to their retreat, the Nazis photographed key locations in the greater Vilna area from the air to ensure that the battle zones were known. These photographs, now housed at the US Naval Archives in Washington, DC, provided excellent documentation of the Ponar site from

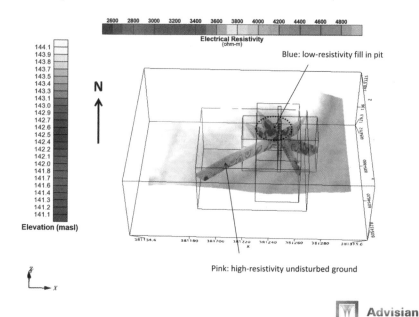

Fence diagram with ERT data sliced to an elevation of 141.5 metres above sea level, northward view

Three-dimensional grid and GPS designations of a mass burial, its size and depth clearly marked without having to open the burial area. (Courtesy of Paul Bauman, Worley-Parsons, Inc., on behalf of the Vilna Excavations Project at the University of Hartford)

a time before the growth of the tree canopy that now covers the entire site. These photos, along with the lidar study carried out by Lithuanian geophysicists, provided an excellent visual perspective.

Three days of work in June of 2016 also allowed the team to identify one massive, seventy-two-foot-wide and twelve-foot-deep burial pit that sat unmarked in the middle of the nearby forest. Geophysicists estimate that the remains of some seven thousand bodies would have occupied the space in this pit alone. Unlike in the previous archaeology at Belzec, for example, no coring was done. The "invasive" traditional archaeological method of coring, sampling, and analyzing mass burial sites is no longer appropriate or necessary to achieve the goals of identification and marking, as I explained earlier. I use the scans to determine the materials, and then calculate compaction to give a sense of how many bodies (the burned ashes of the bodies) might be in a location like the one in Ponar. A similar calculation might be done in the field when gas and oil reserves are estimated by these same professionals. The difference here is that we were calculating how many people died in that single pit during the Holocaust. The cremated remains indicate that the Burning Brigade work at this site was extensive, the range still not fully known.

TEACHING STUDENTS IN THE FOREST OF PONAR

I feel it's incredibly important to take students into the field, something I have done almost every year for the past thirty years. Education in the field is essentially the opposite of education in the classroom. Students are generally unable to use their cell phones (we do have them in case of emergencies, and to photograph elements before a designated photographer can get to a scene) and computers during the day when working in the field, and I and my colleagues are constantly talking with them. Usually it is small talk, about sports and their families, but sometimes there are moments of discussion about coursework, careers, about terrible things that have happened to them—about their lives. I eat breakfast, lunch, and dinner with them, and we often discuss the day's work, all without books or note-taking. I try to give every student the opportunity to learn each technology in the field, no matter what their major. Although strict note-taking is not required, I have them document everything, usually on their phones. Every student gets a chance to work with the geoscientists and archaeologists, to excavate, clean, do ground surveys, map, set out grids, and learn about geophysics and laser leveling.

Often I have found that students have the desire to know more about something they learned in the field. It takes much longer to do something when you are teaching a student, but teaching is as much the point of the expedition as the research. Reading is no substitute for fieldwork. The students' limited exposure to the Holocaust in grade school or high school is nothing when compared to confronting an actual killing field or forced labor camp in person. Many of these students have never had the sense of real hands-on discovery in their daily lives, but in the field, they get that. I also talk about the Holocaust, a reality that is very hard for many of the students to understand.

While we may not have been digging up actual burial sites in the Ponar forest, it was apparent to the students that they were surrounded by thousands of dead bodies, and that it was their responsibility to try to understand what happened there. Almost every student wrote a geoscience and Holocaust paper for credit about their experience in the field. I think the fact that we usually have both a geoscience experience and a hands-on excavating experience at a site like the Great Synagogue gives them a sense of what was lost in the Holocaust. Then we go to the field to search for sites that cannot be so easily excavated. Most of their papers run to forty or fifty pages, and are often handed in months after the excavations. They are illustrated with their own photographs, and include our official reports and maps. Field experiences are always deeply personal and moving, impossible to duplicate in the classroom.

One Friday at Ponar, after we had finished our work and before we went back for dinner, Jon Seligman and I had a simple "moment of reflection" with the students. We listened to a Yiddish song, and I read the mourner's prayer (Kaddish) that is appropriate at a cemetery. The students stood in a circle in front of the Ponar Memorial monument that stands at the center of the Ponar complex. It was a moment that I shall not forget as a teacher—the moment when you know that your students have understood a deep truth about the world, that you never could have taught them, and yet they "got it." It is one of the reasons why I originally went into teaching, and after thirty years of taking students to the field, it still inspires me.

OTHER WITNESSES TO THE PONAR KILLINGS: 1941–1943

Part of what I am urging in this book is that archaeology take into account the entire "holistic" documentation of a site as part of the plan of excavation. One of the challenges of using testimonies is determining their credibility. I concluded that the clearly marked burial pits at Ponar are only one part of a much larger collection of pits in the forest around them. The area is part of the escape route used by the tunnel builders. The Burning Brigade members were shackled at the ankles and waist, and I assume they had no doubt about their eventual fate. They knew they would be the final victims, and that after their deaths, nobody would be able to tell the full story of Ponar. At the Ponar site today, there are some pits in which the killings took place that have been carefully prepared for the visitors, to make them seem quite pastoral. When I visited, the staff of the Vilna Gaon Jewish State Museum revealed that they suspected there were perhaps as many as five more burial pits, as yet unidentified, in the forest. I knew what my project would entail. I took two days to establish the existence of one massive burial pit. I decided to spend the documentation time to identify and scan what were known as "processing trenches" that led up to the killing and burial pits. The pits, even today, are not as deep as they originally were. This means that additional debris was added during the construction of the visitor areas.

One source I have not mentioned is a single eyewitness. Although he was never in the burial pits of Ponar, he saw them every day from his window. The site was well documented by people who were there, and filmed accounts of the locals' recollections were made after the war. There were prisoners who escaped from the pits in 1941 and 1942, and there were people who lived in the village of Ponar who knew what was going on, and benefited from the clothes and personal items they found in the forest.

One person with a unique vantage point was a non-Jewish Polish journalist, Kazimierz Sakowicz, who lived outside of the camp in the village of Ponar from 1941 to 1943, after which he mysteriously disappeared. He noted in his diary what was going on there from 1941 through 1943, when the diary ends.[1] No one knows exactly what happened to Sakowicz, but his accounts of the events that took place in Ponar were riveting in their banality. They contain the simple journalistic language used when collecting data, perhaps for a longer article or book. It is clear that Sakowicz was concerned by the end of 1943 about his own safety, and began burying the accounts in lemonade jars in the forest, in hopes of retrieving them after the war. He never got to retrieve them, but his neighbors luckily did (thinking, perhaps, that he was burying some treasure), and the diary was published after meticulous research by dedicated scholars. Here are a few of the chilling entries:

> July 27, 1941: Shooting is carried on nearly every day. Will it go on forever? The executioners began selling clothes of the killed. Other garments are crammed into sacks in a barn at the highway and taken to town. People say that about 5,000 persons have been killed in the course of this month. It is quite possible, for about 200–300 people are being driven up here nearly every day. And nobody ever returns . . .

> July 30, 1941: About 150 persons shot. Most of them were elderly people. The executioners complained of being very tired of their "work," of having aching shoulders from shooting. That is the reason for not finishing the wounded off, so that they are buried half alive.

> August 2, 1941: Shooting of big batches has started once again. Today about 4,000 people were driven up . . . shot by 80 executioners. All drunk. The fence was guarded by 100 soldiers and policemen. This time terrible tortures before shooting. Nobody buried the murdered. The people were driven straight into the pit, the corpses were trampled upon. Many wounded writhed with pain. Nobody finished them off.

With the Soviets advancing in 1943, the Germans had begun destroying the evidence of their crimes by burning the bodies of the victims. There is solid evidence for this at sites such as Babi Yar, Fort IX, and Ponar. The pattern was the same: Dig out the corpses and burn them. The burning process included the preparation of the pyres, the cutting of the wood, and the daily routine of digging up "figures." (Members of the Burning Brigades apparently did not want to refer to them as "people," and therefore used the Yiddish euphemism for "figure" to refer to the corpses.) This process required a level of objectification of the victims. The descriptions are chronicled in surprising detail by the men who escaped. Pyres were made of alternating layers of bodies and wood. The burning was done nearby, or in the pits. If you look today, the trees by the pits are not old-growth; the older trees were used for wood to burn the bodies. When people came to Ponar after the war, they reported "ashes covering everything, like snow."

PIT #6

I spent a lot of time at Pit #6. The numbering of the pits will eventually change as more pits are discovered, but currently, Pit #6 refers to the commonly used designation on the map at the site. It is where the workers lived and tried to escape, and is captured in the photograph at the beginning of this chapter. You will notice the sandy soil and the stones used to line the pits in preparation for oil tanks. Remember, the pits were originally dug to serve as part of an airport, which was never built.

The prisoners who planned to escape via the tunnel needed tools to cut the chains on their legs; they also had to cut the barbed wire around the camp. They found the necessary tools to accomplish this among the corpses. This may seem remarkable, but remember that those killed at Ponar were tradesmen rounded up by the Nazis in various *aktions*. To allay suspicions, the Jews would have been told that they were being sent to work camps, and so they would have brought their tools. In order to dig, the prisoners used spoons, their hands, whatever they could. Fortunately, it was sandy soil.

To hide the sand they dug from the tunnel, they would fill their pockets and distribute it as they worked in the pits. The sand made the digging easy, but also increased the possibility that the tunnel would collapse. They needed to scavenge wood for supports, so some of the wood of Ponar was used for something other than burning bodies. They also needed electricity to light the tunnel, which came from a generator that was located in their living pit.

On April 15, 1944, they made their escape. According to the testimonies, they had actually finished constructing the tunnel a couple of days earlier. I have been asked many times why this date is so important. As I have mentioned, it was two days after the Easter Sunday of 1944, when the guards possibly would have been celebrating, and not paying as much attention to the Jews in the pits. Probably more important, it was Passover, the holiday of freedom celebrating the Exodus from Egypt. Even if the prisoners couldn't celebrate the Passover Seder, they were aware of the timing of their escape. Finally, there was more darkness with the waning moon, since this was a week after the middle of the lunar month. Passover begins in the middle of the lunar month, which the Jews were able to track without calendars.

Most of the Jews in the burial pit did not know what was unfolding until the very last moment before the escape. This is revealed conclusively in the survivor testimonies. The main formulators of the escape plan—engineer Yuri Farber (who had the compass, and kept the tunnel moving in the right direction); Itzhak Dugin, a local Vilnaite (and the first to actually emerge from the tunnel); Mordechai "Motke" Zaidel; and others who were in the lead that night—realized that absolute secrecy had to be maintained throughout the digging process, especially when facing the final risk of getting out safely.

While speaking on behalf of the *NOVA* television documentary, I was asked several times why all eighty in the burial pit did not get out. The tunnel was only revealed to everyone during the last few nights before completion. Psychologically, one can understand how devastating it would have been if they had been unable to complete the tunnel; everyone would have blamed the small group of diggers for its failure. I can imagine how devastating it would have been for everyone if the tunnel had collapsed, or if it was discovered. All of them would have had to deal with the added stress and trauma of losing their last hope for getting out.

I also learned that when some of the people in the burial pit realized the difficulty of wiggling through the underground tunnel (which might have collapsed, and was clearly a claustrophobic experience, at just two feet by two feet), and the need to remain on the run for days, if not weeks, after the escape, they decided they were not up to the task. Some were too weak, frail, or debilitated by the daily work of burning bodies to attempt the escape. All survivor testimonies are consistent: In the end, the whole group knew about the plan, even if many did not leave through the tunnel.

The eighty prisoners divided themselves up into groups of ten. They all resolved to scatter after the escape, to prevent a mass capture, and the leaders urged each other to keep going no matter what happened to the others. Silence was critical. There was only a sliver of moon that night to light their way in the forest, but this also made it more difficult for the Nazi guards to pursue them. They cut their chains with a file in the tunnel and started to go, between nine and ten p.m. Suddenly, they heard the cracking sound of a breaking stick when they got out of the tunnel. The SS officers heard, shone a light, and saw the road filled with prisoners. They must not have known who they were right away. Everyone ran. Of the eighty in the Burning Brigade bunker, only twelve men made it to the nearby partisans in the forest, and eleven survived the war to tell their tale.

Here is how I found the tunnel which now marks their courageous work: I knew that they had started from the bunker, the details of which were actually part of the Soviet trials of war crimes. The location of the beginning of the tunnel was known from that point. It was excavated by a Lithuanian archaeologist, V. Urbanavicius, in 2004. I also knew what was in the tunnel because of Urbanivicius's work, which shows the types of metal, sand, wood, and artifacts that he found when he opened the entrance to the tunnel. I compared that to the ERT discoveries in the field beyond. It was not as easy to ascertain the direction of the tunnel. A standard archaeological survey and cores would have desecrated most of the burial sites around the tunnel. The route of the tunnel, therefore, remained difficult to track until 2016, when I came with ERT and GPR to perform a massive grid search over the top of the entire area. I cannot imagine how any earlier expeditions could have found and tracked the tunnel without destroying it. In fact, while many researchers began using GPR in the past decade, since I began using it at Sobibor, I have found that the use of ERT and GPR together yields the most exacting results without excavating.

HOW I CAME TO KNOW THE DESCENDANTS OF HOPE

I close this chapter, and the book, with some insights about a group of people I refer to as the "descendants of hope." This group, the descendants of the survivors of the escape tunnel, emerged almost as an afterthought, because of the media coverage of the discovery of the Holocaust Escape Tunnel in July 2016. Dr. Seligman, and the entire network of Bet Vilna in Tel Aviv, began tracking down the families of survivors almost immediately after the newspaper accounts were published in Israel, in late June and early July of 2016. The children of survivors often provide key details about their parents. Every discovery, artifact, map, survey, and project is the result of testimonies provided by survivors and their families.

I have expressly championed the idea that archaeology is related to *people*. Some of the people to whom I refer in this book are the students and staff who did the work, and who were themselves affected by the experience of working on the archaeology, and provided insights that changed our work. I also refer to our donors, many of whom shared the complex histories of their extended family members. Some of the *people* I refer to are those who currently reside in the same places in Rhodes, Lithuania, and Poland. There are others who wonder whether these events really took place, and want to see "the evidence," even as the last survivors of the Holocaust pass away. I also include the survivors and the victims whose stories were buried amid the debris of the past.

One group of people became, for many of us, the most compelling reason for our work: the descendants. The descendants include children, grandchildren, and now great-grandchildren of Holocaust survivors and victims, who live with many unanswered questions. I did not set out to bring them all closure; that would have been impossible. Nevertheless, the work provided a special measure of closure to some, including myself, because we made the effort to look for their loved ones. The stories these descendants shared about their parents and grandparents showed me that people deal with the trauma of the Holocaust in different ways.

I learned from Abe Gol that his father, Shlomo Gol, wore his foul-smelling Burning Brigade clothes to the Nuremberg trials so that everyone in the courtroom could experience what he had lived through. I learned from Sabina Dombe, the daughter of Itzhak Dugin that he chain-smoked, and rarely spoke about what happened to him. I learned from Hana Amir that her father, Motke Zaidel, would obsessively wash his hands and make his children and grandchildren do the same—trying, she said, to get rid of the unseen dirt. I learned that the escapees in Israel gathered on the last night of Passover and reminisced about the escape, a group experience that none of us could truly understand. These men who escaped through the tunnel went on to lead productive lives, to hold jobs, to raise children—never to forget where they had come from.

In the case of the story of the Holocaust Escape Tunnel, which had passed into the category of near-mythic status among historians, the work provided a different measure of closure for their descendants. Thanks to the widespread publicity of the event, *NOVA* did find some of the descendants of the tunnel survivors, and gathered them together in Israel so I could personally tell them of the discovery. I have made scholarly presentations at professional conferences on the tunnel, but it was this group of descendants who mattered most. In a way, they owned the discovery even more than I, since they owed their very existence to the tunnel.

I traveled with Jon Seligman to a Tel Aviv suburb, a little over a month after I had finished in Lithuania, to meet with a group of Israelis whose parents and grandparents had escaped from the tunnel. It was a chance for me to explain simple elements that they had heard about most of their lives, made real by the proof of the tunnel's existence. Some remarked that they had been back to Lithuania with their parents, who had expressed frustration at not being able to show their children the tunnel that saved their lives.

As mentioned, the entire camp has been radically reshaped over the years, and the original entrance no longer is used. The orientation of the Ponar park—the pathways and pits themselves—are so different today that even the survivors who returned to Ponar could scarcely get their bearings. It must have raised questions about one's own memory of even the most traumatic of events, when you cannot place them clearly at the places where they occurred. Not being able to show to their children, and the locals, exactly where everything happened must have created a whole series of new questions. It was not their fault. The parks have been strategically created for tourists, which makes archaeologists' work even more fraught with problems.

For me, meeting these descendants of the tunnel escapees was the highlight of my career. I have spent thirty years in the field working on sites where the people are long gone, and the artifacts and architecture have to speak entirely for them. In this one moment in Tel Aviv, I united the artifacts and architecture of the past with the people whose loved ones *lived* that past. The descendants appear in the *NOVA* documentary, thanks to the wisdom of the directors and producers, who wanted to show how science can often bring new meaning to human existence, not just solve arcane problems. The descendants were transformed that day, but I was transformed along with them. I watched as they asked about the details of the technologies used, the soil where the tunnel was built, the bracing of the tunnel walls, the depth and size of the tunnel; I knew that they found in this presentation much more than just a random series of answers from a nearly forgotten forest in Lithuania. For them it was a nearly miraculous tunnel construction project done by their parents and grandparents, followed by a nearly miraculous rediscovery project done by a group of unrelated scientists coming from countries around the world, with no agenda other than doing good science. The descendants are, by and large, secular Israelis, but it was hard not to feel, sitting with them that day, that they had achieved a moment of what can only be called "enlightenment" that transcended the events themselves. It was a moment when geoscience, archaeology, and history merged into something much more than the sum of their parts.

FINAL REFLECTIONS ON HOLOCAUST AND HEROISM REMEMBRANCE DAY 2018

I am writing the end of this book on Holocaust Remembrance Day, April 2018, in the United States. In Israel, the television documentaries on the tunnel (*Holocaust Escape Tunnel*) and on HKP 562 (*The Good Nazi*) were shown as part of the limited schedule of television presentations aired on this day. In the United States, PBS stations nationwide will rebroadcast *Holocaust Escape Tunnel*. The mid-April date on the Jewish calendar of Holocaust Remembrance Day (*Yom HaShoah*) is purposeful. The Hebrew name for the Holocaust is *Shoah*, which means "destruction," in contradiction with the more theologically weighted term "Holocaust," which is a biblical term for a "whole burnt offering." Early on after the Holocaust, Yiddish writers did not know what to call the event, and preferred the Hebrew rabbinic term of *Hurban* (which also means "destruction," but is typically reserved to describe the destruction of the Temples of Jerusalem, so again, problematic). It was decided

The descendants of some of the tunnel escape survivors, gathered in a suburb of Tel Aviv, Israel, August 2016. (Courtesy of the Vilna Excavations Project at the University of Hartford)

that the non-theologically weighted term of *Shoah* best fit the circumstances, and *Yom HaShoah* has been assigned to the twenty-seventh day of the lunar Jewish calendar month of Nisan. The complete name of the day is "Holocaust and Heroism Day." The timing of the remembrance is related to the uprising of the Jews in the Warsaw Ghetto in 1943, but the term was intended to encapsulate the history of escapes, courageous uprisings, revolts, and acts of martyrdom that were known to have happened during the Holocaust.

Growing up, I never quite understood the meaning of the two terms together: *Holocaust* and *Heroism*. Today, I do. After working in the killing fields of Europe, and searching for the remains of the HKP camp and Karl Plagge's "apartments" in Vilnius, I understand why the two terms need to be grouped together. Working on the Great Synagogue, and learning from the synagogue's creation, destruction, and its unearthing, I believe it serves as a monument to the audacity of the people who built it. I am charged as a scientist with documenting both the carnage and the courage of those who lived through this period. If I can say that geoscience and archaeology have a goal in Holocaust studies, it is to search out the artifacts and sites that will provide a fuller picture of the era.

I know now, after listening to Florence Post talk about her father, Itzhak Nemenchik, why I am motivated to work at Fort VII in Kaunas. I understand Ada Gens's and her daughter's anguish over the search for her father's grave. I understand why Karl Plagge is so fondly remembered by the survivors; why finding Matilda's burial site is as important as finding the Fort IX killing fields. I can speak proudly about the amazing strength of character of the tunnelers of Ponar, which gave us the incentive to uncover sections of the Holocaust Escape Tunnel in the forest. I have learned from archaeology and geoscience, and from the testimonies of the descendants of hope, what a discovery can do for them, and the world. The staff and students involved in this work were inspired by learning about the lives of the escapees in their testimonies. I think this is what lies at the heart of the archaeology of the Holocaust—to give context, background and details of the physical evidence of the events.

Many of the people profiled in this book were ordinary human beings placed in extraordinary circumstances. Learning about Yuri Farber, Itzhak Dugin, Motke Zaidel, Zalman Matzkin, David Kanterovich, Joseph (Blaser) Kagan, and Shlomo Gol, in particular, made me contemplate the work of the tunnel in a new way. It was from the children and relatives of the tunnelers, and the ex-pat Rhodesli, that I learned about how we pass on the lessons of a place. Hearing the voices of the Jews of Rhodes—from Isaac Habib, Aron Hasson, Giuseppe Mallel, Esther Fintz Menascé, Benjamin Avzaradel, Benjamin (Capuano) di Liscia, Benjamin Turiel, Gareth (Amato) Kanthor, Arthur Benveniste, Marcelo Benveniste, Selma (Franco) Jaffee, Rachel (Israel) Goodman, Dean Goodman, and from their children—about their "Paradise Lost" makes my search for their lost legacy even more significant.

When I teach my course at the University of Hartford on geoscience, archaeology, and history, I include historic people, but often not the most famous people. Rather, I include micro histories of a time based on real people that have given testimonies, or were the subject of my research. I have come to understand the true mission of science and what I need to teach based upon my own encounters with people. My encounters with, and the writings of, Toivi Blatt, Selma Engel, Philip Bialowitz, Esther Raab, and Yoram Haimi (who originally wanted to understand what had happened to his relatives killed in Sobibor), the survivors of the Sobibor revolt, helped to document our discoveries at Sobibor. It is the stories of real people that make the archaeology more meaningful. Without this background, the artifacts would be mere hunks of clay, stone, metal, and glass.

Thankfully, I did not live through the Holocaust. I was a post–World War II "baby boomer" who never heard the stories of my relatives who experienced the Holocaust. I realize now that this was a conscious effort by my parents to shield me from the realities of Europe, and the sadness of the loss of whole segments of my family. There is rarely a time when I am in the blood-soaked fields of Europe that I do not think, there, but for the grace of God . . . If my ancestors had not been able to leave Europe before the Holocaust and come to the United States, I would not have been able to do the work I am doing today.

There are critics who think that a study can be scientific only if it is completely objective. This may be true for physics or chemistry; archaeology, as I have said, is about people, and cannot be divorced from the human component. My Jewish heritage impacts my study of the Holocaust; it would be impossible for me to separate the two. The science can still be "good" science even as I elucidate the lives of those who experienced the Holocaust at the sites I am investigating. I risk coming up with far less significant work when I ignore the backstories and information provided by oral and written accounts.

Many communities commemorate Holocaust and Heroism Remembrance Day with events held in synagogues and churches. As a child, and later as a student, I remember listening to Holocaust survivors speak of their personal tragedies. Today, there are fewer and fewer Holocaust survivors available to speak about their experiences. The mantle falls on their children and grandchildren to tell the stories, but it is also the obligation of archaeologists to corroborate these stories with the evidence of history. Whereas before I would simply attend Holocaust and Heroism commemorations, now, I am often one of the major speakers at some of these events. I speak not as a firsthand witness, or even as a child of a witness, but as a steward of the evidence.

Today, on Holocaust and Heroism Remembrance Day 2018, I am finishing the first complete draft of my book on the archaeology of the Holocaust. The work is not finished—not in the field, and not even on this book—but I hope this book serves as a fitting tribute to those who perished and those who survived, and whose stories must never die.

Notes

CHAPTER 1. WHAT IF: GEOSCIENCE AND ARCHAEOLOGY

1. Although the quote used in funeral services is "Earth to earth, ashes to ashes, dust to dust," the origin is most likely from Genesis 3:19: "By the sweat of your brow shall you eat bread until you return to the ground, for out of it you were taken, and to dirt you shall return." Adam's very name is a play on *adamah*, the Hebrew word for ground, or dirt.

2. Caroline Sturdy Colls in her book, *Holocaust Archaeologies: Approaches and Future Directions* (New York: Springer, 2015), provides a good overview of the field.

CHAPTER 2. DISCOVERIES IN THE ARCHAEOLOGY OF THE HOLOCAUST

1. If the reader would like a general introduction to the history of the Holocaust, I suggest the following books which influenced my own teaching (a more-specific bibliography is included at the end of the book): Michael Berenbaum, *The World Must Know: A History of the Holocaust as Told in the United States Holocaust Memorial Museum* (Boston: Little Brown, 1993); Lucy Dawidowicz, *The War Against the Jews, 1933–1945* (New York: Bantam, 1986); Raul Hilberg, *Perpetrators, Victims, Bystanders: The Jewish Catastrophe, 1933–1945* (New York: HarperCollins, 1992).

2. Lucy Dawidowicz traced the history of the Holocaust from the late medieval anti-Judaism of Christianity, and especially that of Martin Luther, to anti-Semitism that led directly to the Holocaust (*The War Against the Jews*, p. 23).

3. The so-called "functionalist" approach to the history of the Holocaust can be found in Karl Schleunes's book, *The Twisted Road to Auschwitz* (Urbana and Chicago: University of Illinois, 1970).

CHAPTER 3. AN ARCHAEOLOGICAL
DISCOVERY "HIDDEN" IN PLAIN SIGHT

1. J. F. Shroder, H. M. Jol, and P. P. Reeder, "El Araj as Bethsaida: Spatial and Temporal Improbabilities, in R. Arav and R. A. Freund, eds., *Bethsaida: A City by the North Shore of the Sea of Galilee*, vol. 4 (Kirksville, MO: Truman State University Press, 2009), pp. 293–309.

2. For more on this, please consult our four volumes: *Bethsaida: A City by the North Shore of the Sea of Galilee* (Kirksville, MO: Thomas Jefferson Press, 1995, 2000, 2004, 2009).

3. Richard Freund, *Digging through the Bible* (Lanham: MD: Rowman & Littlefield, 2008), pp. 250–99; *Secrets of the Cave of Letters* (New York: Prometheus, 2004); Carl Savage, Harry Jol, Philip Reeder, and Richard Freund, *Dead Sea: New Discoveries in the Cave of Letters* (New York: Lang, 2018).

4. Freund, *Digging through the Bible*, pp. 30–59.

5. Freund, *Digging through the Bible*, pp. 103ff.

6. Hannah Arendt, in her book, *Eichmann in Jerusalem: A Report on the Banality of Evil* (New York: Penguin Classics, 1994 reprint), makes the point that if the Jews had not been as organized as they were, and so compliant with the Nazi efforts to use their own organizations and leaders to help facilitate their systematic "selections," fewer Jews would have died during the Holocaust. The criticism of Arendt's position is that it seems a little disingenuous to blame the victims. Even fifty years after the book's publication, the *New York Times* (November 26, 2013) contends: "To a Jew this role of the leaders in the destruction of their own people is undoubtedly the darkest chapter of the whole dark story."

CHAPTER 4. THE SIGNIFICANCE OF TUNNELS:
GEOSCIENCE AND ARCHAEOLOGY FROM THE
ANCIENT WORLD TO THE HOLOCAUST

1. M. Aviam, "Distribution Maps of Archaeological Data from the Galilee: An Attempt to Establish Zones Indicative of Ethnicity and Religious Affiliation." In J. Zangenberg, H. W. Attridge, and D. Martin, *Religion, Ethnicity and Identity in Ancient Galilee: A Region in Transition* (Tubingen: Mohr Siebeck, 2007), pp. 115–32.

2. Ibid. The information on the "secret hideaways" is found on pages 126–27 of the article.

3. It is apparently not the same tunnel described in Yitzhak Arad's book, *Belzec, Sobibor, Treblinka: The Operation Reinhard Death Camps* (Bloomington: Indiana University Press, 1987), p. 311.

4. A 1962 Lithuanian film chronicles the Fort IX escape and its far-reaching effects in Lithuania (www.lrt.lt/mediateka/irasas/2420/zingsniai-nakti), accessed June 19, 2018.

CHAPTER 5. WHY I CAME TO RHODES

1. Many of the photos provided by Esther for the exhibition at the Museum of Jewish Civilization at the University of Hartford are found in Esther's book, *A History of Jewish Rhodes* (Los Angeles: Rhodes Historical Foundation, 2014).

2. The name of the nearby island is spelled either "Kos" or "Cos."

3. This is all found in my book, *Digging through History* (Lanham, MD: Rowman & Littlefield, 2012), pp. 154–78.

4. For a specific history of the Holocaust in Rhodes, I suggest, Isaac Benatar's book, *Rhodes and the Holocaust* (Bloomington, IN: iUniverse, 2010).

5. Aron Rodrigue of Stanford has written excellent volumes on the history of the period. See *A Jewish Voice from Ottoman Salonica: The Ladino Memoir of Sa'adi Besalel a-Levi* (Stanford, CA: Stanford University Press, 2012), edited and with an introduction by Sarah Abrevaya Stein; translation, transliteration, and glossary by Isaac Jerusalmi; see also *Sephardi Jewry: A History of the Judeo-Spanish Community, 14th–20th Centuries* (Berkeley: University of California Press, 2000), with Esther Benbassa; and *Images of Sephardi and Eastern Jewries in Transition, 1860–1939: The Teachers of the Alliance Israélite Universelle, 1860–1939* (Seattle: University of Washington Press, 1993), paperback title *Jews and Muslims: Images of Sephardi and Eastern Jewries in Transition* (2003).

CHAPTER 6. THE SECRET OF JEWISH RHODES

1. R. Arav and R. A. Freund, *Bethsaida: A City by the North Shore of the Sea of Galilee*, vol. 3, (Kirksville, MO: Truman State University Press, 2004).

2. Donald T. Ariel, "Stamped Amphora Handles from Bethsaida," in *Bethsaida: A City by the North Shore of the Sea of Galilee*, vol. 4, R. Arav and R. A. Freund, eds. (Kirksville, MO: Truman State University Press, 2009), pp. 267–92.

3. See, for example, Richard Friedman's *Who Wrote the Bible?* (San Francisco: Harper, 1987).

4. F. Zervaki, "An Inscribed Altar of the Hellenistic Period and Evidence of the Jewish Presence in Ancient Rhodes," *Dodecanese Chronicles* 26 (2015), pp. 86–106.

CHAPTER 7. THE ORIGINS OF THE "FINAL SOLUTION" IN A FOREST AND A FORT IN LITHUANIA

1. Most recently: David Cesarani, *Final Solution: The Fate of the Jews 1933–1949* (New York: St. Martin's Press, 2016), p. 451ff.

2. Anthony M. Platt and Cecilia Elizabeth O'Leary, *Bloodlines: Recovering Hitler's Nuremberg Laws, from Patton's Trophy to Public Memorial* (New York: Routledge, 2016).

3. There are even those who hold that the Khazars, a non-Jewish group that converted to Judaism in Eastern Europe, were the ancestors of many of the Jewish groups in Europe. See: Dan D. Y. Shapira, "Jews in Khazaria." In Mark Avrum Ehrlich, *Encyclopedia of the Jewish Diaspora: Origins, Experiences, and Culture, Handbuch der Orientalistik* [Handbook of Uralic Studies] (2009), 1. ABC-CLIO, pp. 1097–1104.

4. Laima Vince's article, "The Silenced Muse: The Life of a Murdered Jewish Lithuanian Poet" (https://deepbaltic.com/2018/05/08/the-silenced-muse-the-life -of-a-murdered-jewish-lithuanian-poet/), accessed August 3, 2018.

CHAPTER 8. THE ROAD TO VILNA

1. "Archaeologists Find Holiest Part of Vilnius Synagogue Razed by Nazis, Soviets," *The Times of Israel*, July 26, 2018 (www.timesofisrael.com/archaeologists-find-holiest-part-of-vilnius-synagogue-razed-by-nazis-soviets/), accessed October 11, 2018.

2. "YIVO Announces Discovery of 170,000 Lost Jewish Documents Thought to Have Been Destroyed during the Holocaust," Edward Blank YIVO Vilna Collections Project (vilnacollections.yivo.org/Discovery-Press-Release), accessed April 8, 2018, reporting on the opening of the display at the Center for Jewish History, October 24, 2017.

3. Stuart Miller, The Intersection of Texts and Material Finds: Stepped Pools, Stone Vessels, and Ritual Purity in Roman Palestine (Göttingen, Germany: Vandenhoeck & Ruprecht, 2015).

4. The spelling of *mikveh* differs in publications, based upon different transcription styles. Singular: *mikve, mikveh, miqve, miqveh,* and *mikva*; and plural: *mikvaot, miqvaot.* All refer to the same institution.

CHAPTER 9. AN ALTRUISTIC NAZI
AND THE DESCENDANTS OF HOPE

1. Richard A. Freund, *Digging through the Bible* (Lanham, MD: Rowman & Littlefield, 2008), pp. 323–37.

2. Irina Guzenberg, *The H.K.P. Jewish Labor Camp: 1943–1944* (Vilnius, Lithuania: Vilna Gaon Jewish State Museum, 2002).

3. Michael Good, *The Search for Major Plagge: The Nazi Who Saved Jews* (New York: Fordham University Press, 2005).

4. Good, *The Search for Major Plagge*, 107–08 (testimony of William Begell, HKP survivor).

5. The exhibition is based on the title of the book: *Tutti's Promise: A Novel Based on a Family's True Story of Courage and Hope during the Holocaust*, by K. Heidi Fishman (Bethesda, MD: MB Publishing, 2017).

CHAPTER 10. WHY THE DISCOVERY OF THE "HOLOCAUST ESCAPE TUNNEL" GIVES THE WORLD HOPE

1. Kazimierz Sakowicz, *Ponary Diary, 1941–1943: A Bystander's Account of a Mass Murder*, edited by Yitzhak Arad, translated by Laurence Weinbaum (New Haven: Yale University Press, 2005), pp. 14–15.

Selected Bibliography

ARCHAEOLOGY

Arav, Rami, and Richard A. Freund. *Bethsaida: A City by the North Shore of the Sea of Galilee*, Vols. I–IV (Vol. I, 1995; Vol. II, 2000; Vol. III, 2004; Vol. IV, 2008). Kirksville, MO: Truman State University Press.

Aviam, Mordechai. "Distribution Maps of Archaeological Data in the Galilee as an Attempt to Create Ethnic and Religion Zones," *Ancient Galilee in Interaction: Religion, Ethnicity, and Identity*. Edited by Jürgen K. Zangenberg, Harold W. Attridge, and Dale B. Martin. New Haven: Yale University Press, 2004.

———. *Jews, Pagans, and Christians in the Galilee: 25 Years of Archaeological Excavations and Surveys—Hellenistic to Byzantine Periods (Land of Galilee)*. Rochester, NY: University of Rochester Press, 2004.

Freund, Richard A. *Secrets of the Cave of Letters*. New York: Prometheus, 2006.

———. *Digging through the Bible*. Lanham, MD: Rowman & Littlefield, 2008.

———. *Digging through History*. Lanham, MD: Rowman & Littlefield, 2012.

Keller, Werner. *The Bible as History*. New York: William Morrow, 1956.

Mazar, Amihai. *Archaeology of the Land of the Bible, 10,000–586 B.C.E.* The Anchor Bible Reference Library. New York: Doubleday, 1990.

Yadin, Yigael. The Message of the Scrolls. New York: Random House, 1957.

———. *Masada: Herod's Fortress and the Zealots' Last Stand*. New York: Random House, 1966.

———. *Bar Kokhba*. New York: Random House, 1970.

———, ed. *Jerusalem Revealed: Archaeology in the Holy City, 1968–1974*. New Haven: Yale University Press, 1975.

GEOSCIENCE AND ARCHAEOLOGY

Conyers, L. B. *Ground-Penetrating Radar for Archaeology*. Walnut Creek, CA: Alta-Mira Press, 2004.

Davis, J. L., and Annan, A. P. 1989. "Ground-Penetrating Radar for High-Resolution Mapping of Soil and Rock Stratigraphy," *Geophysical Prospecting*, 37: 531–51.

Jol, H. M., and Bristow, C. S. 2003. "GPR in Sediments: Advice on Data Collection, Basic Processing and Interpretation: A Good Practice Guide." In C. S. Bristow and H. M. Jol, eds., *GPR in Sediments*. Geological Society of London, Special Publication 211, 9–27.

Jol, H. M., and Smith, D. G. 1991. "Ground-Penetrating Radar of Northern Lacustrine Deltas," *Canadian Journal of Earth Sciences*, 28, 1939–47.

Sternberg, B. K., and McGill, J. W. 1995. "Archaeology Studies in Southern Arizona Using Ground-Penetrating Radar," *Applied Geophysics*, 33: 209–25.

Sturdy Colls, Caroline. *Holocaust Archaeologies, Approaches and Future Directions*. New York: Springer, 2015.

———. "Unearthing the Atrocities of Nazi Death Camps." www.scientificamerican.com/article/unearthing-the-atrocities-of-nazi-death-camps/2016. Accessed on October 17, 2018.

UNIVERSITY OF HARTFORD RESEARCH GROUP PRESENTATIONS AND PUBLICATIONS

* *National conferences or publications*
** *International conferences or publications*

1. 2018. **Beck, J. D., Burds, L. T., Mataitis, R. J., Jol, H. M., Freund, R. A., McClymont, A. F., and Bauman, P. 2018. "Holocaust Archaeology: Searching for Nazi Mass Execution Trenches at Fort IX (Kaunas, Lithuania)." Proceedings of the Seventeenth International Conference on Ground-Penetrating Radar (GPR 2018), June 18–21, Rapperswil, Switzerland, 79–82.

2. 2018. **Burds, L. T., Beck, J. D., Mataitis, R. J., Jol, H. M., Freund, R. A., McClymont, A. F., and Bauman, P., 2018. "Holocaust Archaeology: Using Ground-Penetrating Radar to Locate a Jewish Mass Grave in Kaunas, Lithuania." Proceedings of the Sixteenth International Conference on Ground-Penetrating Radar (GPR 2018), June 18–21, Rapperswil, Switzerland, 70–73.

3. 2017. *McClymont, A., Bauman, P., Jol, H. M., Freund, R. A., Reeder, P. "Geophysics at Ponary, Lithuania." SAGEEP Applied Geophysics to Engineering and Environmental Problems Conference, March 19–23, Denver, Colorado.

4. 2017. *McClymont, A., Bauman, P., Freund, R. A., Seligman, J., Jol, H. M., Bensimon, K., and Reeder, P. "The Forgotten Holocaust in Lithuania:

Geophysical Investigations at the Ponary Killing Site." SAGEEP Applied Geophysics to Engineering and Environmental Problems Conference, March 19–23, Denver, Colorado.

5. 2017. **Katsioti, A., Luczak, J., Workman, V., Freund, R., Jol, H.M., Foglia, P. "A Preliminary XRF Study of Provenanced and Unprovenanced Oil Lamps from Rhodes," *Archaeopress*. Athens, Greece, 2018.

6. 2016. *Seamans, J., Awad, N., Jol, H., Reeder, P., and Freund, R. "High Frequency GPR Investigation at the Kahal Grande Synagogue, Rhodes, Greece." 50th Annual Meeting of Geological Society of America North-Central Section, April 18–19, Urbana-Champaign, Illinois.

7. 2016. *Jol, H. M., Wavrin, T. A., Seamans, J. M., Erickson, J. S., Kleinschmidt, A. S., Freund, R. A., Reeder, P. P., Seligman, J., and Daubaras, M. 2016. "Geo-Archaeological and Geomorphic Ground-Penetrating Radar Investigations in Lithuania: High Impact Undergraduate Research Experiences. University of Wisconsin–Eau Claire's International Fellows Program." Geological Society of America, 128th Annual Meeting, September 25–28, Denver, Colorado, Abstracts with Program, v. 48 (7), doi: 10.1130/abs/2016AM-285735.

8. 2015. *Jol, H. M., Reeder, P., Freund, R, Workman, V. A. "GPR Investigation of Archaeological Sites: Preliminary Results from Rhodes, Greece." Association of American Geographers, 111th year (2015) Annual Meeting, May 12–19, San Francisco, California, Abstracts on CD-ROM, 98.

9. 2015. *Jol, H. M., Freund, R. A., Darawsha, M., Artzy, M., Arav, R., Savage, C. E., Lopez, G. I., Zapata-Meza, M., and Filin, S. 2015. "UWEC's International Fellows Program in Israel: A Transformative Learning Experience for Students." Geological Society of America North-Central Section, 49th Annual Meeting, May 19–20, Madison, Wisconsin, Abstracts with Program v. 47(5), 11.

10. 2015. *Pingel, A., Awad, N., Jol, H., Reeder, P., Seligman, J., and Freund, R., 2015. "Looking for the Great Synagogue of Vilnius, Lithuania: Ground-Penetrating Radar Proof of Concept." West Lakes Division of the Association of American Geographers, 2015 Annual Meeting, October 15–17, Eau Claire, Wisconsin, Program, 10.

11. 2010. **Bauman, P., Hansen, B., Haimi, Y., Gilead, I., Freund, R., Reeder, P., Bem, M., Mazurek, W. "Geophysical Exploration of the Former Extermination Center at Sobibor, Poland." 23rd EEGS Symposium on the Application of Geophysics to Engineering and Environmental Problems, Annual Meeting, Session on Urban and Archaeological Geophysics, April 8–11, Keystone, Colorado, 15.

12. 2008. *McDonald, J. M., Jol, H. M., Reeder, P., Freund, R., and Anati, E. 2008. "Ground-Penetrating Radar Aided Archaeological Survey on Har Karkom in the Southern Negev (Mount Sinai?), Israel. Association of American Geographers, 104th (2008) Annual Meeting, April 15–19, Boston, Massachusetts, Program and Abstracts on CD Rom, 97.

13. 2007. *Pascal, E., Jol, H. M., Bauman P. D., Reeder, P., Freund, R. "GPR Investigation of Archaeological Sites: Preliminary Results from Tel Yavne

and Apollonia Israel." Association of American Geographers, 103nd (2007) Annual Meeting, April 12–19, San Francisco, California, Abstracts on CD-ROM, 98.

14. 2006. *Bode, J. A., Jol, H. M., Bauman, P. D., Nahas, C., Fischer, M., Reeder, P., and Freund, R. A. "GPR and ERT Investigation of a Coastal Archaeological Site: Yavne Yam, Israel." Association of American Geographers, 102nd (2006) Annual Meeting, March 7–11, Chicago, Illinois, Abstracts on CD-ROM, 66.

15. 2006. *Jol, H. M., Bode, J. A., Bauman, P. D., Freund, R. A., Darawsha, M., Nahas, C., Reeder, P., Savage, C., Syon, D. "Nazareth Excavations: A GPR Perspective." 19th EEGS Symposium on the Application of Geophysics to Engineering and Environmental Problems, April 2–6, Seattle, Washington, 10.

16. 2006. **Bode, J. A., Jol, H. M., Reeder, P., Freund, R. A., Bauman, P., and Nahas, C. "GPR Investigation of the Nuestra Senora de La Blanca Church Site, Burgos, Spain: Preliminary Results." 11th International Conference on Ground-Penetrating Radar, June 19–22, Columbus, Ohio.

17. 2005. *Treague, J. J., Jol, H. M., Fisher, T. G., Freund, R. A., Reeder, P., Savage, C., and Bauman, P. "Three-Dimensional Subsurface GPR Visualization for an Archaeological Site (Qumran, Israel) and a Geomorphic Site (Michigan)." Geological Society of America, 39th Annual Meeting of the North-Central Section, May 19–20, Minneapolis, Minnesota, Abstracts with Programs, 37(5): 15.

18. 2003. *Passow, R. H., Jol, H. M., Freund, R. A., Savage, C. E., and Reeder, P. "Ground-Penetrating Radar and Global Positioning System: Archaeological Aids at Qumran, Israel." Association of American Geographers, 99th Annual Meeting, March 4–8, New Orleans, Louisiana.

19. 2002. **Jol, H. M., Broshi, M., Eshel, H., Freund, R. A., Shroder Jr., J. F., Reeder, P., and Dubay, R. 2002. "GPR Investigations at Qumran, Israel: Site of the Dead Sea Scrolls Discovery." Ninth International Conference on Ground-Penetrating Radar, edited by S. K. Koppenjan and H. Lee, April 29–May 2, Santa Barbara, California, Proceedings of SPIE Vol. 4758: 91–95.

20. 2001. **Jol, H. M., Shroder Jr., J. F., Reeder, P., Freund, R. A. 2001. "A GPR Archaeological Expedition at the Cave of Letters, Israel." Eighth International Conference on Ground-Penetrating Radar, edited by D. A. Noon, G. F. Stickley, D. Longstaff, SPIE Vol. 4084: 882–86.

21. 2001. **Jol, H. M., Shroder Jr., J. F., Reeder, P., and Freund, R. A. 2001. "Ground-Penetrating Radar Studies within the Cave of Letters: Geomorphology and Archaeology." Association of American Geographers, 97th Annual Meeting, February 27–March 3, New York, New York, Abstracts on CD-ROM, 464.

22. 1993. **Shroder Jr., J. F., Arav, R., and Freund, R. A. 1993. "Geomorphology of the Bethsaida Archaeological Site on Lower Golan Heights and Lake Kinneret, Dead Sea–Jordan Rift Zone." Geological Society of America, Abstracts with Programs, A-85.

JEWS OF RHODES

Angel, Marc D. *The Jews of Rhodes*. New York: Sepher-Hermon Press, 1978.

Bedford, Robert. *An Introduction to Literature on the Holocaust in Greece*. New York: Sephardic Historical Committee, 1994.

Benatar, Isaac. *Rhodes and the Holocaust*. Bloomington, IN: iUniverse, 2010.

Constantopoulou, Photini, and Thanos Veremis. *Documents on the History of the Greek Jews*. Athens: Kastaniotis Editions, 1997.

Fintz Menascé, Esther. *A History of Jewish Rhodes*. Los Angeles: Rhodes Historical Foundation, 2014.

Fleischer, Hagen. *Greek Jewry and Nazi Germany: The Holocaust and Its Antecedents*. Athens: Gavrielides Publishing, 1995.

Franco, Hizkia M. *The Jewish Martyrs of Rhodes and Cos*. New York: HarperCollins, 1994.

Lévy, Isaac Jack. *Jewish Rhodes: A Lost Culture*. Berkeley, CA: Judah L. Magnes Museum, 1989.

Levy-Amato, Rebecca. *I Remember Rhodes* (bilingual Ladino and English). New York: Sepher-Hermon Press, 1987.

HOLOCAUST

Extermination Camps

Arad, Yitzhak. *Belzec, Sobibor, Treblinka: The Operation Reinhard Death Camps*. Bloomington: Indiana University Press, 1987.

Arendt, Hannah. *Eichmann in Jerusalem: A Report on the Banality of Evil*. New York: Penguin Classics, 1994 reprint.

Berenbaum, Michael. *The World Must Know: A History of the Holocaust as Told in the United States Holocaust Memorial Museum*. Boston: Little, Brown, 1993.

Blatt, Thomas Toivi. *From the Ashes of Sobibor*. Evanston, IL: Northwestern University Press, 1997.

Browning, Christopher. *The Origins of the Final Solution: The Evolution of Nazi Jewish Policy, September 1939–March 1942*. Lincoln: University of Nebraska Press, 2004.

———. *Remembering Survival: Inside a Nazi Slave Labor Camp*. New York: W. W. Norton, 2010.

Dawidowicz, Lucy S., ed. *The Golden Tradition: Jewish Life and Thought in Eastern Europe*. New York: Holt, Rinehart and Winston, 1967.

———. *The War Against the Jews, 1933–1945*. New York: Bantam, 1986.

Fishman, David. *Embers Plucked from the Fire: The Rescue of Jewish Cultural Treasures in Vilna* (second expanded edition). New York: YIVO, 2009, 2015.

Gilead, I., Yoram Haimi, and Wojciech Mazurek. "Excavating Nazi Extermination Centres." In *Present Pasts: Journal of the Institute of Archaeology Heritages Studies Section*, 1, (2009), 10–39.

Hilberg, Raul. *Perpetrators, Victims, Bystanders: The Jewish Catastrophe, 1933–1945.* New York: HarperCollins, 1992.

———. *The Destruction of the European Jews.* New Haven: Yale University Press, 2003.

Kola, Andrzej. Bełżec: *The Nazi Camp for Jews in the Light of Archaeological Sources: Excavations 1997–1999.* Washington, DC: United States Holocaust Museum, 2000.

Mosse, George L. *The Crisis of German Ideology: Intellectual Origins of the Third Reich.* New York: Schocken, 1981 [1964].

———. *Toward the Final Solution: A History of European Racism,* 1st ed. New York: Howard Fertig, 1978.

O'Neil, Robin. "Belzec: The 'Forgotten' Death Camp." In *East European Jewish Affairs,* Vol. 28.2 (1998), 49–62.

Parkes, James. *Anti-Semitism.* Chicago: Quadrangle Books, 1969.

Rashke, Richard. *Escape from Sobibor.* Chicago: University of Illinois Press, 1995.

———. *Dear Esther.* Lincoln, NE: Morris Publishing, 2000.

Roiter, Howard, and Kalmen Wewryk. *To Sobibor and Back—An Eyewitness Account: Memories of Holocaust Survivors in Canada,* Vol. 1. Montreal: Concordia University Chair in Canadian Jewish Studies and the Montreal Institute for Genocide and Human Rights, 1999.

Trachtenberg, Joshua. *The Devil and the Jews: The Medieval Conception of the Jew and Its Relation to Modern Anti-Semitism.* New Haven: Yale University Press, 1943.

Interviews

Interview with Esther Terner Raab, conducted August 27, 2008, by Sarah Rutman, University of Hartford Sobibor Documentation Project.

Interview with Selma Engel, conducted September 26, 2008, by Avinoam Patt and Sarah Rutman, University of Hartford Sobibor Documentation Project. (Written account of Selma Engel: www.holocaustresearchproject.org/survivor/selma%20 engel.html)

Testimonies

Confino, Alon. *A World Without Jews: The Nazi Imagination from Persecution to Genocide.* New Haven: Yale University Press, 2014.

Frank, Anne. *Anne Frank: The Diary of a Young Girl.* New York: Bantam Books, 1993.

Hitler, Adolf, and Ralph Manheim. *Mein Kampf.* Boston: Houghton Mifflin, 1943.

Langer, Lawrence L. *The Holocaust and the Literary Imagination.* New Haven: Yale University Press, 1977.

———. *Holocaust Testimonies: The Ruins of Memory.* New Haven: Yale University Press, 1991.

"New Dimensions in Testimony." USC Shoah Foundation. May 6, 2014. https://sfi .usc.edu/news/2013/07/new-dimensions-testimony.

Wiesel, Elie, and Marion Wiesel. *Night.* New York: Hill and Wang, 2006.

GREAT SYNAGOGUE OF VILNA,
PONAR, FORT IX, AND ROKISKIS

Arad, Yitzhak. *Ghetto in Flames: The Struggle and Destruction of the Jews in Vilna in the Holocaust.* Jerusalem: Yad Vashem, 1980.

Bakalczuk-Felin, M., ed., Tim Baker (producer), and David Sandler. *Memorial Book of Rokiskis: Rokiskis, Lithuania.* Original Yizkor Book. Published in Johannesburg, 1952 [Yiddish]. Translation Project Coordinators: Tim Baker, assisted by David Sandler. New York: JewishGen, Inc., 2017.

Cohen, Richard. *The Avengers.* New York: Compass Press, 2001.

Cohen-Mushlin, Aliza, S. Kravstov, and V. Levin. Giedre Mickuanaite and Jurgita Siauciunaite-Verbickiene, eds. *Synagogues in Lithuania* (2 vol.). Vilnius: Vilnius Academy of Art Press, 2010–2012.

Faitelson, Alex. *Heroism and Bravery in Lithuania.* Jerusalem and New York: Gefen Publishing, 1996.

———. *The Escape from the IX Fort.* Kaunas, Lithuania: Spausdino Gabijos, 1998.

———. *The Truth and Nothing But the Truth: Jewish Resistance in Lithuania.* Jerusalem and New York: Gefen Publishing, 2006.

Jankeviciene, Alge. *The Great Synagogue of Vilnius.* Vilnius, Lithuania: Savastis, 1996.

Klausner, Israel. [Hebrew] *Vilna in the Period of the Gaon.* Jerusalem: Reuven Mas, 1942.

———. [Hebrew] *Vilna: Jerusalem of Lithuania* (2 vol.). Tel Aviv: HaKibbutz HaMeuhad, 1983.

Levin, Vladimir. "Historical Overview." *Synagogues in Lithuania: A Catalogue*, vol. 1. Digital Archives in Vilnius Academy of Arts; Centre for Studies of History and Culture of East European Jews. Vilnius: Vilnius Academy of Art Press, 2010, 17–41.

Leyzer, Ran. *Jerusalem of Lithuania* (3 vol.). New York: The Laureate Press 1974.

The Old Town of Rokiskis in the 16th–18th Centuries [Lithuanian with English synopses] ed. Romana Songailaite. Rokiskis: Tyzenhuzai Hertiage, 2017.

Porat, Dina. *The Fall of a Sparrow: The Life and Times of Abba Kovner.* Translated and edited by Elizabeth Yuval. Stanford: Stanford University Press, 2010.

Vince, Laima. "The Silenced Muse: The Life of a Murdered Jewish Lithuanian Poet." deepbaltic.com/2018/05/08/the-silenced-muse-the-life-of-a-murdered -jewish-lithuanian-poet/.

Zalkin, Mordechai. "Vilnius." In *The YIVO Encyclopedia of Jews in Eastern Europe*, ed. Gershon David Hundert. New Haven and London: Yale University Press, 2008, 1970–77.

TESTIMONIES OF THE SURVIVORS
OF THE PONAR TUNNEL

Davidovich Farber, Julius, and Mordechai Zaidel. www.shoa.org.il/image.ashx?i=79371.pdf&fn=28.pdf, accessed on May 25, 2018.

Dombe, Sabina. "Escape from Ponar: Itzhak Dugin" [Hebrew]. Tel Aviv, 2018.

Dugin, Itzhak, and Mordechai Zaidel, by Claude Lanzmann, for *Shoah* in 1979. http://data.ushmm.org/intermedia/film_video/spielberg_archive/transcript/RG60_5050/912AA0D8-B9F6-4F59-8796-140D69F714C0.pdf, accessed on May 25, 2018. (This page has more detail on content of Lanzmann's interview with Zaidel and Dugin: www.ushmm.org/online/film/display/detail.php?file_num=5767.)

Ehrenburg, Ilya, and Vasily Grossman. "Yuri Farber testimony," in *The Complete Black Book of Russian Jewry*, translated and edited by David Patterson. New York: Routledge, 2017.

Fortunoff Archive at Yale University (formerly the Holocaust Survivors Film Project). In 1979, this organization began videotaping testimonies of survivors and witnesses in New Haven, Connecticut. In 1981, the original collection of testimonies was deposited at Yale University, and the Video Archive for Holocaust Testimonies opened its doors to the public the following year.

Gol, Shlomo. *My Escape from Ponar* [Yiddish]. Tel Aviv: Bet Lohamei HaGettaot, 1953.

University of Southern California (USC) Shoah Foundation. The Institute for Visual History and Education, formerly Survivors of the Shoah Visual History Foundation, established in 1994 by Steven Spielberg, is a nonprofit organization dedicated to making audiovisual recordings of interviews with survivors and witnesses of the Holocaust and other genocides.

Index

Adam (adamah), 245n1
aediculae (shrines), 102, 135–37
aerial photography: death camps and, 22–23, *23, 24*; drones for, 81
Aktion 1005, 7, 96, 219
altruism: archaeology and moral, 204; existence of, 205; of Plagge, 71, 195–202, 204–7, 209–10, 212, 242
Amir, Hannah, 226, 239
amphorae, 119, *120*, 121–22
The Ancient Synagogue (Levine), 137–38
Arad, Ytzhak, 246n3
Arav, Rami, 49, 51, 119
Arendt, Hannah, 246n6
arks: interview on KS, 117; KS anomaly of, 31–32, 101–2, *103*; Sephardic Jewry and, *103*, 103–4; testimonies on synagogue, 117; Torah, 102, *103*, 104, 172; VGJSM with, 172, 177
artifacts, 19–20
Ashkenazic Jewry: Great Vilna Synagogue as, 33, 38–39, 111–12
Auschwitz: crematoria, 90; as death camp, 113–14; Drancy convoy to, 92–93; Fort IX equivalent to, 7; Frank bookending with, 44–45; Nazis destroying, 10; Ponar, Vilnius on par with, 215–16, *216*;

reconstruction of, 13; Rhodes Jews to, 32, 74, 104, 106, 112–14
Auschwitz-Birkenau, 15, 45
Awad, Nicole, *28*, 29

Babylonian Exile, 138–39
Bar Kokhba, 86, 154, 205
Batei-Knesset (gathering places), 138
batei midrash (great study houses), 168–70
bathhouses (*bod*): daily rituals in, 187, *188*, 189; excavation of Vilna Synagogue, 178–92, *179, 185, 188, 191*; Jewish culture and, 109–10, 181–82; *mikveh/mikvaot* different from, 190; of Rhodes, 117; Vilna Synagogue with, 145, 148
Baubonis, Zenonas, 165
Bauman, Paul, *227*, 227–28, 230, *231*
Belzec, Poland, 10–11, 13–14, 232, *232*
Bem, Marek, 11, 18
Bendigamos (Blessed Are We), 116–17
Bensimon, Ken, 84–85
Bernhard, Irene, 75
Bethsaida, Israel, 61; Arav and, 49, 51, 119; Bedouin leader on, 35–36; earthquakes and, 49, 51, 60, 84; GPR for, *48*, 48–51; international

About the Author

Dr. Richard A. Freund is the Maurice Greenberg Professor of Jewish History and director of the Maurice Greenberg Center for Judaic Studies at the University of Hartford. His most recent work in Lithuania has been chronicled in two television documentaries. A *NOVA* science series episode: "Holocaust Escape Tunnel" on the new discoveries made in the Holocaust-era Ponar Burial Pits and at the Great Synagogue of Vilna, Lithuania, and a DISCOVERY channel episode: "The Good Nazi" on the work done at the HKP 562 labor camp in Vilna. He is the author of hundreds of scholarly articles and several books (written or coedited) including *Digging through the Bible* and *Digging through History*.